Guilt

an exploration

First published by O Books, 2009
O Books is an imprint of John Hunt Publishing Ltd., The Bothy, Deershot Lodge, Park Lane, Ropley,
Hants, SO24 0BE, UK
office1@o-books.net
www.o-books.net

Distribution in:

UK and Europe
Orca Book Services
orders@orcabookservices.co.uk
Tel: 01202 665432 Fax: 01202 666219
Int. code (44)

USA and Canada
NBN
custserv@nbnbooks.com
Tel: 1 800 462 6420 Fax: 1 800 338 4550

Australia and New Zealand
Brumby Books
sales@brumbybooks.com.au
Tel: 61 3 9761 5535 Fax: 61 3 9761 7095

Far East (offices in Singapore, Thailand,
Hong Kong, Taiwan)
Pansing Distribution Pte Ltd
kemal@pansing.com
Tel: 65 6319 9939 Fax: 65 6462 5761

South Africa
Alternative Books
altbook@peterhyde.co.za
Tel: 021 555 4027 Fax: 021 447 1430

Text copyright Caroline Brazier 2008

Design: Stuart Davies

ISBN: 978 1 84694 160 3

A CIP catalogue record for this book is available
from the British Library.

Printed by Digital Book Print

O Books operates a distinctive and ethical publishing philosophy in
all areas of its business, from its global network of authors to
production and worldwide distribution.
This book is produced on FSC certified stock, within ISO14001
standards. The printer plants sufficient trees each year through
the Woodland Trust to absorb the level of emitted carbon in
its production.

Guilt

an exploration

Caroline Brazier

BOOKS

Winchester, UK
Washington, USA

CONTENTS

To my children, Catherine, Jenny and Tim
Hoping their childhood spaces were happy ones

Prologue

This book is about guilt.

When I started to write I imagined this would be rather as my previous books, an exploration that set out its subject and explored its themes in a conventional way. It would be arranged in neat and tidy order. There would be neatly manicured lawns of theory between well planted beds of illustration. The subject was a rich one. For months I had been mulling it, reflecting, observing, discussing it in workshops and courses that I ran.

But I reckoned without Joanne; Joanne, the precocious and outspoken kid, whose story has become the heart of this exploration. Originally I had intended to write her story in a few words, a short anecdote of perhaps half a page at most, to start the process of writing with an illustration. But no, as soon as I began to let her in, she strode onto the pages, took over the theme and told it as it was, and I, happy to see her confidence and bravado go where my timidity might hesitate, let her.

It has always been so. I welcomed her, allowed her to take the limelight, gave her space, just as I so willingly let all the other Joannes that I have known, and, in doing so, I discovered in myself new areas of creativity and insight I had not imagined. The book became richer, the conclusions more complex. She showed me that answers are not simple, and perspectives shimmer like mirages as one moves between them. She took me by the hand and led me back, back into the tangled jungle of childhood feelings. She reminded me of how it was, in the olden days when we were young.

This book is a journey. Narrative and reflection mirror one another, leading us along a narrow path, into the darker regions of the spirit. Together on these pages, as seasoned explorers, we will enter the territory where feelings and judgement struggle to find a foothold.

Guilt is a slippery topic, a modern taboo, our sense of justice tangles with the psychological, creating havoc. Beyond the reign of logic, the clarity of right and wrong, vast territories of undefined experience stretch out. Judicial guilt, the proven case, provides an existential backbone to our lives, its recognition forcing us to authenticity. But this is only part of its meaning, for feelings of guilt seep through our bones for all manner of reasons. They bind us into emotional loops, sometimes preserving pride and other times attacking the foundations of our identities. And such emotions draw their power from silence, the closet nature of guilt, hidden shame and secretiveness, which undermine our spirit.

And so, by cutting back the tangled creepers, entering again those difficult spaces of long nights, sleepless churning thoughts, and half remembered humiliation, perhaps we can let a little light into the darkness. Primarily this book is about honesty. In it we will dare to look into the fine-grain of human experience. The truth is friendly and the facts our allies. So let us go forth.

CHAPTER ONE

The Child

Only when we accept our darkness can we feel the light that surrounds us, the light that extends forever and ever and does not judge us, but loves us for our complicated shades of grey, black, purple and vermilion in all their dappled splendour.

****

Joanne at ten years old was tall and lanky, straw blonde hair bunched untidily in rubber bands that did not match. She was a cheeky and, one might say, precocious child, who stood defiantly in jeans and sneakers in the middle of the roadway of the cul-de-sac, eye-balling the lads from the estate down the road, who had ventured into her street. The emphasis was on the *her*. As the oldest child, and the only girl old enough to count, living in the clapper-boarded houses with their neat front gardens, weeping willows and red acers behind white slatted fences, she ruled the other youngsters who lived there with a ferocity that did not invite dissent.

One for adventure, she and the other kids from the street would spend the time when they were not at school or confined to base by parental influence, roaming the neighbourhood, checking out new building sites as the open spaces where the factory had once stood were gradually converted into housing, or playing on the remaining expanses of broken concrete and waste ground that had not as yet been built on.

In particular, they played around the little ditch that ran from the small recreation ground beside the school through a dark concrete pipe and alongside the overgrown footpath behind the scrap yard, no doubt eventually finding its way under the factory site and, so, on into the Thames.

Sometimes the ditch filled with slow flowing water, discoloured by iron deposits and skimmed by swirls of oil. They called it the Amazon. Occasionally after rain, it would flow faster, though it was never a rushing torrent. Other times it ran dry and filled up with litter, rusty cans, and thick foliage of reeds and nettles. To adults such spaces were the forgotten in-between spaces of the city, but to the children they were an unfolding expanse of adventures.

It was a mixed neighbourhood. Middle class professional families rubbed shoulders with the capital's rougher elements. The housing developments were bringing change. Old and new blended in uncomfortable proximity. The cul-de-sac on the reclaimed industrial land was partially sheltered by a row of flowering cherry trees along the entrance road, and abutted on one side by the older red-brick terraces, and on the other by a small estate of post-war flats, set in untidy grassed banks. Generations of urban decay and regeneration fed the uncertain landscape.

The kids knew their limits. The main road to the south created one boundary and the river another. Less certain, the estate, with its population of older lads, who hung out by the lift shafts, smoking furtive cigarettes or kicked footballs across the glass strewn street, that just missed you as you walked by, thumping and rebounding loudly from the un-windowed wall opposite, was somewhere to be treated with care. Parents allowed children to walk to the newsagent that sat, shuttered with wire mesh, in the little row of shops that nestled between the brick and concrete slabs. There you could spend pocket money on sweets or cheap plastic toys. A sixpenny mix-up would last all afternoon, and the rainbow sherbet, which stuck in coloured crusts to the paper bag as you licked, could go on all day.

The terraced streets, where large dogs often wandered

4

unrestrained, and creepy old ladies peered at you between lace curtains, seemed even less welcoming, though these streets had to be crossed to reach the local school that they attended; a great Victorian edifice of the same red brick, whose iron railings backed onto the main road. They did not linger here, except occasionally when they played *knock down ginger*. Ring the bell and run away; watch from a safe distance as the woman at number seven, in her pink nylon overall and curlers, looks left and right along the street, waves her fist, then shuts the door loudly.

Despite the cacophony of cultures, it was not a dangerous area, and the children quickly grew savvy about the small risks.

Sometimes the kids from the cul-de-sac would play in their own back gardens. Some had swings or climbing frames. Mostly though, they would hang out in the scruffy spaces that adults overlooked, away from the houses, beside the Amazon or on the unfenced scrub of derelict land it crossed. They built dens among the furze and buddleias or toasted stolen bread on fires built under metal milk crates that they found dumped by the road side. They imagined worlds.

The scrap yard held a particular fascination for the kids. There were huge piles of old washing machines and fridges, tangled pipes and bits of cars. Mattresses with uneven springs and broken armchairs could become trampolines, whilst huge pieces of metal, curved like boats, would rock sluggishly if you stood at just the right point.

Of course no one told the parents that they had been playing in the yard. The hole in the chicken wire fence where the stream-pipe crossed it was just big enough for a child to creep under after the men had closed up for the night. You could not be seen, for the fence was full of bindweed, and the path that ran alongside was overgrown with bramble and nettles, and in any case much of the yard was obscured from view by stacked sheets of corrugated iron.

They had not been expressly forbidden to go there, but

everyone knew, without it ever being said, that the scrap yard was off limits. Or at least it would be if the question were ever raised. For this reason discretion became the order of the day. If adults never discovered where the kids played, they would never actually be told not to go there. The intuition that it was wrong did not figure. The logic was simple. Don't look for trouble where it doesn't exist. There were some things parents were better protected from, and this was one of them.

It was not long before the men who ran the scrap yard guessed at these evening activities. There were bubble gum wrappers and old football cards stuffed into the old biscuit tin under the outdoor cupboard where they kept the jars of bolts and screws. They couldn't help but notice the imprints of muddy wellies on the furnishings or the way that the large scrap iron fenders had "walked" across the yard as the gang had rocked them, leaving slip marks in the mud. Once they found a blue and white knitted scarf. They grinned good-naturedly. Kids!

Alf and Ray were brothers. They had lived in the neighbourhood all their lives; grown up in the crowded terraced streets that had covered the area where the flats now stood. They knew London kids because they had been London kids themselves. Big families in small houses, they lived on the streets and found their entertainment in the gutters and back lanes. It was a tight community where you could expect a clip round the ear from any of the women in their flowery aprons if you got too noisy or too cheeky. You learned to be bold but to go unseen.

The war had changed all that. Half the houses had been blown apart when the bomb landed in their street. Two more streets were demolished when the re-development came. The factory closed, a casualty of another bomb. Returning from national service, they had started the business on a piece of land by the park that had once been used to store sheet metal for the factory. It belonged to the council, and the rent was low. It had an old but good sized shed and with their de-mob money and a bit of savings they bought a pick-up lorry. It did them OK.

Alf was a big man. Broad shouldered, but slightly hunched, his flesh hung heavily on his arms, filling out at the breast and belly under his grubby vest top. He had tattoos on his hairy forearms and a broad grin on his reddened face. Ray was leaner, quieter. He gave the impression of being the more intelligent, which was perhaps correct. Often he twisted a cigarette in his bony fingers and looked thoughtfully out from under his heavy brows as he sat perched on an old kitchen chair outside the open door of the shed when they took their tea breaks, which happened with surprising frequency.

The kids knew Ray and Alf. Not in the way that people had known one another in the old days before the war, but casually. They were figures in their landscape like the lollipop lady who stopped the traffic outside the school and kept barley sugars in the pocket of her great white canvas raincoat or the man who swept the streets with his little trolley, yard broom and shovel.

They would peer between the coarse stems of the old creepers that wove their way through the mesh and spy on the men from their hiding place, as they worked. The overgrown path afforded a good view of the yard. Sometimes the kids would shout names through the fence as Ray and Alf ate their sandwiches, and would then run away laughing when the men came to look for them. Other times they would just watch and hold whispered conversations and giggle.

It was not long before the kids became bolder. Their conversations grew louder and their name calling more persistent.

"Hey."

Alf had spotted the movement through the fence.

"What're you kids up to?"

The others were ready to run, but Joanne stood her ground.

"Looking at you!" she called back. Her voice was defiant. It said, so what are you going to do about it? You're fat and slow and there is a fence between us. I'm from the cul-de-sac, the rich houses, and my father is a teacher, and you're just a scrap man, so I'm not afraid of you.

Joanne did not know what her defiance said, but she felt it in her bones and it gave her confidence. She was, after all, ten. In the top year of primary school, she would soon be going to the high school if she passed her eleven plus, which she would, as she was clever.

"You lot the ones who've been coming in at night?" Alf's voice was friendly.

"So?" Joanne was gaining confidence.

"We know, you know," Alf grinned. "Got your brother's scarf too. He'll be wanting that back. Chelsea is it?"

"He's not my brother. He lives next door."

"He'll still want his scarf back."

"Can we come and see in the hut?" Joanne was looking past Alf now.

The hut was open, and inside they could see it was full of a glorious assortment of things. There was furniture and bric-a-brac, an old bicycle and what looked like a bundle of army helmets. Deep in the dark interior she could see shelves and boxes. It was where the men kept anything they collected that might be re-sold. It also served as an office for what little paper-work they did.

That day there were three other kids with her, boys; her eight year old twin brothers Michael and Ian, and Philip from number six. They were all younger than her. Seven kids lived in the cul-de-sac altogether, but the two girls from number four, who were five and six respectively, were too young to count. Simon who was nearest in age to her was on holiday.

The younger boys hovered uncertainly, wondering whether to run away, but they wanted to see what Joanne would do.

Alf laughed. "All right then. Come round to the front."

From that day, the kids from the cul-de-sac would often visit Alf and Ray. They would sit on the old sofas and drink strong tea out of tin mugs or they would peep into the shed to see what new items had arrived. When Simon returned from Cornwall, he was introduced and sworn to secrecy. The gang's new hangout would probably not go down well with parents, so they chose not to mention their new friendships, and younger girls, who could not be trusted to keep quiet, were left to play on their own in the deserted street.

Sometimes Alf would buy them comics. They'd chuckle over the stories and the boys would tell the jokes over and over with raucous laughter. Ray was more reserved, less sure how to interact, but sometimes he would pull bags of sweets out of his army rucksack which hung on the shed door. There was a little stove that ran on methelated spirit on which Alf and Ray boiled their kettle and sometimes would cook up meals of beans or sausages. This latter was largely for the kids' entertainment. They would all sit round and share the results of their efforts, mopping up the last remnants with wads of sliced white bread.

As the men worked, the kids had to keep out of the way. If they didn't, Alf shouted curses at them, but good-naturedly. He liked the diversion the kids brought. It reminded him of his own childhood. They were generally well behaved and did as they were told; cheeky enough to be fun, without overstepping the mark.

So it became a habit. Most days they'd drop in after school and stay until tea time. Saturdays, they might hang out there most of the day. When it rained they sheltered under the old canvas tarpaulin that the men had rigged up, stretched between the hut and two metal poles with guy ropes, sitting on old sofas rescued from the pile, and watched the drips form along its edges. This was better than any camp.

****

Let us leave Joanne's story at this point. The story is in one sense fictional. I never knew Joanne, nor did I know the place where she lived. It does not exist. She, and her London home, have grown into being on the pages of this book, on the screen of my computer as I type. But in another sense they are as real as any account you might read, formulated out of reprocessed impressions of life in a world now fallen into history. Her story, like all our stories, is a weaving together of fact and fiction, of experiences and memories. How else could it be? Our stories are always mirrors of our lives and the lives of others who jostle this world with us, shadows, yet with a life of their own, they haunt our dreams and colour our perceptions.

Joanne is like so many kids I knew growing up in south London in the sixties. Those times were different in many ways. Kids were freer. We went out more on our own; were left to our own devices and amusements more often than children today seem to be. We roamed our neighbourhoods in gangs, got into trouble and tested the limits. We did things that adults thought were dangerous or wrong. We got into trouble.

We got hurt sometimes, but mostly we came through unscathed, bearing the scars of our experience with pride. I still have one scar on my hand from the time a pen-knife shut on my fingers whilst I was trying to saw through an industrial size hose pipe, which I had found on a building site, in order to make a swing. I have another that marks where a burning ember fell on me from a piece of wood I was using to heat some wire to brand a felt horse I had made. The scars are fading as I grow older, but are not gone yet.

Other scars linger for longer. The psychological processes of growing up cut deep swathes through our mental structures, giving form to adult experience and perception, distorting our personalities and shaping them. Some good, some bad; like trees twisted by the wind, we are made interesting by adversity. The strength of purpose in our childhood explorations of the world and the creativity which came from improvising playthings, the imaginative worlds we inhabited in our games, and the relation-ships we developed with the many friends and acquaintances we encountered, all shaped our capacity to live interesting lives in the adult world. Memories of childhood create a paint-box from which our adult selves draw colours and imagery to understand and describe life.

My friends and I lived out many hours in a piece of land we called the Jungle. As an adult I can now see that it was just a small strip of untamed woodland at the end of our street; a place where people tipped their garden waste and occasionally their building rubble, the preserve of owls and cats. To us as children, it was a kingdom in which we lived out our hidden lives. There were shared meeting places and social conventions. We each had our territories where we built individual camps. For these we collected wood and brick ends from rubbish heaps behind the adjacent houses and found fallen branches on the woodland floor to construct our shelters. We created shared defences, encoun-tered aliens, mapped walkways and avoided spies or the Gestapo or wicked relatives who might be hunting us down, in free ranging games which unfolded over days or weeks.

We mocked unmercifully the posh kids, whose gardens abutted the Jungle, until their parents would come out to remon-strate with us, an action we took as our sign of victory, as it showed they were sissies who could not stand up to us on their own. We dreamed of wild adventures and we lamented the prospect of growing up, knowing that it would bring with it an end of these days in which reality was infinitely amenable to invention. I feel deeply grateful for the freedom and imaginative space that time and place provided for me.

The Jungle lived in its specifics; in the names we gave it, which still evoke that special feeling reserved for childhood spaces: The Centre Tree, The Elder Grove, The Cat Walk. As I repeat each name I enter once again into that place; see the rough yellowed bark of the elder trees, hear the voices of my friends, running through the damp undergrowth or perched high above, standing, feet wedged into the forked branches of one of the huge evergreen oaks. I smell the dankness of rotting wood; feel the slimy brown fungus growing on the fallen tree trunk as it gradually decomposes. I feel the slither of muddy Wellington boots on its smooth, naked surface where the bark has fallen away, and anticipate again in my imagination the sting of raw cold hands reaching to break my fall.

Children today live more sheltered lives. They are more organized and guided by adult agendas. The times I grew up in were no safer than today, but somehow our parents were willing to accept the uncertainty and let us learn to face danger on our own. That was how childhood was, and had always been, and child protection had not yet been invented.

There are great dilemmas in child rearing. Looking across societies, the rate at which youngsters are left to discover the world and look after themselves varies hugely. Some variety is grown of necessity. Street kids in poorer countries often look after younger siblings from the age of four or five whilst parents scratch a living by begging or scavenging, or abandon them completely through death, disease or poverty. In African villages ravaged by AIDS, children are left in huge majorities, taking on all the daily tasks of household life at very young ages, caring for sick parents or, having buried them, continuing their work in the home and community.

Even in easier times, the responsibilities expected of a three or five or ten year old can be very different in different cultures. A ten year old child in Zambia may go to school in a far away town, living the week in a dormitory where groups of children will cook and care for themselves without adult supervision. I had a friend in another European country whose five year old offspring came home from school each day with a door key on a string round her neck to let herself into the house and make her own after-school snack before her mother, my friend, returned from work. In that country this was normal.

I am not necessarily arguing here for a change in policy, or for children to be less protected than they are in the modern West, though such debates seem timely and are, indeed, beginning to be addressed. This book is not concerned directly with such matters. Rather, I share these thoughts to lay the ground for our main exploration, the purpose of this book. This exploration and the theme of this book is one that takes us into the nature of our moral being as humans. As such it has relationship to our freedom of action. It is grounded in the choices we make and the motivations that lie behind them. Our subject, after all, is guilt.

****

The subject of guilt is complex. On the one hand, at the simple level, attribution of guilt involves the identification of an act as wrong. Guilt of this kind can be legally proven. It is objective, based upon evidence which is, by definition, potentially open to the scrutiny of others. Some such guilt is, of course, known only to ourselves. All of us have conducted ourselves in ways that we judge to be wrong, but have avoided being found out, either by design or chance. In such circumstances, we reflect on our actions and know in our hearts that we are guilty of a misdemeanour or an omission. In our more sober moments, we assemble in our minds a jury of spectators and process before them the evidence on which we are to be convicted. We invite our consciences to judge.

When we know in our hearts that we are guilty, we may react in different ways. Sometimes we try to slip out of the judgement. We pretend to our internal jury that our crime was not so bad, re-writing the story so as to blame others or justify ourselves. Or maybe we invite them to condemn and sentence us, pronouncing us guilty. Thus we may punish ourselves, or feel driven to make recompense. We may long to confess our crime to others or strive to keep our silence. We may forgive ourselves or cast blame on ourselves indefinitely.

Much that we call guilt, however, is not so much a fact of misbehaviour, logically proven, but rather, it is a feeling that creeps between the folds of thoughts, and wracks our minds in the dark nights of sleepless contemplation. Such guilty feeling is not logical, not proven, yet it tortures us with regret and unease. The feelings lie close to other feelings. They transform into shame and regret. They are uncertain, unwilling to relinquish self-blaming, yet not knowing the real object of our crimes. A musty place of un-investigated causes, such guilt erodes the foundations of our lives.

It is into these dark recesses that we will try to shine a torch in this book. We will look into those secret places of the soul, the in-between areas that we shy away from. We will explore those uncomfortable feelings that well up in us when we are unhappy with our actions, our thoughts or our being. We will explore the squirming, dark, creepy feeling that all of us know sometimes and that haunts so many in our modern age to the point of incapacity.

Language is slippery, but so are human minds. We slip between concepts, confusing the feeling of guilt with its actuality; substituting self-criticism, and the longing for things not to be so, with true remorse and a will to make amends. We resent our unsettled consciences and blame others for imposing guilty feelings upon us, whilst clinging to those same feelings and failing to move on.

There is other confusion in words. Guilt is associated with judgement. We set up courts of law within our minds and, when we feel guilty, we feel automatically condemned. So guilt and judgement merge. Yet the word judgement has more than one meaning. Judgement does not necessarily involve condemnation. It may simply mean to make an assessment. If we can make this separation with clarity we can start to look objectively at our actions and see that we were mistaken, or even deliberately doing wrong. Whilst such a perception is a judgement in the sense of being an assessment of the situation, a discernment of truth, it does not necessarily lead to blame. We can be honest without necessarily following it with accusations.

This distinction is important, for the two forms of judgement are often confused. When we think of judgement in relation to guilt, we imagine being judged and condemned. But if we are to explore the nature of guilt and, in particular, to bring this exploration into the arena of our own lives, being able to look with clarity at the truth of things without condemnation is essential. The fear of condemnation leads us to shy away from honesty. Yet all of us are guilty. We all make mistakes. We act with motives that are not altruistic. Our actions are contaminated with all manner of self-interest.

Real freedom in the face of guilt requires us to own such realities. To do this we need to look dispassionately at our thoughts and actions without leaping to self-defence or self-condemnation. Such objectivity grows from a suspension of critical and condemnatory judgements. It involves looking into those areas of our life where we got things wrong, where we were cruel or thoughtless, self-serving or manipulative. It means being honest about our mistakes and our wilful negligence, our dishonesty and our angry outbursts. We can look at all of this and in it see the deeply human normality it represents and our regret at this being so. We can call this radical non-judgementalism.

Radical non-judgementalism is difficult for modern people. Our society is built on jurisdiction and on values which depend on such concepts as justice and mercy, forgiveness and retribution. Judgement is associated for most of us with ideas of punishment and criticism. Condemnation of wrongdoing, of evil, is seen as essential to the preservation of civilisation. Judgement places a cordon round the good and the just, and excludes those who might undermine the social fabric.

Such values are grounded in our religious heritage. Human courts mete out justice, modelled on the divine. Our mind-set is framed with concepts of this kind. We apply these values both in our perceptions of others and in our views of ourselves. We are critical and condemnatory of much that we encounter, and we find it hard to relinquish such attitudes when looking at our own behaviour.

To explore guilt honestly, involves looking without condemning. As if stalking a timid animal, we quietly and sensitively find a still place from which we can see and explore feelings and thoughts. To do this involves being willing to share our bedspace with our discomforts; to ask ourselves what is really true, and in doing so, being ready to hear the answer, whatever it may be. Such receptivity is rarely achieved, however. We should not condemn our tendency to condemn; we should be non-judgemental about our judgementalism. Only then will we understand.

This exploration begins with a story of children, for it is in childhood that our moral sense is born. To some, childhood is a paradise of innocence. To others it is a pit of primeval emotions. In different ages and different cultures, the myths that surround the child are many. For the most part, like myths of creation and golden ages, they echo more the preoccupations of the adult world. The unknown, forgotten territory of the child becomes the space in which we plant our fantasies. Our view inevitably becomes that of the outsider. As adult observers we contaminate our view with interpretation.

It is difficult to look at the child without bias, and, indeed, to be candid in observation can risk transgressing taboos that are grounded in just such myths of innocence. This book relies on memory, the weaving together of background elements from my own past and that of my contemporaries with new events and locations. This mingling of detail creates a fiction, a view of childhood passed, that might have been. Whether it is accurate, you may judge, seeking within your own memories. Let us look into the reality as far as we are able, discerning truth where we can, and bringing to the process the radical freedom from judgementalism that suspends taboo and tries to simply see the reality of human nature.

CHAPTER TWO

Crossing Lines

Yesterday's revolutionary is today's political leader. Pillars of society stand against the tide of popular opinion. Archbishops speak out against the iniquities of democratically elected governments. The fallen star repudiates earlier profligacy and becomes the voice of the oppressed. The line between rebellion and conformity is often a matter of viewpoint. Who is condemned and who lauded is often more a matter of fashion than absolute right or wrong. In such shifting sands, who should feel guilty?

We create our identities through identification and differentiation. We are like some and different from others. We identify. We throw in our lot with particular groups or ideals which in turn give us a psychological home. We rebel, and as we do so we say "I am not this. I am other. I am different, not of your kind. I will find my own way in this world." And in rebelling, we create alliances. We align with the other, the rejected, the outsider. We join a new society, the society of those who stand against the stream, and that society has its own rules to which we conform.

Thus, in rebelling, we conform. So too, in conforming, we rebel, as in our respectability we reject the path of protest and differentiation, so often idealized. Every standpoint has its opposite, its counter-culture, and each its hinterland of support. In understanding a group within society, it may be more pertinent to ask what is being rebelled against and what is being conformed to. Even so, although we may ask which group or alliance a person belongs to, this alone will not determine their virtue.

As we slide between worlds of alliance and rejection, the complexity of the rule books which underpin our feelings of guilt changes. Social groups set their codes, create their priorities, grounded in different values. Whilst some norms seem absolute, common to most societies, there is little that is not acceptable, even lauded, somewhere.

The beach barbecue is innocent fun to some social groups, and po-faced refusal to join in becomes a source of social castigation. To others, a barbecue is distressing, involving, as it does, such terrible carnage. For those who hold this latter view, there is no enjoyment in seeing so many sentient beings basted, fried and consumed, or worse, tossed in the dustbin when everyone is sated. To others yet, the event is a sordid example of Western depravity. The pleasure in which participants indulge is no less than a debauched orgy of alcohol and sexual audacity, where near naked bodies are flaunted in loose association, and morals disregarded in the wine drugged haze. If we feel something approaching guilt associated with having participated or not, it is likely to be socially conditioned, framed by our association with one group's perspective or another.

In the modern world we often have multiple alliances. We slip between mores, fall between injunctions. We are never right or never wrong. When we are confident we blend and contradict our own ideas, manipulate and play off one perspective against the other. When we are not, we feel ourselves to be in the wrong whatever we do. Thus we slide between the sources of guilt, sometimes finding solace and justification in one perspective or another, but other times haunted, unable to satisfy conflicting demands of different worlds. We look for a root, an absolute, a guiding conscience that transcends culture, but our experience is conditioned, embedded in our histories and social fabric.

An exploration of guilt in such circumstances risks falling into relativism. Is the apportionment of guilt simply a factor of our failure to conform to the accepted standards of a particular group or society in which we happen to be living? Does the experience of guilt arise from social pressures and social judgements which are only valid in the particular context? Or are there persisting standards by which guilt can be determined, standards which persist in all circumstances? Is guilt a feeling or a measurable state?

****

A little while ago I was standing in the bookshop at Gatwick Airport. We were about to board a plane to North America and David, my husband, was with me. He had been looking for a book and was lamenting that he could find nothing interesting in the whole shop that he felt like reading on the long flight ahead.

"Pick something you'd never normally choose to read," I suggested, as he gloomily surveyed the shelves of religious, psychological and political books.

At that point I heard a voice behind us.

"Read this one, this'll tell you what life's really about."

I turned. A man in early middle age held out a book to us. He was pleasant looking, neatly dressed, with light brown hair and an open, friendly face. He had, perhaps, a certain urgency in his manner of speaking.

I did not immediately recognize the subject of the book, but I saw that he had taken it from the section of military and war books, beside which he was standing.

"You have to read something that is different from your usual view. It keeps you on your toes. Get different viewpoints. Remind yourself not everyone thinks the way you do." He paused, "That's why I read *The Guardian* sometimes; to remind myself that some people think differently to me. It's important to do that. Otherwise you think you're right all the time."

He waved the book at us. "This will tell you the real way things are."

The man was insistent that we look at the book. His manner was so urgent that it dawned on me that this was probably not just a casual enthusiasm for this book. I wondered what his involvement with it was; could he even be the author? With this thought, I suddenly felt a new level of interest. Was there potential for fellow feeling, writer to writer? I was fascinated.

"Sounds like you've a personal interest in this book," I commented, testing the water.

"Yes, that's right, I'm in it." His face lit up and his voice became even more animated. He clearly wanted to tell his story. He opened the book to the pages of photographs in the centre, sandwiched in the middle of the text. We looked.

The images were mostly pictures of crowds of football supporters. Many of them were fighting. Some were clashing with groups of police. "That's me, and that, and there." He turned the pages, pointing to various pictures, identifying a young lad in the midst of the fray. The photographs must have been taken some time ago. They were black and white and, from the clothes and hairstyles, looked as if they belonged to the early seventies.

"That guy getting arrested, that's my friend. He's a good guy. He's a social worker now." He paused.

"We had some good fights," he continued. "Mind, we were quite moral really. We had codes, ways of doing things. We looked after the young ones."

I believed him. I thought of Joanne and her gang, and of other gangs of youngsters I have known. I knew something of the culture of gangs, albeit less violent than that of the soccer fans the book depicted. The ones I knew had a strong ethos of loyalty and concern, and a sense of justice and honour, even if to the outside world they looked lawless and threatening. Gangs look after their weak members and expect unreserved allegiance in return. Their ethic may not conform to adult perspectives, but it has its own code of expectations. It is an unsubtle and rough culture, like the heroic code of the warrior. It is powerful.

I thought about the way that groups can be so similar even when their intentions and attitudes are apparently opposite. Freedom fighters and football hooligans, political activists and military units; all thrive on camaraderie and internal discipline, shared values and loyalty. Whilst differences between such groups might be significant, some things seem universal.

Images from the book brought echoes of my own experience to mind. The photographs of police cordons and crowds reminded me of peace demonstrations and protests. Many campaigns against cruelty and oppression in which I have taken part have involved standing facing the police lines and an array of black uniformed photographers. There must be galleries of pictures of me and my Buddhist activist friends in the police archive. Despite our peaceful intent, it is easy to slip into seeing that line of uniformed men as the opposition and the state it represents as the problem to be confronted.

The irony of these similarities brought energy to my response. I felt myself wanting to say "I know how that feels."

But he continued, "We learned to be tough. I joined the army. I've done lots of crazy things, bad things."

He went on to talk of the different things he had done since those days of football gangs. He described how he had taken risks, lived on the edge, outside mainstream society. He had been a mercenary. He had fought for whoever would pay him. He had fought in the Middle East and in Africa. There had been so many different wars, and he had fought on different sides. He hadn't cared about the rights or wrongs of the cause, just about who would pay his wage. Most recently, he had been a sniper.

"But I haven't killed anyone for two years now," he ended.

He had grown tired of killing. Now he ran an ecological business, tackling climate issues.

"The planet's in a terrible state and this country won't do anything about it," he commented, bitterly, "not while it's got this wishy washy socialist government."

He had just finished planting thousands of trees to offset global warming. He was travelling to continue the work.

He recognised us as Buddhists. That was a good thing to do, he

22

said. He wished us well. It was too late for him. He had done too many bad things in his life. It was too late to change.

"Looks like you already have," I commented.

He smiled wryly and went on his way.

I sat down on one of the black vinyl seats in the vast waiting area, among the crowds of holiday makers and business travellers, and felt privileged to have met him. I felt moved by his honesty and by the wistful quality of his voice as he parted. I sensed the intimation of regret and an intuition of another way, but also a pride in what he was. To glimpse into another's life often leaves one with a feeling of deep appreciation. I would have liked to know more, to understand more, yet I felt that even in the brief exchange, I had been permitted a window into a world I had never seen before and the experience had changed me. I could not judge.

What had motivated his engagement with us? Perhaps some curiosity, even some arrogance, a devil may care desire to shock or demonstrate the narrowness of these religious folk, had lain behind his revelations. Or maybe, even beneath the surface bluff, recognition of something else that might have been or could be still, drew him to speak with us. Perhaps we represented something ideal, something we were not, yet something that to him seemed tantalisingly innocent. I wondered if we were confessors and if he sought some absolution, or if we had simply been an audience.

For those who live unconventional lives, the stakes can be high. Good and bad coexist in the extremes. It is no coincidence that there are so many examples in religious writings of scoundrels and murderers who saw the light and became saints. Buddhism has its own history of mass murderers, villains and profligates turned holy men; Anguilimala, Asoka, Nagarjuna and others. Here was a man who was evidently capable of deep caring and loyalty to his gang members, his team. He knew discipline and had lived it both in his gangs and later in army life. He was a man of intelligence and enterprise. Now reflecting back on his life, he voiced both pride and regret. Maybe he felt guilt.

****

So what of Joanne? What of her experiences of guilt or regret? Her life was in some ways very different from that of my airport acquaintance, but in other ways it echoed his early experiences. Did she, did he, in those childhood years, experience regret or feelings of guilt? Did they cross a line within their own code of behaviour? Did they struggle with bad conscience? Or did they simply act in accordance with the morality of their own groups, even when adults might have been shocked or angered at discovering what they were up to?

An aspect of such behaviour is heroic. The kids from the cul-de-sac were a tight knit group. They were Joanne's gang. A source of identification and companionship, the gang created its own world, its own accepted ways of acting. Joanne leads, and leads well, concerned for the welfare of the younger members, but she is also resolute in her demands of them. She expects loyalty and obedience. Mother and commander, she is author of many of their plans and orchestrates their games. A rather isolated figure in some ways, her power goes unquestioned because it bears the stamp of confidence.

Joanne has learned to be a leader. Even at ten years old, she already carries the authority of experience and a style gleaned from a variety of sources. How has she learned to be this way? Who is her role model? Joanne's sense of her position probably owes much to the heroic deeds of history and literature. Stories imbibed from home and school create a backdrop to her life. From these she learns her role.

The sixties were a time of transition. Tradition was respected and its associated values were still revered. Radical new ways of thinking, already established in intellectual circles, were by and large still to sweep the general population. Those who grew up in that time were still inspired with stories of imposing figures, often drawn from earlier ages. These stories exuded a sense of justice and moral strength that owed its passion to the post-empire ethos that still persisted in England well beyond the granting of independence to most of her colonies. Children like Joanne inherited a system of thought that placed honour and the pursuit of what was right, albeit in the paternalistic manner of the occupying class, high in its ideals.

In this context, her leadership, whilst appearing rebellious, was in some of its aspects obedient to the predominating culture which she imbibed. She was a true disciple of Baden-Powel and of those women explorers who roamed the globe in tweeds and flannel petticoats, converting natives and spreading civilized values to the ignorant. Thus is morality instilled in the young.

In spite of these heroic role models of empire, the Britain of the sixties was reluctant to trust authority unquestioningly. The legacy of the rise of Nazi power in the nineteen thirties had brought Europeans to distrust the imposition of ideas or behaviour without criticism. There was a climate of opinion that saw morality as standing against blind obedience. People learned to question and not to accept easy solutions to social dilemmas. The trickster and the independent minded, who rebelled against the accepted standards also became the hero.

Within this frame, the stories that children of that time read offered role models who demonstrated a spirit of independence and self-sufficiency. Richmal Crompton's *William*, the lovable rogue, outwitted adults and revealed the pomposity of polite behaviour. Enid Blyton, so often despised by adults, was loved by children. Her stories of adventuring gangs of children, who frequently escaped from adult control and got up to all manner of adventures, instilled in the young reader a spirit of the camaraderie and sense of adventure. E Nesbit's Edwardian tales of young people were still popular. Though in some ways models of respectability, her characters undertook all sorts of great feats of ingenuity in situations where adult supervision receded into almost complete absence. Swallows and Amazons inspired us with stories of outdoor adventure, of camping under the stars and messing around in boats, most of the time without an adult in sight.

Joanne was perhaps, even in her time, a little old fashioned. Her parents had moved to London a few years earlier from a sleepy Oxfordshire village, which had been her mother's childhood home. Her father, a school master, taught at the private grammar school, a new appointee, struggling to integrate himself into a staff room filled with men who had become caricatures of themselves, all chalk dust and bluff, good humour one moment and louring, bombastic tyrants the next. Her mother did not go out to work, but was active in the community, helping out at a school for blind children, and running the local company of Girl Guides. Their world was the settled world of English propriety which was just beginning to be swept away by new values. As adults, they struggled to accommodate the new regime, sometimes clumsily extending a foot into it with a fashion item, or a risqué book. Mostly they continued in the life they had been brought up to.

****

Joanne and her gang were skilled at finding the gaps in an adult landscape, creeping like ground ivy between the slabs of adult spaces and proscriptions. The parameters of their world were partly set by adult limits: the demands of school and family meals, restrictions on wandering beyond the main road, teachings on good manners and behaviour. Their territory is marked by injunctions, psychological fences, which are sometimes accepted but often scaled through mental ingenuity. Their navigation charts are a complex web of messages learned from teachers, stories, heroes and observed behaviour.

Adult control is accepted in one sense unquestioningly, but in another is regarded as an implicit challenge to be overcome. The battle lines between adult and child become a game of cat and mouse, itself part of the heritage of ideas and role models which they have acquired. The stories of childhood literature are peppered with out-doing wicked uncles or boring family friends, cruel teachers or evil step-parents. Dissent is lauded. Deviance is rarely a direct assault. The child outwits the adult through stealth, through crafty reinterpretation of the rules. It is a war of attrition and the subtle undermining of positions, yet there is a sense of fair play. It is part of the natural opposition that was assumed at that time, the time before adults needed children's approval.

Children create their own parameters. Within the gang, a more or less benevolent dictatorship holds sway and creates its own set of rules. Trust and honour, loyalty and courage are valued. The snitch or the sissy is despised and taunted. Rough justice is meted out. In the dog eat dog world of playground politics, children, forced to spend hours of time in each others company, find their own forms of misery or fulfilment. Within such relationships, views of right and wrong, acceptable and non-acceptable behaviour crystallize. Peer pressure coerces and pulls toward conformity. Sometimes wise, sometimes not so, much is pragmatic.

The children have learned to judge situations for safety and comfort. They test their limits, but generally do so with a measure of caution. Childhood is the time of experimentation. Finding your capabilities and taking risks are programmed instincts; the drive to fly the nest and stand alone is probably genetically based. Kids mostly know how close you can run to a passing car, or whether a roof is safe enough to climb on. They assess risk by their own standards and experience. Some get stupid, but, when they do, their friends usually tell them so.

To cross an adult's boundary means getting into trouble. Children avoid being found out when they are being disobedient. They are frightened of punishment and disfavour. Getting into trouble is painful and sometimes shameful or humiliating. It can leave one feeling angry and resentful or embarrassed and unloved. It can leave one feeling guilty, smarting at the adult condemnation. Such feelings are unpleasant and deterrent, but they mostly arise from being discovered in one's crime, or the anticipation of such an event, and not from the act of disobedience itself.

To cross a line determined by one's own anxiety means encountering potential danger. When children do things that they find frightening, whether or not an adult has forbidden them, they are much more wary, checking out the nature of risk to a degree that depends upon their own levels of caution or foolhardiness. Often eager to prove their courage to themselves or to their friends, children stretch their comfort zones to test their capacities.

Sometimes the stretch is small enough to be exciting. Other times it goes beyond the child's natural limits. Taking such risks and sensing that one has had a near escape from danger is all right in moderation, but if the sense of danger is too great, it is a source of nightmares and anxieties. Not all children have the same thresholds, though. An act which brings terror for one, may offer another the feeling of exhilaration that comes from having survived against high odds.

In this context, disobedience, whether actual, or based on a supposition of what the adult would approve, is a form of risk taking, of courting danger. Without the adult's discovery, one child may be haunted by the fear that their action will come to light. Such a child may anticipate the parent's anger and reproachfulness, even before it happens, and in doing so, may feel its impact. Another child, however, may take pleasure in getting away with the wrong-doing and may find the process of daring to misbehave exhilarating. The child who is not found out may relish the victory, or, conversely, may nurse fears or feelings of guilt.

Some guilty feelings arise as a result of experiencing adult displeasure. Others from anticipating a response that has yet to happen. But are such feelings of guilt really to be equated with a feeling of having done wrong? Is it the child's own assessment that they have behaved badly, or are they simply reacting to the parent's condemnation, or an internalised sense of the parent's view? Is the locus of evaluation the child's own conscience or is it a learned response that anticipates punishment? Can we disentangle guilt from loss of face; remorse from shame? When do we feel regret for our actions because we judge them wrong, and when do we feel regret simply because we feel condemned and squirm uncomfortably before that judgement?

Beneath the fear of punishment by the parent, there often lies a deeper, more generalized fear of parental rejection. Being found out might lead to a complete withdrawal of love and approval. If the secret is discovered, the parent may no longer be willing to forgive. Love is conditional.

At our deepest level we fear rejection. Cut off from the light of parental approval and protection, the child falls into a hellish realm of shades. Inviting such disapproval is like spiritual suicide. It lets dark clouds of guilt seep into the soul. It eats away confidence and hollows one's being. So children hide the unforgivable aspects of themselves.

****

Fear of rejection is a strong factor in the child's relationship with other members of the gang. The culture of the group has its own moral structures of loyalty and trust. Even when one member of the gang has doubts, group pressure often over-rides the fear of punishment or sense of danger. The attraction of sharing an adventure and the deterrent of losing face in front of friends by chickening out are coercive. Children comply with the group's plans, even against their better judgement.

The child, caught between worlds, fears the parent's wrath and at the same time fears rejection from peers. The heroic possibilities involved in the escapade and the excitement of a new adventure tempt him. In this confusion of impulses, the temptation to ignore the voice which tells him that it is wrong to join in the activity is strong. After all, probably no-one has actually forbidden the activity. It is relatively easy to convince oneself that no harm will be done. Less said the better.

So the inner voice of dissent is suppressed. It is a solution of a kind, but it is a solution that may involve a kind of personal dishonesty. The child feels discomforted. Superficially the discomfort comes from fear of discovery but this discomfort, perhaps masks a deeper discomfort. This deeper discomfort arises from knowing that one has lied to oneself. One has pretended that all will be well, when patently it won't. Such dishonesty requires us to make internal barriers of pretence which eat at the soul and cut us off from the favour of the universe.

Sometimes, though, the motivation which leads a child to hide its actions is simpler and even protective. Children do not want to alarm their parents with unnecessary information. From a very young age, children can sense what adults want to be told and what is best left unsaid. Just as adults protect their children, considering their welfare and capacity to absorb certain unpleasant or awkward facts, so too, children protect parents from things that might worry or upset them.

When he was five, my brother fell out of a tree in *the Jungle*. I wasn't there, but I heard about it afterwards. His friend, younger than him, ran to find my father.

"Don't worry Mr Bates," he gasped, "He's all right. He just can't get up!"

Of course, the child's attempt to avoid creating worry

backfired. My father ran to find out what had happened, fearing the worst. Yet we can see the impulse that my brother's friend had to protect my father. Even in seeking help and despite his own anxiety, his first thought was not to worry the parent with this alarming situation. So it may be for the adults' protection that silence is preserved.

Often, though, it seems simply a matter of the child exercising what he sees as common sense. It is a bid to avoid unnecessary trouble. A pragmatic solution of discreet silence is adopted.

****

As she crept into the house, Joanne could hear sounds of movement from her parents' bedroom. Drawers opened and closed. The wardrobe doors scraped along their metal tracks; open, then closed again. The sound of footsteps followed, crossing and re-crossing the floor. Her mother must be putting away freshly washed clothes.

Joanne made her way as quietly as she could to her own room. She did not want her mother to know she was back yet. She sat on the bed, looking out of the window at the road outside. It was quiet. Simon and Philip had gone home some time ago and her brothers, who had left the scrap yard ahead of the others, were downstairs playing with their model fort, which they were extending into a full battlefield with bricks and plastic trees, vehicles and several cardboard shoe boxes. They had now covered the whole living room carpet and Joanne could foresee arguments about clearing it up at tea time.

It was over a week since the children had first been into the scrap yard at Ray and Alf's invitation. Ever since that day she had felt some anxiety. It was not strong, but it nagged away at her in moments like this when she was on her own. The trouble was that she was not sure that she could trust the younger members of the gang to keep quiet about their new friends.

Of course she had sworn them to secrecy. She had taken that precaution as soon as they left the scrap yard on that first afternoon. She knew that they were scared enough of the consequences of going against such an injunction not to talk about their escapades deliberately. She also sensed that they understood. That was more important. When someone understood in their bones, even without knowing why, they would not do the wrong thing. They would not give the game away.

"Oh, hello, you're back." Her mother came into her bedroom carrying a pile of neatly folded school shirts.

Joanne jumped, startled. "I was thinking," she said.

Her mother paused in the doorway. Joanne held her breath. Was she going to say something? Did she suspect? She felt herself colouring.

But her mother laughed.

"Well, don't do too much of that!" she joked, "and put those clothes away. Don't leave them on the bed to get crumpled after I've spent all afternoon ironing."

Joanne put her hand to her burning cheeks and felt cross with herself.

What if one of the others let something slip? She didn't think any of them would say anything deliberately. They were too scared of her, and anyway none of them wanted to face the consequences of their parents finding out, but the situation felt risky, and if one of them did let the cat out of the bag, they would all probably get it, as parents in the cul-de-sac knew each other and were bound to talk. She could just imagine her mother on the phone to Philip's mother next door, or worse, talking over the fence as they both hung out their family washing.

Of course there was nothing in what they had done that had actually been forbidden. She imagined herself standing in front of her parents in a posture of righteous indignation.

"But you never said. We never thought you would be cross." As the words ran through her mind, her face expressed the feigned innocence, but it felt hollow.

So, did she know they would be cross? At least now they had Ray and Alf's permission to visit the yard. There was no longer any likelihood of being caught trespassing or of being brought home by the strong arm of the law, the local bobbie with his navy uniform and helmet marching her home, her elbow firmly held in his big inescapable hand. The image had crossed her mind occasionally in the previous weeks, but it had not worried her unduly. The risk had only been there whilst they were actually in the yard. Once you left, they couldn't prove you'd been there. The important thing was not to get spotted. Trespassing was something she was used to. It was part of being young, and hardly something to get heated about.

So what was it about spending time with Ray and Alf that left her feeling so uneasy? Of course they had all been told since they were very small that talking to strangers was dangerous. A stranger could lure one into a car with offers of sweets. A stranger might steal you away and do bad things to you. When she was small, Joanne had been quite anxious about such things and had always walked past quickly when a car stopped by the roadside anywhere near to her, but over the years she had become gradually less concerned and now she sensed that if it ever happened, she would be able to outrun any threatening stranger. Just let him try! She muttered.

But Alf and Ray weren't strangers. They were part of the community, people they had known by sight for years. They weren't shady characters like the ones on the poster the police man showed them when he visited their school. Talking to them was no different to talking to the shop keeper at the newsagents when you bought sweets.

Perhaps there really wasn't anything wrong in what they were doing. If there was, perhaps it was just another strange quirk of adult thinking, like not putting your knife in your mouth, or hanging your coat up when you come in, even if you know you are going out again in half an hour.

Joanne still felt troubled. Despite her rationalizations and excuses, she sensed that there was something about the new friendship that would be worse in her parents' eyes than trespassing would have been, were they to discover the truth. It felt imperative that they kept the matter secret, yet she couldn't really explain to herself why. Perhaps she sensed that differences of class or profession mattered to her parents. Perhaps she recalled some vague injunction that she should not interfere with people who were at work.

Perhaps even, there was nascent intuition that friendship with the scrap yard men might pose a threat as yet undefined, but darkly disturbing to a ten year old girl.

Joanne sensed something of danger in the friendship. It was perhaps this edge of danger which made it both deliciously exciting and scary. The feeling of fascination and anxiety would compel her to keep returning to the yard, hiding in the strident confidence she cultivated, but as she did so, her sense of unease continued to grow.

CHAPTER THREE

Simon

Being guilty and feeling guilty are not the same thing. At a simple level, guilt and responsibility are linked. A legal perspective does not allow for guilt without the person having, through action or negligence, caused a harmful occurrence to unfold. Such guilt presupposes an element of intention, even if that intention was simply the misdirected attention that led to warning signs being ignored and a disaster left unaverted. Being guilty means being subject to culpability. It is objective. It requires an arbiter, an observer, a judge. Sometimes others proclaim us guilty. Often we judge ourselves and find ourselves to be in the wrong. We step back, watch, reflect, seeing our actions as if viewing a shameful other. We reflect, and in reflecting learn to criticise. We learn to see by seeing how others see, and so create internalised view points.

Yet, as we have found, there are different rule books. The path of childhood exposes us to different value systems, different views. Learning to live with such moral uncertainty is the process of maturation, of growing up. Or perhaps the child, through some innate sense of right and wrong, knows deeply what should and should not be.

When different sources conflict with one another, this leaves space for manoeuvre, for playing one voice off against another, for reconciliation and for silencing. In their everyday adventures, the children blithely skip between the injunctions they have learned. Sometimes they are troubled, but often more by fear of discovery than by true guilt. They take what is useful and ignore the rest, reinforcing their views with the comfort of companionship in crime. Yet even silenced voices can stir trouble in the heart.

In childhood, adult voices are powerful sources of direction for action, but also shape our thoughts. Parental directives create lines across the psyche that are not easily erased. The teacher's unquestioned assertions implant moral knowledge that forms strong currents in the mind. Yet adults have their own stories, their own biases. Shaped by their own histories, they plough uncertain directions and often are in conflict in themselves and with one another. How does this impact upon the child? How does the child develop in such circumstances, living amidst the impossibility of reconciling the opposing perspectives that lie within the heart of his world?

And so to Simon; a boy caught in just such cross-currents, just such turmoil. Let us see how Simon's world gives birth to guilt.

****

Simon was at his grandmother's when the children were first invited into the scrap yard. It was the Sunday of the spring half term break, a day when the roads would be quiet, and Simon's parents wanted to try out their new car, a second-hand Renault.

It was a boxy, noisy vehicle, with a nauseating smell of old leather and stale cigarette smoke. His parents did not smoke, but the previous owner had, and the aromatic legacy hung like a heavy spectre in the interior. His mother said it would soon go, and cheerfully sprayed the seats from an aerosol can of floral bouquet air freshener, but somehow that only seemed to make it worse.

A somewhat delicate child, Simon disgraced himself by being sick on a grass verge just past Basingstoke, and again just before Andover. When his mother pointed out signs to Stonehenge, he could raise little enthusiasm, but the raw wind of the Salisbury Plain, which whipped around them as they sat huddled on the lea side of one of the great grey stone slabs, eating tinned salmon sandwiches and Golden Wonder crisps and drinking turgid brown tea from the flask, did make him feel a bit better.

Back in the infernal belly of the car, though, his stomach was soon heaving once more, distributing its churned up apology for the picnic at a number of undefined locations between Wincanton and Oakhampton. At Launceston his mother suggested that he try to sleep, and so, lying curled up on the back seat of the car, he dozed fitfully for the remainder of the journey, jolted to and fro as the car swung round ever more twisting corners and over increasingly steeply valleyed terrain.

His grandmother lived in a small flat. It was in a new block of sheltered housing, purpose built for old people, with a warden and bell pulls in all the rooms. It looked out on a little courtyard, just off the main street in the middle of town. You couldn't see much out of the window except the other flats across the way, and the cats, though you could hear the cries of the herring gulls down on the fish quay.

The cats, of which there were four, belonged to different people in the flats. They didn't seem to like each other much, Simon thought, but stalked around with hunched shoulders, glaring at each other sideways, or sometimes stopping abruptly to spit and snarl, claws flailing for a brief moment, before skulking off to a distance where they would settle on a window ledge or plant trough to sun themselves in solitude on a fine day, or to lurk behind the dustbins or in doorways on a wet day. Otherwise the yard contained nothing except for the four bins and an old sack of compost that someone had left a long time ago, judging from its slouched, faded appearance. It was not a promising prospect for a young lad.

Simon's family couldn't stay at the flat. It only had one bedroom, which was Grandma's. They stayed up the road at a bed and breakfast run by one of the ladies from the chapel. The bed and breakfast had pink candlewick bed spreads and Simon had to sleep in the little put-you-up bed in the corner of his parents' room. He didn't like the way that Mrs Gurbidge referred to him as "your little boy", but she did cook good sausages for breakfast and there was tomato sauce.

Cornwall was going to last five days. Simon sighed as he tried to calculate what that would mean in hours and minutes and seconds, but he lost track of the noughts. It was grey and damp outside, a rain storm having blown in overnight. He tried to think how he could pass the time, but each thought only led him deeper into despair. If only Joanne were with him. That would change things. She would know what to do. He imagined them exploring the town together, ducking through shops and searching out alley ways. She'd get him out of here.

"Why don't you get out your puzzle book?" his mother asked anxiously, noticing his gloomy face. "Daddy will be back soon, and then we can go to the shops for Grandma's groceries."

His father had slipped out to get a newspaper, but he was taking a long time about it, Simon thought ruefully.

"I haven't got a pencil," he muttered.

"There's one by my bed, dear." Grandma was quite deaf, but sometimes she could surprise you and catch you unawares by hearing things you didn't intend her to hear. It made Simon uneasy.

He went into the bedroom. It was an old lady's room. It had cream walls with photographs of people Simon knew to be relatives, all looking much younger than they were now. A dressing table stood opposite him, with green glass pots and brushes on it, and trays of hair nets and safety pins and other mysterious old lady things, an open box of pink face powder, which had spilled untidily onto its dark varnished surface. Beside it, facing the window and sticking into the middle of the room, so that it seemed to take up all the space, was the bed, with its floral flounced eiderdown and heap of pillows. The whole room had that indefinable smell of the elderly, a sort of sweet mustiness that Simon imagined to come from some sort of decomposition that began before you died. It felt overpowering, as if it sapped his youth and wanted to swallow him up and make him old too.

The bedside table did indeed have a pencil on it. A short stub of yellow wood, sharpened with a knife. It also had Grandma's bible and a copy of the Frances Gay Friendship Book which had a glossy purple cover with a bunch of flowers on it. It looked like the picture on a bottle of toilet cleaner, Simon thought idly to himself.

Grandma was religious, a Baptist, but religion wasn't something they talked about in Simon's family because his father's side were all Catholics. He knew that his father had wanted him to go to the Catholic school, but his mother had prevailed, arguing that that would have meant a long journey on two buses which would be much too tiring to do every day. He knew she would win when he saw her fold her lips shut in that narrow way she did when she was angry but didn't want you to know. She hated religion and said so often at home when she thought Simon wasn't listening, but at Grandma's she did not say anything like that.

So as it was, Simon had gone to the local school, along with the other children from the cul-de-sac. He was in the same school year as Joanne, but not in the same class. There were two classes in each year. His birthday was in August. Hers was in April, making her a whole third of a year older than him. Often it felt much more.

Simon had been to the Catholic church occasionally. His father used to take him to Sunday morning mass at the big red sandstone church that was a twenty minute train journey away. They had to get up especially early to go, before even his mother was out of bed. The building was very tall and smelled of incense, he remembered, and there was a statue of the Virgin Mary with candles you could light, and a little red light hanging high up over the big altar that was supposed to be God. The priest had patted him on the head as they left the last time, and talked to his father about something called "first communion", and "classes", and some long words Simon had not understood. That was the last time they had gone and it was some time ago now. Simon didn't know what had happened, but he did sense that his father was uncomfortable about the whole episode, so he chose not to ask questions.

Back in the lounge, Simon sat at the gate-legged dining table under the window with his puzzle book. They were too easy, kid's puzzles. He felt cross as he did them, so that the pencil gouged channels in the cheap rough paper. If only they could go out and watch the men fishing on the quay, or peep into the dark interior of the penny arcade with its bright lights and whirring slot machines. Sometimes on previous visits to Grandma's, Daddy had taken him there when they went out alone. He sensed it was a man's place and that his mother did not approve. His father had given him a handful of loose change and shown him how to feed the pennies into the slot above the glass, and to watch as the coin rolled down the little ramp, fluttered chaotically for as long as you could hold your breath and settled on the moving metal bed, to be swept unrelentingly into the mass of other coins. It was all a matter of timing, his father had said, and he had showed him how to send one coin after another down the chute until enough coins lay flat on the shelf to push a cascade of pennies over the edge into the collecting bucket with a satisfying clatter. His father could win handfuls of pennies that way, but they always got fed back into the machine in the end. Then they would buy candyfloss from the vendor on the corner and walk home eating it. Those times shone like the bright fog lights in the harbour against the rest of his time at Grandma's. Perhaps they did for Daddy too. Simon thought he caught something conspiratorial in his father's look as he picked a stray piece of candyfloss off his Snoopy T-shirt before they went back into Grandma's flat.

"Must get you tidy before your mother sees you," he had said with a wink.

But this time, somehow, even that didn't happen. There were no special outings with Daddy on his own, just lots of time in Grandma's flat with the puzzle books and a couple of old Beano Annuals, and the occasional foray out to the shops.

So the five days passed. One afternoon his parents took him to see Thunderbirds at the town's cinema, but it was an old film and Simon had seen it before. Another day they drove the Renault, which seemed to be using rather more oil than it should, to a little cove nearby. Grandma came too that time, wrapped in blankets and protesting all the way that she was too old for this sort of caper, so Mummy had to sit in the back seat with Simon. They had tea in a little café on the sea front and Simon and his father went for a walk along the shoreline whilst Mummy and Grandma watched them through the window. The waves were grey and the wind was still very cold, blowing spray in their faces, but they skimmed stones and collected great horsewhips of sea weed, which they dragged along the sand leaving strange alien marks. Mostly, though, they did what they had come for and spent time with Grandma. After all, they had come to see her, and this wasn't really meant to be a holiday, as his mother had told him on the third evening when his frustration and boredom had boiled over into humiliating tears back at the bed and breakfast.

On Saturday they had set out once more to crawl back across the breadth of Southern England, belching substantial quantities of black exhaust as they went. Mummy had given Simon a pink pill that tasted of synthetic strawberries before they left the house because she said it would stop him being sick. He felt nauseous as soon as he swallowed it, and thought he was going to throw up then and there, but it lulled him into a drowsy stupor in which the journey seemed to pass more quickly than before.

Home was a relief. Hardly had the car crawled round the corner and into the tarmac driveway of the family house, than he felt better. It was as if a shadow had lifted from him, a spell, a curse; as if he had awakened from a deep mysterious sleep and found himself back in human form. He wanted, needed, longed to be back with the gang, to cast off this dragging, turgid child-self that hovered gauche and timid like an alien that had invaded his body and to find once more his better, bolder, independent self reflected in the company of his friends.

"I'm off out," he shouted as soon as he was out of the car, starting down the drive.

"But we're not even unpacked, dear," his mother protested

"Let him go," said his father.

Simon knew he would find the others in the Amazon. If they were not there, they would be on the factory ground. It was late afternoon. Soon the men would be packing up for the weekend and they would be able to get into the scrap yard. He felt his body, cowed and hunched from five days indoors, wanting to spring and leap on all those old mattresses, to jump and stamp and punch his way clear of the fog of the last week.

Nearing the fence, he heard voices. It was Joanne and the others. But where were they? It was too early to be in the scrap yard, yet it sounded as if they were already there. Maybe the men had finished early. It was odd though. Puzzled, he made the gang's dog bark, the call they used to summon one another. He waited for the familiar echo to answer. Where were they? To his surprise and relief, Joanne's face appeared at the hole in the fence.

"It's OK," she said, "you can come in. Alf and Ray know about us. They're friends now."

****

So Simon struggled to reconcile his conflicted worlds, and to find in their mirror a reflection of who he was. Identity, our fragile protection against raw exposure to life's unpredictable harshness, is so much a reflection of the conditions we inhabit. Illusory, it quickly scatters in the confusion of new circumstances.

The child, learning to adapt that sense of self to changing situations, tries to accommodate to the various pulls of different environments, and to the natural processes of growth and change in his own body. As adults we have more choices, more freedom to select our mirrors. The child has mirrors put before him not of his own choosing.

Simon was an only child. His parents, sober and respectable people, lived within the particular and often difficult parameters of their wider families. So Simon became the focus of many pressures. His ordeal unfolds. He is pulled first by the wishes of one parent, then the other, his grandmother entering the scene as a third and powerful influence, so there are three conflicting gravitational fields in his life. Theirs were generations where much was said with few words. Subtle messages were conveyed with a look, a frown, a raised eyebrow that could stop a child in its tracks. Respectability was the outward form, territorial battles often the real agenda. The child was both victim and beneficiary, caught in the cross fire, but learning how to manipulate the game.

In Simon's family, one area of conflict revolves around religious allegiances. Even with the liberalization of Catholicism that was going on during the sixties, a mixed marriage was still problematic. The scenario is complicated. Simon's mother is the daughter of a God-fearing chapel goer. She has no doubt had her own experiences of religious conflict, as she, for her own untold reasons, has broken away from Christianity of any form into an angry rejection of religion. So Simon is caught between the three: his father a guiltily lapsed Catholic, his grandmother, the Bible reading Baptist, and his mother who rejects both sides. Much is unspoken. The family visit is purposely timed to avoid Sundays. Appearances are preserved.

Beneath these deeply drawn lines, in all probability, lie other areas of dissonance, worn over the years through a thousand small failures of intimacy and the disappointments that all relationships deliver when their initial promise fades. Religious flags simply provide rallying points for unspoken conflicts.

It is the same with nations. The potent symbol of religious iconography adds venom to ordinary conflicts. Religious struggle rarely owes much to God or spirit. Far more deeply is it buried in our ordinary human nature.

****

Simon inhabits a difficult space, caught between worlds. At ten, he is already looking over the terrain of childhood with disdain, ready to step into adolescence. In his last year at primary school, like Joanne, he sees himself soon moving on, leaving the safety of that familiar territory. A bit of him longs for that move, resents the forces that pulls him back. He is angry with the childish puzzles and the fact that he does not have the courage to refuse to do them. He hates himself for being car sick, squirms with embarrassment each time he has to ask for the car to be stopped, humiliated as he stands retching by the road-side in full view of all the traffic, but circumstances conspire to infantilise him. He cannot escape the cloying company of his parents or find other ways to reassure himself of his maturity. Even where they stay in the bed and breakfast, he is treated like a baby, put in a bed that is little more than a cot in his parents' room; he is the "little boy". How hard it is not to fall back into childish ways, so recently been left behind, when such conditions are put in place. How easily such regression leads us into feeling shame.

Even as adults, it is not uncommon for people to regress when visiting their parental home. Capable people with responsible jobs become helpless and dependent. Some expect to be waited on, forgetting to do simple household tasks. Others are unable to assert themselves, putting up with criticism or bossiness. Yet others shrink from seeing their parents' vulnerability and cover their perceptions with a false heartiness and reassurance that nothing has changed.

Seeing our parents' weaknesses shakes our sense of our

parents' dependability. We hate to see that they are no longer the invincible, dependable anchors that we believed they were in childhood. Worse, we fear a future where we might be the carer and they might be old and defenceless. We fear the day when they may be gone.

How much greater the tendency to regression is for children, so recently infants, completely held in the parental space. Yet, how much more strongly to be resisted when the cost is to lose one's newly established independent identity, falling back into childish dependency.

Simon winces with shame and inwardly curses himself each time he uses the babyish terms "Mummy" and "Daddy", yet he cannot bring himself to throw them off and call his parents by any other name. It is not easy. Although he tries to imagine calling them "Mum" and "Dad" as his friends call their parents, each time he flunks it. He can only use the names he knows. They are, for him, simply Mummy and Daddy. The names are stuck in his mind like chewing gum on the pavement.

Even in naming his parents, Simon is pulled back. He feels younger, less confident. The walls of his home-world are tightly constructed, keeping him firmly in the role of child. There is no foothold on which to pull himself into his older self whilst confined in his family's company. Vainly he looks out of the window, but even the cats are hostile and imprisoned. The four miserable creatures seem to mirror the humans in their antagonism and lethargy.

Simon is also caught between the adults. He straddles the worlds of his parents just as he straddles childhood and adolescence. Sometimes he is stifled by his mother's constant attentiveness. Her irrefutable logic leaves no space for dissent. She is always ready to offer support and guidance. When he escapes, it is to join his father in his subversive jaunts. Two men together, he is drawn into a plot to participate in and enjoy activities of which his mother would disapprove. It is a common scenario. Fathers and sons bond through such shared escapades, a conspiracy of mutual benefit. The father feels young again, the son more grown up. "Your mother wouldn't like it. Don't tell her what we've been up to. We're lads together."

Simon is stranded in a world of forces which pull him back into childhood and also threaten to twist him apart on the rack of his parents' differences. He becomes a pawn in a genteel war of nerves, just as much as any child caught in a bitter divorce process. In some ways it is harder, for being unacknowledged and hidden in the shadows of politeness. The conflict is never quite visible. He cannot know for certain it is happening. He has no markers to steer by, no solid points of reference. An only child, he has no siblings with whom to compare notes or against whom to pit his perceptions. He only has the view presented by his parents. They are the adults, he the child.

How much of a relief then it is for him to leave that claustrophobic nest. Thankfully, he looks to Joanne to create a different role model. Her confidence and defiance exemplify all he wishes he could be. Her courage reflects the courage that he wishes he could muster. He does not see her frailty or her self-doubts. His feeling of shame and remorse at his own inability to remain confident or strong, cloud his vision so that she becomes the opposite, the example that guides his search for self-respect. He looks to her for guidance and follows her lead. He cannot allow her to be weak.

Even when she is not present, he imagines her there so that he can know how he should act. In this he gives to her even that part of him that is strong and courageous. It is his sacrifice to her. He could be different, but he does not recognise it. He attributes to her all the knowledge and power he finds in his heart. In this way he not only maintains his own familiar identity as loyal acolyte, but also hers as the leader and example. He holds her in the idealised, perfected state, keeping for himself the possibility that she will always, infinitely, be able to come to his aid.

The self, a fragile fortress, created from such distorted views, is our protection. The mechanisms by which we construct it are found in our relationships. By relating we find identity: the child, the parent, the friend. Sometimes we find similarities to those around us, sometimes distinctions. Creating roles that mesh with others, we seek out players to reinforce our ideas of who we are. Since childhood is the time when identity is built, relationships with others are important to the process of growing up. The child has much imposed, but also seeks out friendships, finding those who will protect the parts of himself that he values.

The identity is primarily protective, warding off a sense of vulnerability and our knowledge of the instability and unpredictability of life. Identity, however, changes as the child grows older and this is alarming. The same experience of fluidity and changeability which urges us towards maturity, also adds to our anxiety. The shifting sands of growing personality reinforces our experience of life's impermanence, frightens us and leads us to depend on others' stability. In our desire to escape the childish roles and find independence and adulthood, we create new anxiety that can drive us back into cycles of regression. So we try to find a fixed point, a guide, a mentor. And so Simon tries to escape through his admiration of Joanne. It is a common process. Such is the origin of adolescent adulation.

And what of guilt? Enmeshed in this complex of adult interests, Simon feels shame, and he also feels guilty. He feels guilty when he obeys his mother, because in his heart he knows he resents her and harbours anger. He knows that he is being inauthentic; that he is complying because he lacks the courage to do otherwise. He knows that he is not the willing child that he pretends to be.

At the same time he feels guilty because sometimes he enjoys colluding in his father's rebellion. His father gives him the strength to do the things he wants to do, but lacks the courage for. He feels guilty because he relies upon his father's help in escaping his mother, so that sometimes, although he does not enjoy what his father offers, he pretends to do so to keep his favour and displease his mother.

He feels guilty because he does not know how to tell his parents who he is, or what he wants out of life. He feels guilty because he is jealous of his grandmother because she gets so much attention, and very guilty that he sometimes thinks about her dying and wonders if she will leave the family any money. He feels guilty that he sometimes suspects his parents are not happy or that they are pretending things, but this he denies even to himself, creating a guilt of self-deceit.

This is not all. His father feels guilt that Simon is not being raised a Catholic, and his mother feels guilt that this choice has come about through her opposition. She senses that her opposition was not quite honest, that it was not really an opposition based on buses or practicalities, but on her unresolved religious war with her mother, who made her own childhood such a misery, leaving her all but damned by the age of eleven. How can the child not imbibe such guilt, curdling from his mother's breast, and swallowing it, make it his own? This was Simon's inheritance. Thus was the mire from which Simon struggled to free himself.

CHAPTER FOUR

Magazines

The children continued to visit the scrap yard regularly. In the initial excitement of their new adventure, they were hardly away from the place, turning up at the big chicken wire gates as soon as they were released from school, but gradually over the next weeks, as the days began to lengthen and the first new growth of spring began to push uncertain shoots of green among the tired fronds of ivy in the fence, the kids would sometimes go back to the Amazon to recover their old camps, renewing them with treasures begged from the scrap yard.

A symbiosis developed. The men would put by items that they found among their gleanings which they thought the kids would like, and the kids in return amused them with their brash cheek. The evening fry-ups remained a popular diversion, and happened with fair regularity, often on a Friday when school was finished for the week. Alf would tease the kids when they arrived.

"Sausages?" he'd say with feigned puzzlement, "who said anything about sausages? You'll spoil your dinners."

"But you've got some, I know you have,"

Michael could not contain himself, leaping up to plunge his hands into the bulging pocket of Alf's old tweed jacket where he knew he would feel the cold damp fleshy paper parcel that he knew Alf had picked up from the butcher's on his way back from his round.

Alf laughed. "OK, fair game."

There was time to cook on Fridays. School finished early, and, the next day being Saturday, evening meals at home tended to be later, more casual. It left just time to get the stove out, watch the sizzling, spitting sausages in the old aluminium frying pan turn from soggy pink fingers into tight shiny brown parcels, swelling to bursting point and sometimes breaking with a loud bang that spattered hot fat everywhere. They wrapped them in slices of bread and smothered them with Daddies sauce, impatient to sink teeth into the crusty, oozing sandwich, not caring that the hot fat burned their tongues and the juices dripped onto their anoraks.

It was one day while the boys were engrossed in preparing the sausage sandwiches that Joanne discovered magazines in the shed. She had gone into the shed to poke around in the pile of clutter. She didn't know what she was looking for, but she felt a little bored with the younger ones, who had resorted to lavatorial humour. Someone had suggested that the sausages looked like willies and they had all started to roll about giggling and pointing and the younger ones were threatening to have a look and see if their own or each other's anatomy was still intact. Sometimes such romping was amusing, but right now she found it rather trying. She needed something new to distract her until it was time to go home for tea.

She saw the pile of magazines tucked under the old table that served as a desk. The sun slanting in at the doorway caught their glossy covers.

At first her eye was attracted to the brightness of the pictures but she did not really look to see what they were. She thought they were women's magazines like the ones her mother read. She wasn't really interested and turned to carry on searching through the cardboard boxes piled beside the desk, wondering if there was anything she could put aside for her camp. As she turned, something caught her eye again and she looked back at the top magazine on the pile. Suddenly she noticed that the image on the cover, rather than being, as she had first thought, a woman in a swim suit, was actually of a woman with very little clothing on at all. In spite of herself she blushed. Then she saw the title, *Playboy*.

Joanne's breath stopped. She swallowed. Instantly she felt both naïve and embarrassed, realising in a flash what she had stumbled on. She knew enough to know that *Playboy* was a magazine that some men read that was all about sex, but she had no idea really what it was like. She was both horrified and filled with curiosity. Her heart was racing. She glanced behind her to check that the door was shut, which it was, then tentatively she reached out and picked up the top copy and began to leaf through the pages.

Initially she was shocked. She had never seen an adult woman naked, apart from the rather demure classical paintings of nymphs and goddesses in the local museum and art gallery. She had been there on school outings. Now, the sight of so many women's bodies spread-eagled across the page, naked or near naked, made her want to recoil. Yet, a second impulse followed fast of the heels of her shock. She wanted to see more. She found herself drawn compulsively to the images, compelled to at the, page after page.

There were articles too. She flashed her eye across the pages, but she felt too distracted to read anything. She flipped through, turning the pages quickly with her finger tip as if she didn't really want to touch them, yet unable to stop herself. For a few moments she was completely caught in a different world, a world where she felt a stranger. Those few moments were enough. In a wave of panic she remembered that the others were outside. Someone might come in. Soon the sausages would be ready and they might come looking for her. Red-faced, she stuffed the magazine back on the heap and started sorting through the pile of old biscuit tins on the desk, making a clatter as she did so.

"Look casual," she told herself, pulling herself up straight, she slipped out of the hut.

Ray was unloading the scrap metal. An old sink, and a water tank topped the load and he was struggling to control them as he pulled pipes and hoses from round them. Alf, cooking sausages, looked up.

"Hey, gi' us a hand 'ere," Ray shouted at him.

Alf took the pan off the stove and put it on the ground beside the loaf of bread. The sausages were cooked, charred on the edges, but still pink where they had erupted out of their skins. They still spat occasionally as they settled in the fat, jerking around as they did so.

"Here Joanne, stop messing around and come and sort these out," he shouted. Then he sauntered over to where Ray was.

Joanne stood still for a moment blinking. Alf was looking her way, looking to see why she wasn't dealing with the pan of sausages. She blushed. Did he know what she had been doing? She turned to the boys so he wouldn't see her face and made herself busy sorting out their sandwiches.

That night Joanne lay in bed troubled by what she had seen. Whenever she shut her eyes she saw again those pictures of naked women. She had stayed home after dinner. The others had called round, but she told her mother to tell them she had belly ache, so Michael and Ian went out without her. It was even partly true. She did feel strange in her stomach. Sort of quivery and sick all at once, like she'd been too long on the waltzers at the fair. She'd tried to read in her room, skimming a book she had read before, but her mind wouldn't settle. She kept thinking about what she had seen.

As she lay in the dark, Joanne tried to reason with herself. Alf and Ray hadn't changed. She knew them. They were fun to be with, her mates. They were up for a lark and knew what you were thinking more than you did sometimes. They were not bad. Perhaps the magazines were not theirs. Maybe they had just been given them with a pile of junk collected from an empty house. Maybe they were storing them for someone.

But try as she might, in her heart she felt dirty. She felt a dark, cloying, panicky feeling deep in her body that seemed to creep through her guts like slime and whispered of something dangerous. She felt the sweat rising through her and though she tried to turn away and bury her face in the pillow, she could not escape it. She could not think of Alf or Ray in the same way she had done before. The memory of the smell of sausages lingered in her nostrils, making her feel nauseous. Her throat gagged, but she swallowed hard. She was not sure that she would ever be able to face going back to the scrap yard.

"Get a grip. Don't be a sissy," she told herself angrily, biting her lip as she breathed the words into the darkness.

She couldn't lose face and refuse to go out with the others, so she forced herself to think of Ray and Alf in the way she had before she found the magazines. She imagined the time before she went into the hut, before it all changed. After all, they had not changed. She had to get back to feeling comfortable. She had to be able to go back to the scrap yard.

"They are just the same men. They are just the same men. They are just the same...." Her mind repeated over and over, "Don't be a scaredy cat, they're Ray and Alf. They find interesting things for our camp and cook sausages. They're just ordinary. They're just the same men."

Gradually the fever subsided, and she relaxed. They really were still Ray and Alf. Nothing had changed. As the rush of anxiety faded, in its wake the other feeling began to grow: curiosity. Almost as compulsive as her fear, it rushed in, tugging at her thoughts. Her body still felt charged, edging between the anxiety and something else, something completely new and compelling.

"They're just bodies," she told herself, forcing herself to recall the pictures. "That's what grown ups look like without their clothes."

The images floated, now seductive in her mind. Curious, she strained to remember what she had seen. Languid women, stretched out on rumpled red satin sheets. Breasts impossibly big, pushed forwards toward the camera, or squashed together between hands, whose outstretched fingers ended in scarlet talons. She placed her hands on the flat expanse of her own rib cage and wondered how it would be to have something grown there, something that didn't exist yet but that one day she would have to accept as part of her body. Could that really be how her body would look when she grew up? The photos were luridly pink and fleshy. They reminded her of the great carcasses of meat that hung in the butcher's window. She saw a pig, pink and naked with tiny eyes and a round open snout.

Having once thought of that great pig with its fixed smile and tiny eyes, she couldn't get the image out of her mind. She felt disgusted. She did not want her body to change that way. Why did it have to happen?

Of course she knew about growing up. A girl in her class had "started" early, and she had told the others all about how it felt. She said you could feel it slipping out. It just happened. You couldn't control it. They had all huddled in the corner by the kitchen door in the bit of the school yard that was officially out of bounds, and whispered about it until the boys found them and wanted to know what was going on. Joanne didn't like the girl, but on this occasion she hovered on the edge of the group to hear what she could. She didn't like the sound of growing up.

Joanne did not really fit in very well at school. Most of the other girls in her class were from the area immediately round the school. They clacked along in slip-on shoes with little heels, and back combed their hair and licked pencils to draw their eye brows darker or to line their eyes, peering into the brown speckled mirrors in the girls' toilets. Sometimes they bought real make-up pencils or pale peach colour lipsticks from Woolworths, which worked much better, making them look like ghosts.

She'd see them in the cloakroom at the end of the day, surreptitiously trying to put on make-up before they went out of school. Of course, sometimes they got caught and sent back to wash that muck off their faces. They would smirk and mince past the windows of the secondary modern, hoping to catch the attention of the lads as they sat out the last hour of the day in the school on the adjacent site, then run back giggling stupidly. Joanne thought they were silly, so she avoided them as much as possible. She had got a job as milk monitor, usually a boy's job, to avoid having to go out at playtime, but at dinner time she had no choice.

Of course none of the gang talked to her at school. You couldn't be seen associating with boys or with children from other classes. That would be akin to suicide in the playground. The kids from the cul-de-sac walked past one another with lowered eyes in school, acknowledging each other with a sideways look or muttered greeting.

When she was not carrying milk crates, Joanne hung around with a couple of other girls who were also on the periphery of the main crowd. Sarah wore blue plastic glasses and had a squint and Wendy was in love with Paul McCartney. Both were misfits in different ways. Sarah was quiet and read a lot. Joanne liked her because she had lots of ideas and wrote stories about them in hard backed exercise books which she bought from Smiths. She also always knew answers in class, which the other children didn't like. They teased her for it. Wendy lived with her mother and two older sisters and didn't have a Dad. She didn't talk about her home life much and was more Sarah's friend than Joanne's. They both lived in the semi-detached houses across the main road, so Joanne did not see much of them out of school. If she was honest, this did not worry her over much. She secretly hoped that when she went to the grammar school, she'd leave them all behind and find some better friends. In the mean time she whiled away the time as best she could, half engaged in their conversations, and half thinking about what she would do that evening.

As she lay with her churning thoughts, Joanne wished for a moment that she had a real friend. If only there were a girl she could really trust. Somehow, Sarah and Wendy just wouldn't understand. She wanted someone whose opinion she could ask. Suddenly she felt very alone.

****

So Joanne struggled with her discovery, caught between the feelings of shame and revulsion that the images had evoked in her, and her tentative curiosity about the changes which lay ahead in her life and, in particular, for her body. Still innocent, yet knowing enough to recognize the forces which she was unleashing, did such feelings constitute guilt?

Her discovery was accidental, but in some senses it was already embedded in the secretiveness that underlay much of her life outside her home. The seeds of guilt were ready to sprout. She shouldn't have been in the scrap yard. There were already layers of self-deception in the reasoning she used to justify this to herself. She was acting against what she knew to be her parents' wishes. Her arguments were built of sand. She knew that she would be in trouble if she were ever discovered there by her family.

On that particular day she had gone into the hut to escape. In some ways she was taking advantage of Ray and Alf's good nature. It wasn't exactly dishonest, but she shouldn't have been there. She was avoiding the ennui of the boys' conversation, but also she was probably testing the limits of what she could get away with. She might try to wheedle some special favour from the men, a small item for her camp maybe. She was taking advantage of her privileged access to the hut, which gave her a special entrée into the space where the men kept their personal items. She was pushing the limits and playing with the possibilities.

She had already crossed several lines. Her first entry into the yard, her cheeky defiance when she spoke back to Alf, had both been wrong. She was fascinated by the roughness of the men, their tattooed arms and hairy chests, the folds of Alf's beer gut. She had smelled their sweat and thought it disgusted her, yet, without even being aware of it, had noticed its masculinity. She enjoyed bantering with them. She liked being the only girl. Liked the way it made them treat her differently, the way that she could get away with more cheek, more innuendo. All this brought extra excitement to her visits to the yard. Mostly the feelings were unrecognised, but perhaps they meant that she went more often than she otherwise would have, and that she put up with the younger boy's irritating habits. They were, after all, her alibi. In its unacknowledged potency, such excitement may create the seedbed of guilt.

****

The last year at primary school marks threshold. The child, standing on the verge of adolescence, is ready to launch into the undefined future. That last year, in the familiarity of the school that has been the focus of life for so many years, new possibilities start to appear on the horizon. There is a restlessness, a readiness to move on, feelings that can quickly spill over into frustration.

So it was. Girls tried on make-up, flirted with older boys, innocent, yet precocious. The children grew arrogant and bored, ready to throw off the childish stigma of the small school. They were bored with class mates with whom they had already spent what seemed an eternity, bored with teachers whom they had known since infancy, bored with the same structure of lessons that they had had right through the junior school. Everything seemed small and narrow minded. The class rooms with their small chairs and desks, the toilets with their low basins, the small children who ran about screaming and shouting and falling over one another, or clasped your hand adoringly in the playground, gazing up with big eyes. They were all boring.

A surly conspiracy of resistance grew.

It was humiliating too. A growing consciousness of approaching puberty made children shy away from their bodies. They resented the gym classes, where, in those days, boys and girls had to change together in the same cloakroom and climb on apparatus wearing gym knickers, side by side, too close for comfort. Swimming lessons were embarrassing too, but then, so were singing in choirs or performing arts. It was not just bodies that were embarrassing, but anything that threatened to single out or expose the child. In the big school it would be different. The children looked forward to proper sports facilities, to showers and team games, to specialist coaching, and to choice.

Strange that within a matter of weeks those same children would become the "little first years" at the big school, but in those last months of junior school they became monitors, supervised the classes of younger children, ran errands, and took mugs of tea to staff on playground duty. In such tasks the pre-teen child preserved dignity, and, though still locked in the junior school, discovered a more comfortable identity as they were trusted with leadership.

So it was that Joanne, struggling with her feeling of alienation from her class mates, bored with trying to reconcile differences with children whom she had little affinity for, looking forward to new opportunities for different friendships, found solace in responsibility. She tested her strength, lauded her boyishness, demonstrated her capability, as she shifted milk crates, and deferred the difficult feelings that were stirring in her. Her mind struggled to rationalize, to hold back the tide of inevitable change, whilst at the same time longing for things to be different.

****

Amid the pressures of this dark pre-adolescent world, where shadows as yet undefined hint at a future world of new excitements and concerns, Joanne accidentally encountered a powerful new energy. It both scared and excited her. Already latent, to this point her interest in such matters had been distant, confined to small incidents and fragments of information. Now it could not be kept in the shadows any longer. The door was open. Once open, there was no closing it. Her feelings, which had been tentative and experimental, were suddenly thrown into confusion when she discovered the magazines.

At ten, Joanne inhabited the in-between land betwixt childhood and puberty where sexuality is still uncharted territory. Dawning interest presses the child to search for information. Knowledge is scattered, but comes from a surprisingly number of sources. Disjointed and ungrounded in experience, the child gleans whatever information is available. The girl who started menstruating early shared her experiences with the other girls. Joanne listened in. No doubt there were other sources too: older sisters, books in libraries or on the shelves of family friends, medical dictionaries. Such were the contributions that were shared in playground conversations.

We girls wanted to know what it was all about. Back in the sixties it wasn't always easy, but it was surprising what you could discover. At lunchtimes my class mates and I sat on an iron staircase outside our classroom, sharing our knowledge. The pooling of information cut across the limits of friendship groups. Even girls who rarely spoke to each other joined in such conversations. It was our final year at primary school. We were a small class, with just eight girls, so it was easy to get together and talk in giggles and whispers. One girl had a book that her brother had given her. I guess it was some sort of biology textbook that described the technicalities of reproduction. We listened in rapt attention as she passed on information, explained the diagrams, and shared the details we were hungry for.

Yet knowing about sex was not necessarily an advantage. It could be embarrassing to be too knowledgeable. If older friends told you too much, you could be left in cringing agony when naïve questions were raised by others.

"What's a prostitute?" asks a class mate, putting up her hand.

The teacher turns and looks at us before answering.

It is my first year in the new secondary school. I am a new girl, shy and quiet. I feel my throat lurch in horror. I know the answer because my friend, who is in the year above me, told me. We spent hours together scouring the dictionary for definitions of words like that. You went round fruitless circles. A prostitute was a harlot. A harlot was a whore. A whore was a prostitute. What use was that? Then my friend asked another girl in her class who knew, and she told me. So it was we both knew. But we knew not to ask the teachers about words like that.

So now, how can this girl be asking? Does she not know what it might mean? Should I not know? I feel the blood rising to my hair roots; I want to hide. Please don't ask me. Don't see that I know. Don't see I am not innocent. I am contaminated by knowledge that cannot be unlearned.

Yet, in that in-between world, to adult eyes, all is innocence. The scraps of knowledge are just small excursions into the adult world that lies ahead. The slow, steady accumulation of experience is just a normal part of growing up, but sometimes something intrudes before the child is ready. The child is shocked, recoils.

Seeing the images in the magazines was just such a shock for Joanne. It would have been for any of us at that age. Of course, she knew such magazines existed. Perhaps a girl at school had talked about a brother keeping such magazines under his mattress. She knew in theory that such magazines had pictures of naked women in them. She knew they were something some men read. Not nice men like your father or uncle, but other men, men in dirty rain coats who scampered furtively along dark alley ways with brown paper parcels, or who might even, so Wendy had told her, if you were unlucky enough to meet one, open their rain coats and expose themselves to you (though what exactly they would expose they were both uncertain.)

Both repelled and fascinated, Joanne's interest was caught, guilt and her natural curiosity inflaming feelings she barely recognised. This so often is our early introduction to our sexual nature. Confusion and secrecy mask spontaneous pleasure, and the certain knowledge arises that this is the danger which parents have hinted at but not dared to speak directly. Hidden in the secret spaces of the mind, where stories we tell ourselves conflict with our deeply known truth, we feel guilt rising. In the first scent of excitement and danger as our sexual instincts start to emerge, conflicted and silenced, we sometimes wish we could return to childhood innocence.

And so Joanne lay, tossing and turning. Now she longed for a real friend. A friend could share the secret, and be the mirror that reflected her dilemmas and found answers. A friend could reassure. Caught in a boyish world, Joanne lacked female allies. The girls she knew at school provided a modicum of social companionship, but pride held her back from really confiding in them. She did not share her home world with anyone at school, nor did she acknowledge her friendships with Simon or the others. Their friendships cut across the natural lines of playground society, and revealing them would lead to ostracism. Joanne, the leader, was cornered by her strength, restricted by her burden of assumed authority, preserving her independence at the cost of real friendship. So she looked forward, hoping for opportunities that her new school would bring; a fresh start, new people, more like herself.

****

One source of anxiety for the growing child comes from parental messages. In the sixties, when sexuality was just being invented, few parents talked openly with their children about sexual matters, especially when the children were still in primary school. Later they would probably convey to their children rudimentary information about "the facts of life". Meantime, their hesitance, embarrassment, and fear of questions conveyed in silence a message of danger and forbidden fruit. Two decades later the advent of AIDS changed that and sex education was high on the agenda.

In what was not said, parents often conveyed their fear and shame. The child should not see, not know, and above all, must not participate. Some children took heed of this, becoming timid, and developing other interests, immersing themselves in sport, childhood pursuits, horse riding and tennis. Others felt the attraction of forbidden fruit, and dared themselves to venture secretly into the territory beyond the line, experimenting with one another or alone, talking in whispers about boys, and perhaps becoming fast girls, the ones "who would". Thus another source of guilt is born.

Parents, in the craziness of human unconscious wishes, in part at least, hoped against nature that their children would remain children for ever. They longed for them not to know and to grow up in innocence. They wanted to draw a line between themselves and their offspring where such matters remained secret and unspoken. Some maybe even wanted to deny their own sexual nature, though it was irrevocably proven in the child's existence. Such motivations, of course, lie beneath the surface of the mind, currents which direct the flow of thought, but are themselves unseen.

Thus, in the tangled complexity of human relationships, it is impossible to please. We face the contradictions of other people's minds and their illogical expectations. We are bound to fail. So we are born to guilt. The person that the child becomes cannot conform to the contradictory ideals which they would like us to fulfil. In the face of their child's hormonally changing body, the parent has to change their view, but also, in doing so, faces a challenge to their identity. They are no longer the parent of a child. Their role has changed, and we are the cause. Our natural process bids us grow and explore, but parents long to wrap their children safe and secure in the habitual family ways. And so for all these reasons, completely unjustifiably, guilt grows.

****

Sexual guilt pervades the Western psyche and cloaks the female form. Eve tempted Adam with forbidden fruit. Since then women have embodied original sin. Potent and feared, female sexuality lurks in the darker recesses of the social mind. There are many precedents, mythic and cultural. In Western minds the female archetype is frequently ensnared with taboo and magic; the seductress, the predatory emasculator, the sexual woman, voracious, dangerous, and powerful.

For containment, male authority is summoned. The woman becomes tamed, held in the sway of her father, brother or husband. Free and independent she would find her basic nature; become the wild woman or the whore, a loose cannon, unpredictable and frightening. The virgin, maiden goddess, mother of Christ, becomes the ideal of feminine innocence, non-sexual, adored and worshipped for her purity. She is to be emulated. The sexual woman, on the other hand, nurses within her body the guilt of human kind, and in her womb, swaddles the legacy of The Fall.

And so the young girl learns to fear her sexuality and feel it as contamination. How strongly is it woven into our culture and our collective knowing, this web of guilt, that our sexual nature becomes our sin.

****

Even today, society is far more outraged over explicit sexual images in cinema or books than over violence. Children are meticulously protected from pornography, with censorship and internet restrictions, yet parents often happily collude as they slaughter each other in war games or pore over cartoon books of torture and destruction. Naked bodies are censored from imagery for the young, whilst dead or mutilated bodies are commonly portrayed in comic books and television drama. What inconsistent logic views the act of love as more corrupting than the act of callously taking life?

It is uncomfortable for adults to recognize that children, even from an early age, far from lacking interest in these subjects, are often drawn, fascinated, to seek them out. Why else are fairy tales so full of themes of love and death?

This is not some aberration but simply a natural unfolding of instincts. But adults are not happy knowing that their children are not the innocents they would wish. Small wonder Freud was so shocking to his time. A state of separate development grows up. Children find their own ways to investigate. They experiment tentatively, away from parental eyes. Children's bedroom doors are shut. They play in hidden spaces away from adult eyes.

So Joanne, young and innocent, stands at the fence, defying and taunting the men with her girlish cheek, her youthful confidence, experimenting with her ability to charm. She is alluring in her childish ways, challenging them with her independence, trading on her special status as the only girl. Labelled by millennia of female images and myths whilst still oblivious of the implications, she straddles childhood and adolescence and tests her power.

Joanne was tempted; caught by forbidden fruit of knowledge that had as yet been hidden from her; caught by a rising tide of feelings, undefined and unacknowledged yet inviting, that surged up in her, even as she felt fear. So her instincts drove her on. Hardly aware of the implications she wanted to return to the yard.

CHAPTER FIVE

Wendy's Story

The child's capacity to see the emotions of others varies. Even quite small children sense the feelings of their parents, and are deeply affected by the grief, the anger, and the disappointment of those around them. They learn to read the signals and to anticipate the response. They learn to manipulate, to choose their moment. Survival depends on it.

Empathy is an early mechanism by which we maintain our safety. Incidentally, through empathy, we learn to establish relationships. From the first rewarding smile, the baby learns to please, to entertain, to seduce. And so the mother falls in love again, and loving, cares selflessly, even to her own detriment.

But children can also be unaware of others' feelings, lack insight. Sometimes they need to preserve ignorance. Locked in the grandiosity of the infant self, slowly new ways of interacting grow, chiselled from experience to fit new circumstances, yet still emergent. Through these experiences, new identities are created. The child breaks out of the rigidity of his initial grandiose state through bruising encounters with others he encounters, but also through meeting their love and seeking to give it. He learns to adapt to the needs of those around, and even to care about them, but this can be at a cost. Sometimes it is better to retreat into ignorance. The first glimmerings of compassion fight for space with fears of annihilation. The child sees and does not see, on occasion astute and wise, but at other times oblivious to others' state.

In the misery of social isolation, pride, the protector of the self, throws up walls of ignorance. How can the child let herself know or understand the other, without relinquishing the fortress? The failure of friendship, itself a deep source of shame, masked by more utilitarian companionship, hides many lonely children. Back to the wall, they coexist, go through the motions of playground chatter, but keep the secrets within their hearts a closed book.

To Joanne, Wendy was a companion of this kind; another girl who tagged along, Sarah's friend, someone for her to wile away lunch hours with, a representation of a friend, but not really known. Joanne kept her privacy, kept her private world intact, lived for the time when she could rule her own kingdom. It never occurred to her to let Wendy into this world. So, what of Wendy?

****

Wendy had no father. She lived with her mother and two sisters in a semi. This Joanne knew. Wendy had dark kinky hair, pale brown skin with freckles on her face and arms, and a chubby flat nose, unlike her older sisters and her mother who all had coppery gold hair and pale skins. Their father had left soon after Wendy was born. They didn't talk about him because he never wrote and had stopped sending money ages ago. Wendy's mother had had to go back to work when Wendy started school and she now managed a hairdresser's shop on the high street. It was a trendy hairdresser's, with stands of brightly coloured costume jewellery on the counter top and a row of dresses for sale too. She employed two stylists, young women who hovered behind the row of wet haired customers on their stilettos, wielding long pointed scissors and tail combs. Wendy would go to the salon on Saturdays to help out with the sweeping up so that her mother could keep an eye on what she was up to. Her mother gave her two shillings pocket money out of the till for doing it, which made her feel important.

The older girls were in their teens. They went to the secondary modern next door to Wendy's school and until last year she had had to wait for them in the yard every day so that they could see her home across the main road, but now she walked back with

Sarah, crossing the busy lanes of traffic with the lollipop lady. There was always a crowd of boys crossing too. They shouted insults at one another and liked to try to hit the lady's round stop-sign as they passed it. Wendy was nervous of them, but Sarah just put her tongue out if they made any comment to her.

Of Wendy's sisters, Maureen, the eldest, was in her last year at school. She wanted to go on to college to learn hairdressing and work with their mum in the shop. Kerrie, a year younger, wanted to be a secretary, but she had to pass some exams called "O-levels". Wendy's mum worried that she wouldn't pass, but Kerrie just laughed. She was confident. Wendy thought both her sisters were beautiful, and she envied their straight hair. They would spend hours combing it out and curling the ends to create flick-ups so that they looked like the women on the adverts in Mum's magazines. Sometimes Mum would let them do it in the salon. They filed their nails into long, smooth ellipses and they painted them bright red on days when they did not have to go to school.

Although later in life, Wendy would discover that men found her unusual looks attractive, her long limbs and afro hair coming into fashion by the time she hit adulthood, and her honey coloured skin and freckles giving her a disarming charm, at eleven she felt self-conscious and ugly. In particular she felt acutely aware of her difference from the rest of her family. She could not have articulated the reasons for this, but a feeling of shame pervaded her life. Whether this was of her own making, a sensitivity to instinctive forces that she did not understand, or whether she had learned it from others, whose reactions suggested curiosity and even pity, was uncertain. People would look at her sisters and her mother and then look at her and their eyes would ask questions. Sometimes these would be articulated.

School had been difficult for Wendy. She was conscious that her appearance was different from others around her. Although there were black children whose families had come to London from the Caribbean, she was not one of them. Her family were

Irish on her mother's side, and she didn't know who her father was. When she was in the infant school, other girls had been curious about her hair, fascinated by her matted crinkles, sometimes patting them or trying to pull them straight. This was only childish interest, and felt friendly and she quite enjoyed being an object of attention, but it still made her aware that she was different.

As she got older, things took a turn for the worse. She was in the second year of junior school when she became aware that a couple of girls in the class were whispering about her. They would be huddled together in the corridor or in corners of the yard and would giggle as she passed. She did not know what they might be talking about, but this made her all the more uncomfortable.

Eventually the girls could no longer contain their secret. "My mum says your mum was a bad woman. That's why she got you," Sharon sneered. She was a big girl with dark brown hair in a pony tail and a red face. Wendy was frightened of her, as, probably, were many of the others in her class.

Wendy went home that night and cried, buried deep under her bed covers where no one could hear her. She did not know what Sharon had meant but she felt deep in her being that she was right and that whatever was wrong was her fault. Perhaps that was why their father had left. Nobody had said. She knew now that she was somehow bad, flawed; different from others in the depth of who she was. She had no idea why or how she knew it, but somehow she was shameful. She did not want her mother to know what Sharon had said; that her mother was being tarred as bad and somehow it was because of her. Her instinct told her that if she talked about it to her mother or her sisters they would be badly hurt. More than that, they might hate her. Telling them might make it true. Keeping quiet stopped the shame, kept it within her. It contained the demon that had been set loose.

So Wendy became silent. In class she shrunk away from the company of the other girls. She had always been shy, and now, as she lost confidence, her tentative friendships dissolved. She imagined that whatever Sharon knew, they now all knew. She dared not try to find out the truth. She felt ill at ease, out of place, as if she were inhabiting a life to which she did not belong. When the teacher read the story of *A Midsummer Night's Dream* to the class from *Lamb's Tales of Shakespeare*, she heard of the changeling and wondered if she were one such creature, switched by the faeries with the legitimate child of the family, a wayward half-being from another shadowy world.

For most of the year Wendy was desperately lonely at school. At home her sisters still spoilt her and let her watch them as they experimented with new make-up and hair styles and shortening their hem lines with the new fashions. There was always pop music playing on their radios or Wendy would put their records on the red box gramophone. In particular she liked *The Beatles*. Kerrie bought her a big poster of Paul McCartney for her wall. Wendy would look at his kind dark eyes as she lay in bed. He understood how she felt.

But Wendy was still very sad inside. She never told her sisters what Sharon had said, or how she and the others still taunted her, putting nasty notes in her gym bag and making up names for her. She felt deeply humiliated, and hoped against hope that the teachers would not notice and find out about her unpopularity. She always tried to look busy whenever an adult passed by in the playground or school corridors so as not to draw attention to herself.

Eventually Wendy got to be friends with Sarah. Sarah had also been the butt of Sharon's ridicule because of her glasses and squint, and because she didn't join in with the other girls in the yard. Wendy encountered her hiding in the cloakroom one lunch time, crying. It was a moment when suddenly, profoundly, she realized that she was not alone. The two girls sat there talking, hiding among the anoraks and gym shoes on the wire framed hangers until the dinner lady shooed them out into the yard.

Sarah told her how she hated playtime and couldn't wait to get back into class.

As they talked, Sarah wanted to know more about Wendy. What did her Dad do? What did her Mum do? Did she have brothers and sisters? Wendy was surprised at how little Sarah knew about her, because she had imagined that everyone in the class was talking about her. Surely Sarah had heard that she was bad, responsible for the family troubles? Surely she knew.

She took a deep breath. Suddenly an expanse of possibilities opened up. What were the facts? She knew nothing, nothing for sure. There were only stories, other people's stories. But Sarah did not know these. As far as she was concerned, the past was a vast white piece of paper. Wendy could use it to write her life the way she wanted it to have been.

"My Dad died when I was a baby," she said. "He was a famous rock climber and he fell when he was on a mountain. They tried to rescue him, but he died."

****

So Wendy struggled with the truth she did not know. Deflecting an invisible opponent, she manoeuvred her way around unseen obstacles in the darkness. She felt shame in the depth of her being, but did not, and indeed, could not know its roots, which had been sown in the adult world before her birth.

Within the turgid waters of her experience she sensed areas of danger. Her looks spoke of her difference, her father's departure after her birth linked her for ever to this abandonment. Was she responsible? Surely, she must be.

Moreover, she was not like her mother or sisters, so maybe she was like him. Maybe she was of his flesh and blood, his line of descent. The talk of his irresponsibility, his bad influence in the family, coloured her sense of the heritage he had left her. Perhaps this is why she felt the need to defend him. With what relief

Wendy created a story to tell Sarah, seizing the opportunity to allay the rumours which she imagined were circulating in the class, and in doing so, gave herself a new, more positive history.

Much was unknown, and in such circumstances, the child builds its own fiction. The story may be positive, as that which Wendy told Sarah. This is rare. Often the story is far less benign. The child, reflecting on its troubled sense of its own history, forms a hideous explanation, which lurks, half conscious, colouring the growing identity.

Wendy created a dramatic story of her mountaineer father intentionally, but this was not the story that she told herself within her head. That tale was different. There she imagined herself to be a profligate, a good-for-nothing wastrel like her father. This private story, instigated by her shame, was assembled out of a thousand nuances. Adult conversations, reactions half caught in the corner of the eye, Wendy felt the story embedded in her bones and from it drew little comfort. Against this deep-felt knowledge, the tale of tragic death was just a hollow foil.

The sense that Wendy had of her real story was not created from an empty slate. Wendy had not had the same early experience of family that her sisters had enjoyed. As two small girls with two parents, they had been a normal family. Such a foundation was not part of her experience.

In the sixties, single parents were fewer than they are today and the single mother, the broken marriage, was still a source of stigma. Reactions were varied. Some pitied Wendy, the child abandoned by her father. Others regarded her with suspicion and disdain, a faulted child born of a faulted union, offspring of irresponsible parents. Adults related to her according to their view. She was an object of sympathy or critical regard, but was never ordinary.

And whilst Wendy was baffled by the difference of her own appearance, adults cynically speculated. Why had her white, Irish father left with not a word? Where had her mother found the money to set up in business? How had she moved to the street of semis on the better side of the main road? Why were her girls so unalike? The better mannered wondered in silence, but the loud mouthed speculated more publicly.

"We can all guess what Aileen was up to," they would say. "Small wonder Patrick left. Any self-respecting man would. Giving birth to that half-caste, what did she expect? A man doesn't want his nose rubbed in it every day, over the breakfast table."

And they would look and shake their heads, as they stood at the school gates. Wendy, the little girl, clutching the painting she had brought home to show mummy, did not know why they looked at her in that way, or why her mother stood a little to the side, away from the other mothers.

The child does not see or understand in ways an adult might, but the feeling of wrongness still creeps into its heart, tearing apart confidence. It is hard to grow tall amid such unspoken rebuffs.

The story of her conception was a mystery. We can surmise in Wendy's arrival, evidence of her mother's indiscretion. We can surmise that her mother may have felt ambivalence towards her. We do not know. She may have been a love child, or perhaps the focus of regret, a source of embarrassment, perhaps a symbol of defiance, or a bid for freedom from an abusive marriage. We are not told. Wendy's mother keeps her secrets. But we can imagine complex emotions a mother might have had surrounding this child and how these might have manifested in her manner of mothering.

The relationship Wendy had with her mother may have been difficult for other reasons. The other daughters look like their mother. They look alike, reflecting each others' features, and confirming the mother-daughter bond. Wendy was not a mirror to her mother's looks. Just as Wendy notices the difference in their appearance, so too, did her mother - so like her father, and so different from me, her colour, her hair, all alien, not the fruit of my own flesh at all. What a psychological challenge to raise such a child. So in that earliest meeting, beneath her mother's gaze, the nurturing influence within which the child-mind grows, the early message grows "you are not of me, something is wrong".

So Wendy created a story, a cover, to plaster over the murky uncertainty of her origins. It is a common strategy. In a sense it is what we all do, perhaps not in such an obvious way, but subtly adjusting reality to make a coherent and flattering truth that we can show to others without shame. We call it spin. As we struggle with anomalies and uncomfortable facts, we find respite in justification after the event. We use logic. We create stories. Without such a tale, we thrash in mental turmoil between understandings that don't fit together or that show us in a bad light. We long for it to not be so. With the tale, we settle into a created reality, polishing it until, eventually, we believe it ourselves.

Such tales are part of our process of creating identity. Our self becomes the reflection of such stories, forged out of carefully selected images and iconic events. In this way, these fictions defend us against the onslaught of experiences which would otherwise erode our confidence and destroy our sense of well-being.

Stories protect us from shame and guilt, but deluding others, we delude ourselves. In our hearts we know that we have created something of a sham. Maintaining identity often comes at the cost of honesty. Built on self-delusion, as we create our peace of mind, we break faith with ourselves. The fiction intended to keep the feelings of guilt at bay, binds us into a position of inauthenticity. So, in protecting ourselves this way, we sow new seeds of guilt.

This is not to say that such strategies are without their reasons, or indeed that they are not inevitable. The whole process of creating such delusions, of forging identities from half truths and impressions, is so much a part of our nature as humans that we cannot imagine a way of being that does not involve such means at least at subtle levels. This is our ordinary nature. So are we bound by virtue of our humanity to struggle to efface our guilt, but, through doing so, to create further layers of it.

****

The sins of the fathers and mothers fall upon the child. The guilt of our parents becomes our blood legacy. Trans-generational scripts are powerful. Often, unknown to the conscious mind, they haunt us all the more strongly through their mystery. So, commonly, the child lives out the parents' unlived dreams. Patterns repeat. Unfinished stories are completed.

Was it because I abandoned the path suggested by my original training as an archaeologist that my eldest daughter took up geology and now spends her time inspecting building sites and walking flood defences? How did I come to move from that outdoor life to become a religious, pastoral worker and educator, when my father and his father before him had both been clergy, a chaplain and a head-teacher respectively? Not by intention. Nothing was further from my mind as a young adult. The one thing of which I was certain was that I was not going to follow in my parents' professional footsteps. And yet, somehow, I did.

No doubt our paths are cast from many small diversions and attractions down the years, from patterns of thought and action, from world perspectives passed on subliminally in childhood. Some are conscious, expressions of interest and cultural outlook, conveyed in family conversation. Others are more mysteriously transmitted. We swear we will not follow the family pattern, or carry out its business, only to find that it has crept into our lives by the back door.

I remember, most strikingly, meeting a young woman who had suffered all her life from anorexia and bulimia. Her father, it transpired, had been in the concentration camps during the last war. He had witnessed terrible atrocities and been rescued when he was so weak and thin he could not have survived more than a few more days. She hated his bad temper and depression, his stories of his war time experiences, yet still she lived out his starvation, almost giving her own life to his cause.

Did Wendy live out her mother's guilt? Did she feel a reflection of her mother's unvoiced shame? Did she learn to cover such feelings with sweetness and a good face? It was, after all, the family business to create beauty, transforming with make-up, hair products and preening, and creating a warm, girly environment. But such activity cannot cleanse the sense of dishonour that Wendy carries in her being. Even could she straighten and colour her hair to match that of her sisters, she holds her secret difference, ineradicably in her heart.

Children navigate a sea strewn with unseen jagged rocks of adult agendas. The stories of parents' lives, their values, histories and secrets, all lurk beneath the surface of the child's awareness, causing currents and eddies that may only be partially understood. For Wendy, guilt was in the circumstance into which she was born.

****

Wendy's guilt is mirrored in the cruelty of others. Her sense of worthlessness, of badness and humiliation, is reflected in the taunts and bitter comments from Sharon. Sharon, the bully, no doubt has her own story of misery and humiliation lurking behind her blustering exterior. In the hall of mirrors of human relationships, there are no winners, no losers, but only complex reflections and ambiguities. Just as Wendy's story requires a persecutor, so Sharon's requires a victim.

Children's worlds are harsh. Far from the idealized images of childhood harmony, the bitter warfare of playground encounters is fuelled by every human passion. Put any group of humans, randomly chosen, into a closed environment, with regular tasks and pressures to perform, with little respite or recourse to sympathetic facilitation, and struggle will generally ensue. Within the closed group, interactions are magnified, conflicts exaggerated. With no hiding place and no option of leaving, turmoil is forced to simmer into survival strategies.

In groups, people find solutions to these uncomfortable dynamics through various tracks. Some withdraw into isolation and pleasantry, hiding beneath conventions that obscure the truth. Others create alliances, form cliques, building collective identities and reinforcing shared stories, offering mutual alibis. Sometimes such groupings thrive on difference, seek scape-goats, hunting like jackals in packs and picking off the weak. When survival is threatened, particularly, the rough and ready lore of the jungle prevails. In such conditions, the wary keep their presence quietly.

There were times when I experienced such painful taunting as a child. Children seek out differences and I guess I was sometimes the odd one out, a bit different from the others. It is often so for the child who writes stories or plays crazy imaginative games, who does not conform to the ways of the crowd or to teachers' wishes, who confronts and challenges and speaks out inappropriately. Such a child does not have an easy ride. Beset by feelings of self-righteousness and guilt, I remember feeling terrible shame on the occasions when I was teased. I hid it as far as I was able. Yet, remembering some of the incidents that occurred on different occasions, I can still feel the vulnerability of being the child who was picked on.

One day, I remember finding a catty note left anonymously in my desk. I guess little girls do that kind of thing quite often, but for me at the time it felt like the end of the world. It could have been from any one of a number of tormentors. Even now, forty years on, what I remember most is the feeling of shame. Part of me says, no, do not write it. Edit it out. Do not speak of such things. Then, I hid it as fast as I could, before friends or teachers could see it. I didn't want them to know that I had been humiliated in this way. How could I let them see this evidence of my unpopularity?

And will you judge me now? Now I have spoken, have I exposed my weakness after all these years?

Our persecutors are successful because they reflect our deepest fears. Whatever our cover story, beneath the smooth exterior we have weaknesses and feelings of guilt. There the persecutor will find a foothold on which to sink the grappling hook. Probably we all have such vulnerabilities, we all harbour secret guilt and fear. For some it is less defended, more easily located. Such children make good prey. So Wendy felt shame for her origins and with it felt guilt for her part on creating them.

One can speculate that Sharon was also vulnerable. Did she feel guilt? Likely her power, her vindictiveness, in some way reflected her own pain. The victim becomes perpetrator, the tortured becomes torturer. Such malevolence does not spring up without the seed of injury. But once accepted such a role relies upon control. The oppressor controls external criticism and dissent with an iron will. She gathers the timid, the compliant and those who would attain similar power around her. She viciously attacks the dissenter and intimidates the uncommitted.

The same is true of her behaviour towards her own thoughts and mental processes. Such voices of dissent must be silenced. Confusion and regret are not tolerated. Guilt and doubt must be banished to the darker levels of the unconscious mind where they can be suppressed. Thus the bully will not listen to the voice of conscience.

Between the ages of seven and eight I attended a school on a housing estate in inner London. Coming from a close-knit village community in Kent, I found the children in my new environment baffling and different, their lifestyles contradicting everything I and my previous friends had been brought up with. In my confusion and loneliness I found it impossible to form friendships with children my own age, whose interests in pop music, fashion, and hanging out around the flats where they lived, were so alien.

Details made a big difference. They had ten shillings a week pocket money, more than I could ever imagine. My mother said they wouldn't learn the value of money. They wore patent leather shoes with pointed toes, in contrast to my sensible Clarks lace-ups. My mother said I would get bunions if I wore pointed shoes whilst my feet were growing. They stayed up until ten o'clock at night whilst I was expected to be in bed by seven thirty. My mother said I needed my sleep or I would not be able to learn in school the next day. So everything I wanted in order to be like them and be liked was impossible. Not surprising. The details of difference were symptoms of more structural differences in our lifestyles. They were bridges that could not be easily crossed.

Eventually I befriended a little boy in a younger class. When I first met him, he was being teased by other kids in the playground. He was crying bitterly and they were taunting him for it. I think I identified with his plight. He was called Peter. Having rescued him, we became companions for a while, spending all the playtimes together. Sometimes another boy from my own class, who was also quite timid, joined us.

After a while, I must have learned to attune better with the girls of my own age. Although I never really made close friends at that school, I did get to know a girl I shall call Debbie. Looking back, I think she must have wanted my friendship too. Eventually this led her to demand a show of loyalty from me. Debbie gave me an ultimatum. To get her friendship, I had to stop being friends with Peter. It was a choice. I chose her.

This led to an incident for which I still feel guilty. Debbie demanded that I tell Peter to his face that I didn't want to be his friend any more, then I had to kick him to show that I meant it. Obediently, I followed her instructions, wanting her approval. I remember his face, crumpled up with misery as he looked back at me. I remember hating myself even as I rejected him. I remember knowing that I had to do this for my own survival. I wish that I could say that I had the courage to say no, to refuse to comply with Debbie's wishes, knowing them to be cruel and wrong, but I did not. To do so would have meant enduring more months of being on my own. I was miserable and lonely and my own unhappiness counted more than his, at the end of the day. I'm sorry Peter.

Of course, the fact that I feel guilt and shame as an adult reviewing these incidents does not necessarily mean that I felt guilt at the time. I have no clear recollection of any such feelings relating to the incident. I do remember very clearly seeing Peter's hurt expression. I remember then the feeling of wretchedness it evoked in me at the time. Was that guilt? Does the child learn to feel guilt through seeing how others are hurt by its actions? How is our conscience created?

CHAPTER SIX

The Bonfire

Saturday morning, Joanne was up early. It had been raining in the night and the sky was grey and heavy. Her parents were in the kitchen, sitting over breakfast. Her father had the morning paper spread out in front of him and the radio news droned on in the background, a male voice monotonous and sober, talking on and on about the election and something called Vietnam. Why were adults interested in such boring stuff?

Michael and Ian were still in their bedroom. Joanne could hear them squabbling over the Scalextric set. Squabbling was a hobby for them. Who had the blue car or the yellow one, the inside or outside track, who had won the lap, all became sources of contention and bickering. Usually it stayed verbal, descending into name calling and abuse, but sometimes it got physical, the two boys pushing each other and rolling over and over on the toy strewn carpet, impaling body parts on sharp corners of Dinky toys, Lego bricks and car track. Usually they were careful not to roll onto the controls and actually break anything. No fight was worth winning that much. But occasionally they would accidentally fall badly onto something that was not sufficiently well engineered for boisterous young males, and a piece of plastic would break or metal would bend, leading to further recriminations.

Joanne could smell eggs frying.

"Give the twins a shout, will you," her mother called. "Their breakfast is ready."

Joanne went to the bottom of the stair case and yelled. The voices overhead stopped momentarily as the promise of food registered, then her two brothers came tumbling out of the bedroom door and down the wooden stairs, seating themselves at the table, still squabbling without let up.

"Stop that and eat!" their mother chided, putting plates of eggs, bacon and fried bread before them.

The bacon was limp and fatty. Joanne really liked hers crisp. She liked the salty, crustiness of rind that had been frazzled in the pan for a long time, but her mother was in a hurry that morning. She wanted Joanne's father to drive her to the supermarket before it got too busy. That meant leaving soon. Joanne cut off as much fat as she dared with the rind, eating the pink meaty part, dipped in the oozing yolk of the egg.

The kitchen clock said eight thirty. Finishing her breakfast, Joanne put on her anorak and her canvas baseball boots, which were a little muddy from last night, and went to call for Simon. She stood outside his drive, giving the dog bark until an upstairs window opened and Simon's head appeared.

"OK, I'm coming!" He shouted. "Just got to tidy my room up first. I'm not allowed out otherwise. I won't be long."

Joanne sat on the kerb, twisting a willow wand that she had found in the gutter into a bangle, and waiting for the others. The concrete was still damp and she felt the coldness seeping through her jeans. Since last night her mind had cleared. Like the fresh air after the rain storm, she felt bright and settled. She wasn't going to be fazed by those magazines. How pathetic could you get? It was good to get back to normal.

Philip came out into the street first. He crossed the road to where she was sitting.

"Where are Michael and Ian?" He asked, looking at Joanne and then beyond her towards her house.

"Just finishing breakfast," she replied, hardly looking up. "They'll be here in a minute."

Philip sat down, hands in his pockets, whistling between his teeth. Joanne kept twisting the willow.

"They're having a bonfire today," Philip continued, "all the old boxes that were piled up by the shed, if they're not too wet."

Joanne said nothing. An image had flashed into her mind of burning the magazines, of getting rid of them and making things as they had been before, as if she had never found them. With the image of burning pages something deep inside her relaxed. Then, quick as it had arisen, the thought was forgotten, replaced by a new thought, that of the fire. New images formed in her mind of the roaring flames leaping into the sky and the gang helping out.

The twins and Simon arrived at the same time. She had seen her parents leave already, and Ian and Michael followed shortly after, carrying half a loaf of sliced bread and a bottle of tomato sauce.

"You'll be in trouble. Mum will notice that's missing when she gets back!" Joanne said, but Ian just stuck his tongue out at her.

"We can toast it on the fire," Michael said.

Joanne was doubtful, but she didn't want to argue. It wasn't worth it. They could get in trouble if they liked. She'd keep out of it. Her mother would know it was them, because she had already seen Joanne leave the house earlier. Anyway, she knew the twins' liking for ketchup, so it would be bound to be them.

At the scrap yard, Ray was already pulling boxes out from under a tarpaulin beside the shed. They were fruit crates: light, coarse wood that splintered easily if you tried to sit on them. Some were whole but many were already broken. There were some old bottle crates too, more solid, with the company names stencilled on the sides. The men only burned the broken ones of these. The others made useful seats and tables because they were strongly made.

Alf was over by the fence, shifting some old bed frames onto a heap of other scrap metal to make space for the fire. He grinned as they approached.

"Hi kids!" he said. "You all ready?"

Before they could answer, he reached behind the bed frames and hauled out a couple of car tyres that he sent rolling towards the children. The first wobbled its way on a circular path, then toppled in the middle of the yard, but the second ran more speedily towards them. Simon had to jump out of the way, but Michael, behind him, caught it. It hit him with such force that he hurt his hand. He shook it wildly, swearing as he did so.

"That'll make it go!" said Alf. He laughed, and the boys joined in. They were very excitable. It was going to be a big bonfire.

Ray piled the boxes round the tyres, stuffing cardboard and newspaper into the gaps. He brought over some old sofa cushions that had gone mouldy and leant them against the heap. A broken tea chest and a chair without a seat went on top. It was a big heap, perhaps eight feet tall, certainly bigger than even the men.

"Who's going to light it, then?" asked Ray, taking a box of smokers' matches out of his pocket.

There was an immediate clamour from the boys, but Ian pushed himself forwards first. "Me, me, me," he shouted, pulling at Ray's arm.

Ray laughed and handed over the match box.

The match heads were soft and perhaps slightly damp, for the first one fizzed and spat and flew off onto the ground. The second match struck properly though, and with Ray's help, Ian crouched down beside the pile, lighting the newspaper charges in several places.

Fortunately, despite the recent rain, most of the boxes had been covered by plastic sheeting and were very dry. Being light weight pine, they went up quickly, sending a shower of sparks high into the sky. There was a roaring sound as the fire drew wind into its vortex. The children jumped back as the heat and sparks became intense, hovering in a semi-circle round the windward side of the conflagration to avoid its intensity. They were getting hot. Simon peeled off his anorak and threw it onto the old mattress pile. Others followed suit, strewing coats in various places around the yard.

By now the cushions and tyres were catching light and a pall of black smoke was replacing the ferocity of the first sparks. Ray and Alf began to throw on other items from around the yard: more broken furniture, soggy mattresses, more boxes. Some items burned well, causing more rushes of sparks, but many were damp, sometimes even waterlogged and sent up clouds of heavy grey smoke that smelled musty and rancid. The men were careful to add these gradually so as not to put the fire out by smothering it, but the car tyres kept burning steadily, exuding their particularly nasty smelling smoke and maintaining the fire.

Michael found a long stick. He wanted to toast the bread on the fire, but Ray laughed at him.

"That'll taste foul toasted on that fire, even if you could get near enough to do it. Save it for later," he said.

Eventually the men had cleared all the rubbish that they wanted to burn. They began sorting through the remaining items that were strewn around the yard, creating heaps of different sorts of metal and other scrap items. The fire burned down to a heap of embers, tangled bed springs and wire, still glowing and emitting a soft grey line of smoke. The children stood around, watching the last tiny flickers of flames die out.

As the heat of the fire waned, the boys began to retrieve their discarded outer garments which had been scattered round the site on convenient posts and surfaces. Joanne sat on the old sofa watching the scene. She felt at ease again. Ray and Alf were fun to be with, and they were kind.

"Where's my anorak?"

Simon's voice sounded suddenly anxious. The pile of mattresses on which he had thrown it had now gone, most burned on the fire, one or two that were in better shape leaning against the side of the shed under the shelter. His jacket was nowhere to be seen.

"Dunno," said Alf, "where was it?"

"I put it on the mattresses. It got too hot with the fire and everything."

Simon put his hands on his head and looked desperately to and fro across the yard. It was pretty empty now, all the accumulation of rubbish from the last couple of months having been burned. All he could see was empty space. Suddenly he felt helpless. He could not see a way that his anorak could be found. There was no where to look.

"Oh no," he moaned, "oh no..."

The others, who had not taken much notice till this moment, suddenly jumped into action and started to scurry round the site, looking into all sorts of unlikely places; in the water butts and behind a pile of metal fencing, under the shed and by the heap of car parts, on the sofa backs and among the old cookers and electrical equipment. Simon knew it was to no avail, but everyone sensed his predicament and knew what it meant to be in trouble for a lost coat. They could not let themselves believe that his anorak might have gone for good.

Ray and Alf looked too, though rather half heartedly. They strolled up and down, peering into corners, behind the remaining mattresses, behind the hut. They shrugged as they looked in each place.

"Where did you last have it?" Ray asked again. "Think, might you have put it somewhere else?"

Simon shook his head forlornly.

"Look in the shed, Joanne," Alf called.

Joanne was still sitting on the sofa. She couldn't think how to help, so she just sat and watched the others. Now she stood up.

She hesitated for a moment before approaching the shed door. Then, putting the fragment of a thought aside, she opened it and peered in. It was dark and she could not really see that well, but she knew she would not find the anorak. She just looked because to do otherwise would have been to admit to the hopelessness of the search, to confess her certainty that the anorak would not be found. It was to voice the unthinkable, that Simon's anorak was gone without trace, with all the implications that such a loss would carry. So, out of loyalty to Simon and the others she went through the motions of looking.

The space under the table was dark and she did not intend to look there, but she couldn't stop her eyes wavering towards the place where the magazines had been. What if the men had burned them? Perhaps they would be gone after all. She was surprised to find that, rather than the discomfort of the previous night, her main feeling was curiosity. A bit of her hoped that the pile would still be there. It was.

"Nothing in here," she called.

"Well," said Ray, turning to Simon, "I think you might have lost that one." He shrugged his shoulders. "Sorry mate." He slapped Simon on the back.

Simon sank onto one of the wooden crates. He knew Ray was right. He didn't want it to be so, but wanting things to be different changes nothing. The others stood round, looking at him in horrified silence. They sensed that, of all of them, Simon was probably the one who would be most deeply in trouble. Not that it would have been easy for any of them. Each child secretly felt relief to feel their own garment zipped securely round him, and in feeling it felt grateful not to have to find words to tell his mother of such an unspeakable loss.

Simon looked hopelessly into the distance. There was a slight tremor in his lip. Then, saying nothing, he got up and started to walk out of the gate.

Joanne, seeing him go, went after him. The others, unsure what to do, made to follow but then thought better of it. It was nearly lunch time, but they held back to let Joanne catch up with Simon before they too slipped away, grunting goodbye to Alf and Ray.

Simon was trying not to cry when Joanne caught him.

"They'll kill me," he said.

Joanne did not know what to say. What could you say? It was unthinkably awful to have to face your parents and tell them you'd lost something big like your coat.

"It was new," he went on forlornly.

"Shit!" Joanne said, speaking slowly and deliberately so that the word whistled out through her teeth. Joanne was not allowed to swear, so the expletive, deliberately voiced to express the seriousness of the situation, carried extra weight. It told Simon she understood.

A few tears were spilling over and running down his cheeks in spite of his efforts to stop them. He cursed inwardly and tried to wipe them on his sleeve before Joanne could see him crying.

They walked in silent companionship back towards the cul-de-sac.

"Come round this afternoon, if you can," Joanne turned to him. "My mum says I can do some baking. She's getting stuff to make chocolate crispies. If you come round we can do it together. The kids can go out and play football or something."

Joanne stood at the fence outside Simon's house and watched as he walked up the drive and rang the front door bell. She felt especially close to Simon at that moment. She wanted to be there and to be visible, so that his mother would see her as she opened the door, so that she would see that Simon had friends, that he was not unsupported, and so that she should not be too hard on him. She wanted to offer a distraction at the moment when the missing coat became apparent, to soften the first impression and to make things ordinary. She did not know if this strategy had worked. Simon's mother ushered him in without comment.

Joanne turned and, feeling heavy, went into her own house. Michael and Ian were already back, standing round in the kitchen watching their mother making the last of the preparations for dinner.

"Have you been hanging round bonfires too?" her mother greeted her, "What a stench! Take your clothes off so I can hang them on the line."

Her mother was always fussing about clothes. "Where was this fire anyway?" her mother continued. More trouble; another crocodile to be avoided; she should have thought of that one.

"They were burning stuff at the scrap yard. We were in the Amazon outside the fence. The smoke was blowing all over us," Joanne responded quickly before the others could answer.

****

There are those moments when we just wish we could turn the clock back. There are times when, despite our best efforts, the universe catches us in its web, bundles us up, and dangles us by a thin thread. There are times when we watch others struggle like some unfortunate fly against the sticky threads of inevitability.

It is ironic that so often our worst disasters arrive unannounced, accidents of circumstance, unforeseen and unpredictable. Despite even our best efforts to control our living environments, it is often when we feel most at ease, with all our bases covered, that the unexpected interrupts our lives. How are we guilty for what we do not foresee? Theory suggests that intention is the real creator of karma, but do we through our negligence create guilt? And when events are completely beyond prediction, what karma can we call on for explanation? What should be foreseen, and what cannot reasonably be expected? What is sensible precaution and what neurosis? What should we anticipate, and what of the disasters, the acts of God, that strike without any precognition?

Simon, as we have already seen, was caught between different circumstances which made it well nigh impossible for him to act without some degree of deceit. He inhabited that familiar human space of fudged relationships and selective truth, managing the conflicting pressures of a solitary childhood in a strict home against his need for friendship, and his growing desire to find a place in the world, independent of the pulls of childish identity. His involvement with the gang epitomised and amplified whatever guilt accrued from this, both offering the attraction of complicit companionship, and drawing him into activities that on his own he would not have entertained. In the process it also drew him into further layers of dishonesty.

The involvement with the men at the scrap yard was something that Simon's mother would certainly have forbidden, and he had to act with considerable caution to avoid her finding out about what he was doing. For the most part he did not directly lie, but he became an accomplished dealer in half truths and implication, expert at covering his tracks. Such behaviour left its inevitable residue of discomfort, especially in a lad whose conscience was sensitised by the mingling religious streams of his past. It also created a precedent, making it likely that, as situations compounded, at some point the fabric of inferences he had built up would take him into deeper water.

As well as living with small everyday deceptions, Simon also struggled with the uncomfortable feeling that his life was constructed of many small everyday failures of courage. This knowledge was a constant assault on any pretence he had towards manhood. He felt guilty for this too. He sometimes wished he was brave enough to assert the truth of his wishes, and to be honest about his feelings and impulses, but he was afraid of criticism and punishment from his parents.

As an only child, the pressure to conform to standards of behaviour which other children might have rebelled against was enormous, and many times he reluctantly gave in to family injunctions, or found ways to avoid conflict through silence or through judicious adjustment of the truth. In such situations, not only did the dishonesty eat away at him, but, more profoundly, the feeling that he had chickened out in taking the easier route of lying and deception, instead of saying what was really true, diminished his self-respect and left him feeling defeated and immature.

So, for Simon, losing the anorak was particularly painful. To face his mother and be forced to explain its loss by whatever means, knowing that she would not accept or easily forgive his carelessness, brought all these factors into sharp relief. Would his carefully woven cover story, which had been so carefully crafted by implication rather than direct lies, break down? Would the uncomfortable truth emerge? Or did the situation require a bigger lie, a fabrication on a scale hitherto not envisaged?

Holding the parts of his life separate suddenly became a far greater challenge, and one in which the stakes were raised substantially. To lie about the coat and be discovered would bring serious punishment. To tell what had happened would possibly bring an end to all that he wanted in life: his friendships, his life of fantasy adventures and his independence. His tears, hidden from the younger children, but evident to Joanne, were a shameful indication of his childishness. He felt confusion. He didn't see what he could say to his mother, yet he had to find words by the time he got home. This thought span him into spirals of emotion in which he could only wish that things were not so.

It is in such moments that the helpless predicament of one's humanity becomes evident. We indeed cannot turn the clock back. We cannot undo the mistake. Simon could not hang the garment on a different, safer post, or rescue and reconstitute its material from the grey ashes into which it has turned. It is impossible to make life run smoothly.

Whether it is an untimely death, or an accident that with foresight might have been avoided, the unexpected disaster shakes us out of our everyday tracks. The situation that arises in a particular place and time, when one might have been elsewhere, arrives like a meteorite from a clear sky. We cannot avoid such things.

****

Last night as I sat writing, whilst visiting our friends in Hawaii, the little wooden house in which we were staying suddenly jolted on its foundations, throwing things around the room. I leapt up and rushed out of the building, not knowing what had happened, but urgently, instinctively, needing to be on firm ground. It was, it turned out, a small earthquake. That is how disasters often come. Unexpected and unanticipated, they shock us into acting in ways that may be skilled or not, but are often more instinctive than planned. In this case, the actuality turned out to be a minor event, which raised no lasting damage, and was even somewhat exciting in retrospect. Only chance and perhaps geology made the difference between this and an altogether more serious situation. Circumstances inevitably from time to time deliver painful blows.

When I was Simon's age, I stayed with some cousins for a few days during the summer holidays. They had two pet mice, and we were playing in the garden with them. I was allowing one of the mice to run on the lawn, being careful to guard it by laying my arms along the grass, so that it stayed within a limited area and did not escape. My cousin was carrying the other mouse in her hand. She had not seen what I was doing as she was giving her mouse all her attention. Engrossed in watching that my mouse did not escape, I did not see her coming as she walked quickly towards me. We were just kids, having fun. Then in a moment the whole situation changed. She trod on my mouse, her foot landing heavily on top of it. I let out a scream of horror, and she, stepped back. Seeing what she had done, the bloodied creature lying on the grass, in shock, and probably in part as a result of my scream, she dropped the mouse she was carrying. It broke its back. In a moment both mice were dead.

I remember struggling with the pointless inevitability of the scene. By what dreadful coincidence had we brought this terrible thing about? Surely, somehow, the mice could have been saved? Feeling ill with guilt at my part in what had happened I took to my bed for the afternoon. My whole energy was taken up running and re-running the scenario through my mind, as if doing so could change something, yet each time I saw that same awful result; the two dead mice lying on the grass close by one another.

Helplessness is both the source of human frailty and the fuel of our spiritual being. Our struggling minds, facing our power-lessness against life events, sickness, old age and death, may on the one hand rise to the occasion, taking courage in the face of the inevitable and harnessing our responses so that we grow in spiritual capacity, or on the other hand, may lose courage, so that we fall into deceit and delusion, avoidance and escape. Most of us do the latter most of the time. We are ordinary, frightened beings, struggling for survival. The gift of courage is rare.

To think we can control circumstances is grandiosity. To imagine we can steer our fate or prevent disasters, and then to feel guilt when the unexpected arises, is to place ourselves as gods, all seeing and all powerful. Yet we are often deeply disturbed by events that remind us of our inability as humans to have this sort of divine omniscience. Guilt is a price we pay for preserving our sense of power. It can be easier to feel guilty than to accept our vulnerability to nature, easier to be villain than victim.

We cling to a belief that the earthquake can be foreseen, avoided, averted, rather than letting ourselves know that it may strike without warning. The modern clamour, "This must not be allowed to happen again" speaks against the inevitable. It will.

Once I took my children to a park. We were feeding the ducks, alongside other children and parents. Going to see the ducks is something that small children like to do. It's an ordinary family activity. There were ducklings too, sweet and fluffy. We all peeped and cooed at them, commenting on their cuteness. Then suddenly from the sky a large herring gull swooped down and snatched a duckling, then flew away. The children wailed in shock, and several of the mothers shrieked out in consternation.

"It shouldn't be allowed!" one said vociferously. She was very angry. The sight of a sweet little duckling being gobbled up was not something she wanted her children exposed to. But try to tell that to a herring gull.

We cannot prevent suffering. It is part of the fabric of life. We fear the knowledge that we are incapable of preventing all disasters, and that inevitably things will go badly wrong from time to time. This fear drives us to retreat from raw reality. Instead we construct whatever personal delusion will stave off that knowledge. We seek control. We fantasise about our power to effect change. We want to feel that we are not at the mercy of fate. The cost of such delusion, however, is that if we do manage to convince ourselves that we have control of events and the power to avert disasters, we also then believe that we are responsible for what befalls. When tragedy befalls us, or those close to us, we are then beset with feelings of irrational guilt. Guilt is the cost of feeling in control.

****

As the children stand around the embers of the fire, wondering where the anorak might be, suspecting that it is in the ashes in front of them, everyone recognises the awful inevitability that hangs over Simon's predicament. They feel for the situation he faces. At the same time everyone is grateful that it is not them who must go home and confess to the loss. Such are our imperfect human responses. Such is our compassion. We give sympathy, but it is fuelled by our thankfulness that it was not us. Whilst the others feel sorry for Simon, none of them would willingly swap places with him. In this they too perhaps feel some guilt.

This, then, is the guilt of those who stand alongside but are unaffected by a tragedy, the guilt of the survivor, the person who might so easily have been the one to suffer, but has been spared by fate. The feelings are complex. Perhaps we feel relief. It is hard to see another suffering and know that one's own response includes such feelings. We blame ourselves for not at some deep level being willing to take the other's place (even though logically we know it would not have been possible anyway). We may even feel some smugness, irrational as it is, at our escape, even a gloating satisfaction at the other's misfortune. Perhaps we nurse a sense of justice done, or perhaps of having passed some divine test by being spared. Most of these feelings flit across our consciousness but momentarily, before they burrow deep into our hidden depths. But there they linger. We do not always feel as much compassion as we would wish.

Or maybe we simply think 'there but for the grace of God go I'. We feel the cruel arbitrariness of fate. It could have been any one of the children who had lost their coat. Anyone could have been facing parental wrath. Watching another's suffering, we feel the terror of what might have been. We wait for our turn, almost jealous of those who have already felt the blow of fate.

For some, guilt grows easily. Guilt is a habit of thought, the seedbed is ready. Perhaps a mental strategy of bargains with the divine and the all powerful begins it. Maybe our sense of being already condemned leaves us eager to receive our punishment so that we may proceed in life cleansed. Perhaps we feel that it should have been us who suffered. We feel that somehow we have cheated the fates by not having received the same misfortune. Or maybe we feel that we have been cheated of our opportunity for atonement, our chance of salvation. Maybe we missed our moment of redemption, of glory. Maybe we feel there was some way we could have taken the victim's place, and so become the martyr.

****

Joanne has also been struggling with her own fears. She has been caught in the space between an intense desire to run away, to forget what she has seen, not to know that the men have such material in their shed, and her latent interest in the magazines.

She struggles between her loyalty to the gang, her need for friendship, her memories of good times at the scrap yard, and her new sense of danger and threat around Ray and Alf. The ferment of feelings rise and fall, as Joanne struggles to suppress the cacophony of responses which push her to run away. She too would rather turn the clock back. For all her fascination with them, she would rather that she had never found the magazines, so much have they upset her equilibrium. Yet having seen them, having lost her innocence, she cannot go back, and even, to her own surprise, finds herself wanting to look again.

The currents of emotion, memory and instinct pull us, often running deep below the surface of our reactions. Human psychology is thus an ever changing mirror of circumstance, in which shadows of feelings cast subtle layers of shade across what appear simple responses. So in their silence, Simon and Joanne feel closeness. Old friends, in their growing wisdom, grounded in their brushes with adversity, they start to recognise new levels of familiarity. Seeing Simon's tears, she does not comment. His dignity respected, he is allowed to retain his manhood, and not to be reduced to the snivelling child. Perhaps Joanne sees in him the echo of her own emotional struggle, and doing so feels fellow feeling with him.

So with the chance occurrence of circumstances, the arbitrary allocation of fate, the die is cast and Simon draws the bean. Unhappily he goes home.

CHAPTER SEVEN

Simon's Mother

Opening the door, Barbara immediately noticed that Simon was not wearing his anorak. Fancy having gone out without it! She scanned back through her mind to his departure. Had she seen him leave that morning? Surely she would have said something. It was only March and had rained heavily in the night, so to go out without a coat was asking for trouble. She couldn't actually recall having seen him leaving the house, though he had shouted to her that he had finished tidying his room. That was another matter. There was tidying and tidying. His idea of tidy left a lot to be desired. How did you get boys to be tidier? She was sure a girl would have been more biddable in that respect.

"What happened to your anorak Simon?" she asked, "You know you shouldn't go out without a coat at this time of year."

Simon looked uncomfortable. He hovered on the step as if reluctant to come in. Behind him Barbara could see that girl hanging around. Perhaps a daughter would not have been so easy after all, but then if Joanne were her daughter she wouldn't get away with half of what her parents let her do. She was a bit of a bad influence.

Simon grunted something inaudible and slipped in past her. As he did so, Barbara caught a strong whiff of smoke.

Barbara's first thought was whether he or his friends had been smoking, but she realized almost as soon as she thought it that it was not cigarette smoke she could smell. Her mind raced through other possibilities. Most likely they had been lighting fires again over on that waste land. She'd caught the children doing that before now, and told them off for it. Not that it was that much of a problem. They were quite sensible really and as long as they didn't take risks, she was prepared to turn a blind eye to it. So she had watched the situation from a distance and pretended not to know. It was better that Simon was afraid of getting told off. He was less likely to take risks. Today, however, the smell was hard to ignore. It smelled rubbery, like they had been burning old rubbish.

"What have you been up to Simon, you smell of smoke?" she continued.

Simon, who was hovering at the bottom of the staircase, about to run up to his room, but held by her question, shuffled his feet. He wished the floor would swallow him up.

"Have you been making fires again?"

Simon mumbled reluctant agreement.

"Whatever were you burning? That's not wood smoke. You'll have all the neighbours complaining."

"There aren't any neighbours on the old factory." Simon felt momentarily safe.

"You know I don't like you playing there," his mother said.

Simon felt a wave of relief pass over him. He knew this was an end of the conversation, effectively his mother signing out. In the move and counter move of parent-child negotiation, this was his mother's way of closing the matter. She had voiced her disapproval, but she had not forbidden him to play on the factory site. That was tantamount to approval. It allowed each of them to keep face.

"Yes, Mummy," he said quickly, acquiescing to her terms and thus freeing himself to escape to his room.

"Dinner's nearly ready," she called after him. "Do change your clothes. I don't want to have to sit with that smell while I'm eating… and don't put those smelly jeans on your bed."

Simon threw the jeans on the floor and pulled on his spare pair, which had patches on the knees. He sat down on the bed and took stock. So far his missing jacket had not been noticed. Maybe he could spin this out. It wasn't long till summer. Maybe he could wear his old anorak and his mother wouldn't notice that the new one wasn't around. It seemed like a long shot, but he could think of no other way out.

As he was thinking about the situation, he heard the front door bang. His father had come home. Saturday was his half day at work. Lunch would be ready and his mother would call him any minute. Simon could smell food cooking downstairs; he guessed from the smell that it was boiled cabbage, but he thought he could smell sausages too. That at least was good.

"Dinner!" His mother's voice interrupted his thoughts. He knew better than to be late, so he jumped up as soon as he heard her call, and ran down the stairs, his stockinged feet sliding on the wooden treads so that he had to grasp the hand rail.

Barbara had laid the table already. They had their habitual places. The three of them could sit facing the garden, leaving a gap on the window side of the table, which was nice, as the daffodils were just coming out along the fence opposite. The trellis on the shed would look a lot better if the clematis grew, but for the moment it was at least neat and tidy. Perhaps they could put a seat out there in the summer. They could afford to splash out a bit now that she had taken the part time job working on as receptionist at the doctor's surgery.

She carried the serving dishes in and put them down on the floral place mats: mashed potato, smooth and yellowish white, with plenty of butter and top of the milk, and cabbage, cooked to near transparency. There was also gravy in a china gravy boat that had been in the family for years. She served the sausages straight from the pan onto the plates in the kitchen: three each for the men and two for herself.

"*There are two men in my life, to one I am a mother, to the other I'm a wife, and I give them both the best…*" she found herself humming the tune from the advert, then caught herself and smiled, half amused, half cross. "ITV rubbish!" she thought. But she was proud of her men. In spite of everything, in spite of all the irritations of bringing up a boy, the dirty clothes and noisy games, she wouldn't swap him for anything. After all, he was her son.

Her husband was already sat at the table. Still in his suit, he looked business-like and formal. She wished he would get changed when he came in. It would save his suit, but also it made her feel more at ease when he put on his casual trousers and open necked shirt. She felt then that the weekend had started. Saturday mornings always felt like a continuation of the week when he had to work. That was the draw back of working in the library service. The advantage was that although his job took him all over the borough, he often worked close to home so he could come home for dinner.

Today Terry had been working in the central library. She liked it when he worked there because it was just across the main road. He was able to be back in no time. As she bent to put his plate in front of him, he caught her hand, and pulling her towards him, kissed her perfunctorily on the cheek. She felt herself blush slightly, but she smiled too. She put the other plate in front of Simon and, returning to the kitchen collected her own.

"Had a good morning?" she asked, cheerfully.

"Yes, it was OK." Terry cut a piece of sausage and put it in his mouth before adding, "There was a stinking fire over the way this morning, though. The smoke was blowing all across the road. I think it was at that scrap merchants yard. We had to shut all the windows to keep it out. They must have been burning tyres or something. I nearly rang Mike at environmental health to get them to go over and have a word with the men there."

Simon's heart stopped. His mouth hung open, half chewed cabbage and potato clogging his teeth and tongue. It was only a moment, and he quickly swallowed and continued eating as fast as he could, keeping his head down so that no one could see his face, but his mother had noticed.

"What's the matter Simon?" she asked.

He knew from her tone that she had seen his reaction. He

knew that he had guilt written all over his face. He knew that he was blushing and his expression, no matter how calm he tried to make it, was shifty and evasive. He knew she was putting two and two together and that she already knew that he had lied. He knew that she must be realising that a lie covered another lie and that beneath it all must be an awful truth, a truth too terrible to tell your parents.

"You know something about the fire, don't you? You weren't on the factory site, were you? You were hanging round the scrap yard."

He did not have to say anything. His expression told her that she was right.

"You lied to me, Simon. You know I wouldn't let you go there. This is a serious matter." Her voice was very calm. It always was when he was in trouble.

"I'm sorry," he muttered, almost inaudibly. Not half, he thought, ruefully, sorry I got caught, sorry I'm in this mess, sorry about the anorak.

"How dare you!" she continued. Her voice was now raised somewhat. "How dare you? Do you not think? I've told you enough times about playing in dangerous places. You know very well I'd never let you go and mess around in a place like that. You must have been being a nuisance to the men too. They've got work to do. Do they not mind you getting in the way?"

"We were helping," said Simon, desolately.

"Hmm. Some help you lot would be." said his mother. "Well, you're not going there again."

There was an air of finality in her tone that felt ominous. To disobey such an injunction would be to really court danger, yet not to go back to the scrap yard would be disastrous. Simon could not imagine the loneliness of staying at home while all the others spent their spare time with Alf and Ray.

There was another dilemma. The anorak loomed greatly in his mind. It was another disaster waiting to happen. Should he say something? It seemed that maybe he had weathered the worst of this particular storm, and that, if he appeared suitably penitent and promised not to repeat the escapade his involvement with the bonfire might be allowed to slip into silence. It might fall into the abyss of family history and join the collection of incidents which he always feared might be brought up at any point as extra ammunition when his mother was angry with him. To confess to the loss of his jacket would be to walk back into the lion's den, having once escaped. On the other hand, not to admit to what had happened was to simply postpone the inevitable. It was to add further deception to his list of crimes, and to add nights of anxious misery to his suffering. Could he be brave enough to tell his mother? Would it be foolhardy to do so? What alternative was there?

His mind was whirling. His face held an expression which must have been akin to a rabbit caught in headlights.

"Come on, lad, out with it," his father, noticing the hiatus, had paused in his eating. His tone was friendly, almost supportive. Simon felt it. Now was as good as ever.

"I lost my anorak," he blurted out.

Barbara nearly dropped her cutlery. What had he just said? Disobedience was one thing, she had the measure of that, but this confession took her into new ground. She had been prepared not to ask too many questions, not to uncover how Simon had got involved in this incident. It wasn't necessary. She had told him not to go to the scrap yard again and she knew he would do as he was told on this occasion. This new admission was different. Of course, "lost" could mean many things, but Simon's anxious face told her that she was unlikely to see the anorak again.

"Lost it?" she let the words roll out slowly and deliberately in her best Lady Bracknell tone. "You lost it? And how did you lose it? Are you going to find it again?"

Simon's body recoiled. Had he been a younger child it would have given in to the impulse to wet his trousers at this point. As it was he felt miserably close to doing so.

"What happened, son?" his father was still with him.

"I don't know," Simon said honestly, "I couldn't find it." Tears welled up in his eyes as he added quietly, "I'm afraid it might have got put on the fire by accident."

The truth was out, and a rush of relief went through him like a sudden gust of wind on a hot day.

Barbara sat motionless. A great distance had suddenly opened up between her and her husband and son. The half eaten dinner was going cold, knives and forks abandoned like flotsam on the half emptied plates. Dinner would be wasted. The anorak was wasted. All she could see was the waste.

The anorak was new. She had taken Simon to buy it only a few weeks ago in the sales at Marks and Spencer's. It had still not been cheap. It was a good one, meant to last him for his first few years at secondary school. Barbara was careful with money, but sometimes buying something that was a quality item was a good investment. Quality things lasted, and they told a story. Being well dressed improved your chances in the world. It was true that money was easier these days since she had taken the job. She no longer had to count the pennies quite so carefully, weighing up whether they could afford to buy proper cheddar this week, or whether to make do with the yellow processed cheese, whether they could buy those little chocolate swiss-rolls with their silver paper wrappings or whether she should make her usual coffee sponge cake for tea time. Now she could treat them a bit more, she could spoil the family, albeit in small, controlled ways. But it was still important not to be wasteful. She had always known that. Frugality had been bred into her since childhood. It ran in her veins with her very life blood. Among the many moral and religious injunctions of her upbringing, the prohibition against profligacy had etched itself most deeply into her being and was written on her heart as indelibly as Calais had been on Queen Elizabeth's.

Simon looked at her. His face was expressionless. He was looking to her for a reaction, in limbo. He did not know what she was thinking. He could only hold his breath and wait.

Barbara saw the scene in the shop; the row of thick padded anoraks. There had been thickly quilted ones, rather smart, in navy or black nylon at one end, and rather thinner smooth fabric jackets in maroon or bottle green at the other. In between had been some bright red ones with white trim and others in a dull biscuit colour. They had tried them all. The sales girl had been helpful, holding Simon's old jacket while she got him to try on coat after coat, looking at him, her head tilted sideways.

"Oh, that looks smart! Try this one... maybe the sleeves are a bit too long... but he'll be growing over the next few years... a big lad isn't he!" She'd reach over and pull at a shoulder seam or straighten the hood.

The one they had chosen was not the cheapest. Even then she had had a little tussle in her mind. Both Simon and the girl liked this same one. It was bottle green, with navy and white striped edges. She might have gone for a different one, something more sober, but they were both so enthusiastic that she gave in. It was good quality, but then, so were the others. In the end Simon had prevailed, and the new jacket was duly wrapped and sent home in the green and white carrier bag. She sewed in a name tag before she did anything else so that it could not go missing in the school cloak room.

"How on earth did it happen?" Barbara was thinking aloud more than asking the question to anyone in particular. "How could you let an anorak get burned?"

A bit of her knew that it could not have been deliberate. Simon had been too proud of his new coat. But boys were careless. She had often seen them using coats and pullovers as goal posts in the playground or at the park, never a thought of how muddy they might get or who would wash them.

The tears in Simon's eyes, which had been prickling close to the surface on and off ever since he had discovered the garment missing, and that had been swimming in front of his vision making everything blurred and wobbly, began to spill over. They dripped into his plate of half eaten vegetables.

"Tell us about it," encouraged his father, picking up his fork deliberately. He did not want a prolonged scene.

"I just put it down. When we'd finished it was gone," Simon blurted out between muffled sobs. "I couldn't help it. We looked and looked."

Barbara folded her lips. She felt angry. It wasn't so much that she felt angry at Simon. Mostly she felt angry with herself, but more than that she felt guilty. In some strange way that she could not explain, she felt responsible. Simon's carelessness, if that it was, reflected the multitude of her own failings as a mother. After all, she wouldn't have dared to do something like that herself when she was a child. Her mother saw to it that she behaved herself. If she had brought Simon up properly, with proper values and proper respect, this would never have happened. The incident just showed how bad she was as a mother.

Simon sobbed, now uncontrollably. "I didn't mean to."

Barbara looked at him. She had been a rather timid child, frightened easily. Simon was quite timid too. She knew that he often struggled with things that other children took in their stride. She had sat comforting him at night times when he couldn't sleep because he was worried about things that were happening at school. She listened to his fears about tests and his anxiety when he had to read a paragraph out in the school concert. She heard his worries about friendships with other children, his fears when some of the bigger boys picked on him in class. Sometimes she felt so deeply reflected in his pain that his suffering became almost unbearable to her. Other times she felt frustrated by his weakness, saw him as pathetic and cowardly, wished he would stand up for himself better. She had always seen herself as cowardly. Poor Simon! It was truly awful to have to confess one's shortcomings to one's parents.

Then Barbara remembered the time she ran away to the fair. She had been eleven years old.

The fair had come to the village. It did each year. It was not a big one: two or three roundabouts, swing chairs and galloping horses, the waltzers, swing boats, a haunted house, and some side stalls and coconut shies. All her friends would talk of nothing else all week. They would be going on Saturday evening but she was never allowed to go. Sadly she would sit in her bedroom and try to amuse herself with her toys or books. Sometimes she watched them walking up the street out of her window. The fair was always just at the end of her road on the little area of grass where you could sit on the old wooden benches overlooking the town and the harbour. She could hear the music and smell the sweet scent of candy floss and doughnuts mingling with the steam of the old traction engines. She never asked to go because her mother made it quite clear that she disapproved. "Place of the devil," she would call it, "temptations at every turn." Barbara just knew about it from her friends' accounts, and from the sweet, soft, candy they brought back for her and shared with her on the walk to Sunday school the following morning. She knew they pitied her and she hated being pitied.

The year that she was eleven was the year that a thread broke. It was not that she had not wanted to go to the fair on previous occasions, but that year things were different. Perhaps it was some courage born of her emerging independence, her growing sense of other possibilities in the world. She felt less sure that her friends were wrong or that her parents were right. She felt unconvinced by her mother's predictions of hell and damnation, unable to believe that any god would damn her friends for anything as harmless as a ride on the bobbing wooden stallions.

That night, while her mother was sewing in the front room and her father dozed by the fireplace with his book, she slipped out by the back door and met her friends in the street outside. She had feigned a head-ache and gone to her room early. She said she needed to sleep it off. She intended to slip back to bed without being spotted on her return, and had left a pillow in her bed as a precaution, a trick she had read about in a story that she had borrowed from the library. She hoped her mother would not look too closely for fear of waking her.

It had been a wonderful evening. Without money she could only wander between the rides and watch the others enjoying themselves, but they shared their pink sticky candyfloss and she felt intoxicated by the music, lights and smells. Towards the end, the other girls went for a last round on the waltzers. They piled into the tubs, three or four to a carriage, whilst Barbara stood on the side planks watching. The young men who ran the ride came over to where the girls were sitting and stood on the back of the tubs, spinning them even before the ride had started. There were lots of shrieks and screams and giggles. Then one of the fairground lads looked over at Barbara.

"Are you not coming on, lass?" he asked.

"She's got no money," piped up Deirdre, the boldest of the crowd.

Barbara thought she was going to die of embarrassment. How could Deirdre put it so blatantly? She might as well have told him that her mother went to chapel and thought fair grounds the work of the devil.

"Come on. We'll gi' you a free one this time!" the lad called to her, pulling up the safety bar so that she could get into the tub.

There was a second of hesitation then she ran over and slid in beside Helen and Lizzie. The bar clamped down on her lap. In that very moment the engine started, the barrel organ began to churn out its throaty tune and with a cranking and creaking the whole bed of the machine began to move.

At first the rocking was gentle, but the lads stayed with the girls' tubs, spinning them faster as the ride gained momentum. Round and round they went, a sea of lights and colours swirling before her eyes so that she could no longer make out the fair ground or the town or the sky. Only the music churned on, and the faces of her friends, thrown back, red and excited, the pressure of their bodies, forced together thigh to thigh, and the smell of sweat from the dark haired youth who span them round and round and round. Her breath went from her body. She struggled to catch it, yet threw her head back onto the red leather cushion behind her, exhilarated. They spun on, out into the growing darkness, out beyond the lights into a place where all was light and dark and music and sensation. And then slowly the ride began to lose its pace, the cart to slow its spinning, the lights to reconnect, and the world to take form, and soon they were rocking, gently rocking, gently riding the highs and lows of the wooden deck, slowing, easing to a halt.

The young man gave the car a last spin, winked at the girls, and wandered off to entice new customers for the next ride.

Barbara staggered off the ride, nearly falling over at the wooden steps, her head dizzy and swirling. She could not put what she felt into any set of words that she possessed. It was crazy, it was wonderful, it felt as if she were embracing the universe and laughing in the face of God. She felt free.

The house was in darkness when she got home. Slipping into the backdoor, she hoped she would be able to creep quietly into her bedroom without waking her parents. She had just reached the bottom of the stairs, however, when a voice called out to her. It came not from her parents' bedroom upstairs, but from the front parlour downstairs.

"Is that you, Barbara?" It was her mother's voice. "So you've come home at last, you dirty little thing. Been out flirting at the fair, I'll bet. Devil's work! You're bound for the devil for this."

It was when her mother was beating her that Barbara lost faith with God. She recalled that moment with absolute clarity. With the pain and humiliation of the wooden stick on her back and thighs, she saw with complete precision that there was no justice or love at the base of the universe, nothing that could save you beyond your own wit and conscience. She vowed that she would create her own rules from now on.

Barbara looked at Simon. His face was red and tear-stained. He was frightened. She saw that the object of his fear was herself, his mother.

"Never mind," she said. "These things happen sometimes. We'll get you another anorak before the autumn. You can do with your old one for now."

Simon's mouth dropped open. His father glanced up for a moment, clearly taken by surprise by what he had just heard.

"Now eat your dinner. It's getting cold." She went on.

****

And so the conflicting paths of guilt unfold. In such complex and contradictory ways we form our sense of right and wrong; our patterns of conscience out of the patchwork of memories and history.

Barbara struggles to do right. Childhood experiences forge identity. Layers of archaic responses become the foundations for adult ways of acting in the world. Barbara's guilt rests on a bed of injunctions and disapproval, on silent rebellion and on painful incidents which stand out like lone trees in the wasteland of missed childhood opportunities. The delineated life of sober frugality, which had served well the generations of chapel-going women, left a legacy that focused a girl's attention on what was sensible and on careful attention to detail in day to day matters. It trained young women to be good wives and mothers, to pass on generation to generation the lore of household order and virtue, and to live small lives of devoted service within small communities. It was a legacy which had its own rewards in its own times, but for Barbara, born into a different age that threw loose such restraints, it was hard to set aside, despite her rejection of the religious form which underwrote it. Despite the new values of a modern age, old ways permeated her thinking at every step. Like the patina on an old mirror, it coloured life's reflections, adding a haze of ancient gloom to whatever circumstance she viewed.

Her mother's voice still echoed through her head, commenting on her ways of mothering, both offering direction and criticising its shortcomings. A woman of solid views and unrelenting morality, nothing and no-one was ever good enough for Barbara's mother, at least as far as Barbara could determine (for no doubt her mother also had her story). So Barbara felt that her mothering was always being viewed, always criticised, always challenged, and Simon was always at the centre of that exercise, the measure of her failure, the test of her metal.

Yet, also, within her lay the resources for other perspectives. Her story is not only dominated by conformity. Other possibilities emerge. Certainly she has learned to be the mother, prudent, resourceful, controlling, but also she has the resources gleaned from her experience of being the child. She knows how it feels to be injured and fearful and hurt. And so the shift occurs. In a moment of human contact, she sees Simon's distress. She sees his fear, an echo of a memory, and in it finds a moment of identification. The experience interrupts her. It breaks the seal of her position, shakes her out of her anger and moves her away from a familiar script.

Barbara sees Simon afresh, and doing so, feels identification with his plight. She recognises his anguish, the pain and fear of being at the mercy of parental anger. In that moment of recollection, she knows the passions which the young person feels when the world beckons. She knows the urge to explore, to be free, and go beyond parental limits. She knows the way that such youthful adventures can so easily go wrong. She knows the fear that accompanies the return. She remembers herself, creeping back, like a skulking dog, with its tail between legs, when the adventure was over, hoping against hope not to be found out.

The family dynamics are unsettled. Barbara, who clung to the absolute power of her parenthood, has long been the force of strength in family relationships, her orders often mediated and softened through her husband's somewhat more moderate stance. Meanwhile, her husband plays a careful game, complicit sometimes with her, he provides a united front, a wall of authority that creates limits against which Simon throws his rebellion, such as it is. Other times, showing himself sympathetic to Simon's position, he undermines his wife's more rigid expectations with a dismissive look or muttered aside. So it circles.

There are times when Barbara would have her husband more compliant, she would direct him into particular positions, dress him according to her view of correctness, and have him respond in appropriate ways. Yet in his mild rebellion, he maintains a good natured stance against her rigidity which softens and yet supports her, despite her self-doubts. Likewise her son, despite his disobedience, in his nervous acceptance of her authority, demonstrates not simply subservience, but willing submission.

For beyond it all is love. Barbara loves her husband and son, and they in return love her. There is deep warmth within the family despite its rather formal façade. But love is dangerous. Its free expression is yet more terrifying than anger, for it melts the heart and unsettles the equilibrium. Thus love is meted out piecemeal. It is wrapped in practicalities and concern for right. It is rationed through the everyday details of interaction. But the deep love that never disappears completely is sensed, the ground of family life. Against its presence Simon fears retribution, but he never loses faith, for he is loved.

CHAPTER EIGHT

Biscuits

Simon felt a bit numb as he walked up the road to Joanne's house. The emotion of the morning had left him drained, but more than that, it had left him uncertain of his ground. His mother's reaction had disturbed him. What had it been about? Why had she changed so suddenly? Above all, could he go to the scrap yard again?

He kicked at the gravel in the gutter. It was wet and mixed with bits of twig and fallen cherry blossom which stuck to his feet. He felt uneasy. He understood her anger, braced himself against it. He feared it, yet now that it was absent he almost wished for its familiarity. When she looked at him in that familiar way that she did when he had broken some rule, explicit or implicit, he knew what to expect. Now that she did not react in this way, it was as if a part of her was absent, as if she were weaker, defeated by his shameful behaviour, as if a part of her had died. He felt a gnawing, sudden sense of loss. He also felt guilt. It was as if he had destroyed her.

He could not, of course, articulate all this. His awareness had language only for a vague sense of discomfort, but in his heart he felt a strange grief, a loss of innocence, and a sense of being alone in the world.

Indeed, in one sense, his mother had stepped aside from her appointed role. No longer the powerful matriarch, in that moment in which she recognised his fear, she became his travelling companion, and, in her deep empathy for her son's misery, relinquished her power over him in favour of sympathy and identification. In that moment too, as his mother, she had died. Barbara became something else to him, or he to her. In that moment a new possibility for relationship was born. It was just momentary, a short interlude stolen from the nurturing path of motherhood, but it was apodictic. Simon could never return to his former childhood assumption of her inviolable power. He had glimpsed her frailty.

This frailty reminded him that she was mortal. No longer flying on archetypal energy, she was grounded; a fallen angel. She too would age. Like his grandmother, decomposing before his eyes, he would now notice anxiously the first grey hairs, the tiredness after work, the heavy veins in her bare legs in summer. He would see her living death and know that they inevitably would be parted and he would be left alone, and, knowing this, he grieved in anticipation.

His unease had other sources too. Although he had feared punishment and would have delayed it, or even postponed it indefinitely, covering his tracks with half truths and distractions, this sudden lifting of the sentence left him unanchored. It was as if the deed, the carelessness, the crime, hung in suspension like an unfinished story. Sin required retribution; misbehaviour, punishment. Without its conclusion, the echoes of the crime rang on and on. Part of him longed for the clean sharp end that justice brought. A slap, a harsh telling off, restrictions or deprivations, whatever she determined would seal that matter and wipe clean the slate. In punishing him she would take away his guilt and, in doing so, would hold its burden in her breast.

This new scenario left the guilt uncauterised. Simon knew well the punishable nature of his crime. Indeed, the failure of his mother to punish him came out of its complete awfulness. This awfulness took the crime even beyond the awfulness of ordinary everyday misdemeanours. It was so awful that it had brought about this terrible silence. Like parched ground in the summer heat, he needed, craved, the relief of punishment. His mind rose up and scolded him ten-fold more vehemently than his mother could have. The image of her melting face haunted him like an avenging spectre. The memories of the lost anorak ran over and over in his mind like a voice that could not be silenced.

He kicked at the bruised petals, watching them turn from soft pink to brown, mashing them with his toe and squashing them into pulp, hating them for their delicacy. The rain would wash them into the deep darkness of the drain when next it came.

****

Joanne was in the kitchen when he rang the door bell. The two tone chime sounded too bright. Breaking in on his silent thoughts, it shocked him.

Joanne's mother opened the door.

"Hello Simon. Come on in." She smiled. She was a plump, friendly woman, who liked to put children at ease. Used to organising them, she could be over-familiar and a bit bossy, but Simon liked her. "Were you playing round with smelly bonfires too?" she asked.

Simon did not answer.

"So, what did your mother have to say?" Her look was slightly knowing, but not enough so to be disloyal. She knew Barbara.

Simon looked down at his feet and still said nothing.

"I bet she was none too pleased!" Joanne's mother went on.

Simon was glad not to have to reply.

"You're going to do some baking." she went on. Her sentence felt somewhere between a question and a command. Baking was, after all, a good thing for children to learn to do. "I've put all the things on the kitchen table and I'm going to leave you two to it. I'll take the twins out to the town with me so they won't disturb you, and we'll expect some good results when we get back. Your Dad's working, Joanne, so don't disturb him unless its urgent... you can always call him if you get into difficulties though."

She added the latter almost as an afterthought. She trusted Joanne.

Simon felt relief and trepidation. To be allowed to cook in the house on one's own was novel. His own mother would never have encouraged such a thing. But then, Joanne had been doing baking with her mother ever since she was old enough to stand on a stool in the kitchen. As Guide captain, her mother believed in teaching girls to be independent and to learn all the skills of home-making, as well as those of surviving out doors and being a good, community minded citizen. She believed in stimulating imagination and rewarding capability with responsibility. She believed in teaching young people to lead and to be led, to explore and to be respectful. Whilst many of her values were old fashioned, her spirit was energetic and enthusiastic.

"She let you out then?" Joanne's first words when the door closed after her mother were reassuringly blunt.

"Yes."

Simon paused. He wanted to tell Joanne what had happened, to share with her the burden he was still carrying, but somehow the words just weren't there.

"Something happened..."

The words tailed off. What had happened? He was struggling to voice his experience.

He tried again. "She was going to tell me off. She was really angry. Then something happened. She just stopped. She just said 'these things happen' and 'not to worry'."

He blurted it out, but it sounded all wrong. It didn't sound like anything. Like nothing had happened. Yet he knew it had. The whole world had been turned upside down. How could he tell Joanne something important had changed?

Joanne looked at him quizzically. She couldn't make him out. He was acting as if something really big had happened, something momentous, but all he had told her was that his mum had let him off. It seemed silly to her. Sometimes she found Simon a bit babyish.

"Sounds OK," she said, her tone somewhat dismissive.

"But she just sort of looked….." again, Simon ran out of words.

Joanne snorted. "Come on, lets get on!" she said.

The recipe book was open on the kitchen table. Beside it were the ingredients, laid out neatly, and beside them a large brown earthenware bowl, wooden spoon, a measuring spoon and rubber headed spatula. There were old fashioned scales, with lead weights in a little tower of decreasing sizes, discoloured with age, and slightly encrusted in the recesses of their rims with yellowed flour. There was also a little plastic packet of crinkled cake papers in pastel colours. Laid out on the top of the cooker were dark metal baking trays.

"We can make chocolate crispies *and* oatie drops," said Joanne. "Mum says to make the chocolate crispies first then they can be setting while we make the oaties."

She was as organized as her mother in the kitchen. Simon spooned and stirred and measured to her directions, melting ingredients together in the heavy aluminium pan over a low flame. There was a wonderful chocolaty smell, rich and dark and syrupy. They shook in the rice crispies and giggled as they crackled and popped in the hot sauce. Soon they were spreading out the little paper cases on a tea tray, checking they were really separated, as two or three tended to stick together, then spooning into them the mounds of chocolate flavoured confection. When they had finished, they set the tray of little clusters aside in the cool of the larder whilst they started on making the biscuits.

The biscuits involved melting things in the saucepan too. Joanne suggested that they saved washing up and used the same pan, which was perhaps a mistake as the chocolate burned a bit on the bottom, but the margarine and syrup and sugar were soon melting into a liquid, the last lumps of fat shrinking in little yellow pieces, which could be poured into the bowl with the oats and flour.

"Let's add raisins," said Joanne, fetching a packet from the pantry.

Simon was impressed by her confidence. He would not have dared to vary the recipe. But then, she was a girl. Girls knew about cooking.

They threw in the raisins, one handful then another for luck. Then they greased the trays with old butter papers which Joanne's mother had kept for the purpose. They rolled little balls of biscuit mix, as big as walnuts, just as it said in the recipe book, and put them onto the baking sheet. You had to put them a distance apart because they would spread, Joanne had told Simon. Simon tried to make some oaties into funny shapes, a fish, a tree and a ginger bread man, but it didn't work and they came out of the oven looking like strange misshapen blobs.

"Let's eat the failures," Joanne said, breaking the head off Simon's man. It was still hot and bent languidly as she lifted it off the tray.

Just as they were finishing lifting the biscuits onto the wire tray to cool, Joanne's father popped his head round the door.

"Thought I smelled something good," he grinned, and without being invited came over and helped himself to Simon's fish. It was still hot and he whistled air into his mouth as he chewed it, spluttering a little, "Whooor, very good. Tasty. Yes, that will keep me going." He took another biscuit, shifting it from hand to hand to cool it, and went back to his study.

Simon and Joanne went up to her bedroom. They took some biscuits and a couple of the crispie cakes which were nearly set, and fun to eat as they broke up and left your fingers all coated in chocolate. They also took a jug of lemon squash and plastic tumblers. Joanne had the little box room at the front of the house, so there wasn't a lot of space. They sat on the bed, one at each end, the biscuits between them on the window sill, lemon squash poured into the beakers. They ate quietly.

"These are good," said Simon. He was thinking how clever Joanne was, how grown up. She would soon be able to manage on her own. She always knew what to do.

"Your mum's dead strict," said Joanne, breaking the silence.

Simon looked out of the window. The rain had washed much of the cherry blossom off the trees and new, young, reddish leaves were breaking out of the branch tips, shiny and fragile. He did not reply.

"Did you ever see a picture of a nude lady?" Joanne didn't know why she asked the question. The words sort of jumped out of her mouth unbidden. She bit her lip and wished she had said nothing.

Simon did not answer. It was not even apparent that he had heard.

"Let's get some more biscuits," said Joanne, jumping off the bed and running down the stairs.

****

The gap between experience and words perplexes us and thwarts our understanding. Even to represent to ourselves those deep concerns that echo through our hearts in the long nights of wrestling with our consciences requires facility with language that so often eludes us.

For Simon, struggling with new intuitions of adult thoughts and preoccupations, the intensity of feeling was woefully difficult to express in words. He struggled, isolated in his confusion.

Of course, he could not know his mother's story. The change of heart came unexpectedly, out of the blue; a shift from anger to sympathy, punishment to leniency. It had no context and he had no context with which to understand it. Adult concerns intruding on the child's sense of propriety unsettle the world so recently constructed.

Joanne too, despite her confident and sometimes dismissive manner, still could not quite subdue the feelings that those images which she had seen had evoked in her. Still clinging to that space between guilt and fascination her words broke out of her unguardedly. They sought an outlet, perhaps complicity, perhaps reassurance. The secret knowledge burned inside her, eroding her self-assuredness.

So each child felt the burden of their knowledge, the uncomfortable residue of guilt that rose from experiences which could not be set aside, nor yet easily voiced. Each sought relief. Not least they sought to voice their feelings, break the isolation, unbind the spell. As in the confessional, the secret guilt once voiced loses potency. Guilt hangs over us, contaminating our being, seeking resolution. We long to tell, to release the imprisoned knowledge of our wickedness. We seek a friend, a confidante, a powerful figure, who can hold the force which threatens to overwhelm us, who has the power to give absolution, to comfort and restore us to innocence. We long to retreat into the womb of another's compassion, our naked, evil selves huddling in the arms of our protector, willing to take whatever penance is ascribed in return for surrender. Yet voicing secrets may involve crossing a dangerous edge, entering a vast swathe of open desolation, a no-mans land, territory of barbed wire and snipers, before the safety and comfort of a confidante is reached. Simon attempted such a meeting first. Struggling to make sense even in his own mind of what he had experienced, his words could not explain what had happened. He did not know himself. How could Joanne possibly understand?

But perhaps some communication did pass between them. Perhaps in commenting on his mother's strictness, Joanne acknowledged his earlier distress. Perhaps, even though she could not understand, could not see why he was so upset that his mother had not punished him, she could see that there were pressures in his life which were beyond her experience. These she acknowledged. It was an overture, a partial venture into empathy, an offer of connection. In all probability this tacit support gave partial relief for Simon.

More than this, though, Joanne probably recognised Simon's

attempt to share. She saw his struggle and, despite the part of her that despised and feared weakness, she felt solace in seeing that more personal sharing might be possible. Not consciously, but in the periphery of her awareness, this opening of new channels of intimacy softened some internal wall. It invited sharing of a secret in return. Almost without deciding it, she asked him. Had he seen pictures? Did he know what such images were like? Could he share her burden of knowledge? In a moment the question was out. And in a moment too, it was over. His silence returned her to the safety of not knowing his answer. It aborted the move that might have taken both of them deeper into dangerous territory.

Perhaps the intimacy of the situation; the two eldest, boy and girl, separated from the protection of the gang, having to discover how to relate person to person; had fuelled her question. Perhaps the closeness of sharing domestic pleasures, of withdrawing into her personal space, her bedroom, fuelled her question. Perhaps some emerging curiosity, some new awareness of latent differences, of gender, of sexuality, still unacknowledged and far enough from consciousness to be innocently expressed, fuelled her question.

Relationships at that age hover round such half emergent themes. I search my own memories, aged ten. Recall a fair haired lad, perhaps even a little like Simon, partnered with me in a school play. Noticing, even then, that light frisson of excitement when he had to help me put on a pair of long socks in some unremembered scene. Noticing how that scenario, the feel of his hand on my foot, the look of his tousled blond head as he knelt in front of me, eyes intent upon the socks, appeared in my thoughts in idle moments for long after we had gone our separate ways to single sex secondary schools. Yet never, never, never till many years later, did I consciously make that association with romance, with dawning sexual feelings, which to the adult eye seems so obvious. Or do I lie, even to myself? Even in the memory, some delicious, half permitted awareness of the implications, of the possibilities, glimmers in the background; some fantasy sequel hovers in the air.

So what was Joanne's question? Was it a confession, an expression of disquiet, or a seduction? How it sat on that edge between curiosity and innocence, just as her own internal process swung between discomfort and fascination, the interest that would not be silenced, rising like spring sap through her being.

****

Unburdening guilt in most instances requires a witness. Even silent confession requires a god to hear it. Sometimes seeking the co-conspirator, other times the executioner, the thread of feeling lingers unabated until it finds a resting place in communication. Simon without punishment floundered in uncertainty. His sense of having committed a terrible crime, of having allowed events to unfold in such a dreadful way, could, it seems, only be assuaged through punishment.

The fugitive gives himself up, the suspect confesses. The tension of running is too much to bear. The anticipation of capture and trial grows in the evasion and becomes too great. External threats create anxiety that wears us down eventually, eroding our confidence and our will to persist. We long to conclude, to face the inevitable and get it over with, to bite the bullet and to live again. Some would run forever, but many of us prefer to terminate the chase. We do not have the stamina.

A friend of mine was an attorney, defending prisoners in the United States on death row. The men (for they were generally men) went through appeal after appeal, using the full force of the judicial system to delay their executions. Sometimes an appeal would be successful and a sentence reduced. Often, it just led to another layer of judiciary, another sequence of waiting and collecting evidence and standing trial. For many it took years, and became a career of finding loop holes and navigating the space between conviction and execution with cunning and resourcefulness. For others the running became too much. She told me that a good proportion of executions were actually of "volunteers". They were men who felt enough was enough, buckled under the pressure of continuing and grasped at the release of death. Who can blame them? Better the fast oblivion by lethal injection than the living death of life on the legal circuit of appeals and convictions.

Perhaps too, we sometimes feel that we are only getting what we deserve. Sometimes we want justice, want to feel the security and predictability of the system, even when that system is focused on judging us. Our inner voice echoes the outer forces, bidding them do what must be done. We want to believe in the forces of right and the power of good over evil. We want to believe that good triumphs and to sacrifice ourselves on its altar. Only then do we feel safe, held by walls that cannot be breached.

The inner voice is powerful. Without external threats, its protestations persist. Our minds readily create their own judges and persecutors. Whether from the internalised voices of past moral authorities or from phantoms arising spontaneously from our own consciences, our internal judges can create a regime far more oppressive and harder to resist than external powers. We beat ourselves up, judging ourselves in every tiny misdemeanour, and adding each into the reckoning. We blame ourselves regardless of mitigation, accepting no reason and no excuse.

Punishment is a relief. It creates an end, finishes the process begun by transgression. So, bitterly, did Simon feel his deprivation. Without his mother's anger, the deed's aftermath, the untidy spillage of carelessness, thoughtless action and, before that, disobedience, flowed like an oil slick, un-stemmed across his life. There it would lie like a dark cloak for years to come. Easily re-ignited, the pain of remembering that awful day when his anorak was burned would bring shudders of guilt flooding back into his cheeks and anguished regret into his belly.

Sometimes we even seek punishment. Perhaps we long for the catharsis of another's anger to cleanse us of our sinful nature. Often, such feelings seem rooted in a need for finality and closure, linked to sense of justice and fair play. Sometimes it is simply a desire for a swift clean ending, in which we will be released from the misery of anticipation.

Corporal punishment is now outlawed in schools and institutions in England, and rightly so. When I was nine, it was still a threat, rarely used yet ever present. That year we had a new teacher who came to take our class, a young New Zealander. It was September and we were in a new class room, sorting books and putting them away. Our teacher was directing operations. Opening a cupboard he was surprised to discover a slipper and a wooden rod.

"What on earth are these?" he asked us.

We giggled at his surprise. Perhaps we heard the disapproval in his tone and felt he was on our side. We told him that his predecessor had been responsible for meting out punishment in the school. The cane was for boys and slipper for girls. He looked taken aback, but he closed the cupboard door without saying anything. I never saw it opened again.

I was never beaten, but I did receive the occasional clip, slap or shaking from an angry teacher. Many of us did. I have to confess that as a child I actually preferred the kind of teachers who settled their own scores. Often they were the more idiosyncratic ones, passionate about their subjects, who felt no need to placate children or earn their approval. I loved their enthusiasm and caught their love of learning, but also you knew where you were with them. When they were angry with you it was done and dusted by the lesson end. In contrast, I felt contempt and suspicion for those who did not deal with the matter themselves. I disliked those who reported you to your form teacher or to the head teacher. I suspected cowardice in those who let someone else do the punishing. It felt somehow dishonest. Also it prolonged the whole process and added more layers of embarrassment and adult disapproval. Better the clean ending, the teacher's fury vented in a stream of angry words or physical impact, which brought the matter to conclusion. Such was a child's view.

So Simon sought relief through his clumsy attempts to communicate, his confessions of his guilt. He missed the resolution of his mother's anger and feared the desolation of her sympathy. He craved another who could hold and support him. He sought counsel, longed for the wisdom of the person he admired most in all the world to tell him how to release himself from sordid discovery.

He wanted Joanne to guide him, to make it all familiar and to turn the clock back to earlier, simpler times, but she could not. She was already locked in her own turmoil. Simon's guilt, his complicity in his mother's annihilation, festered on. He could not relinquish the knowing which had come to him, nor understand the mystery of her weakness which had been exposed.

The small child lives in the security of his parents' certainty. This was even more so in the nineteen sixties. In most instances, family relationships seemed firm and unchanging and threats of loss were distant possibilities which happened to other families. Families rarely broke up and death was uncommon among the young. Only time could conspire to end such comfortable continuity. Glimpsing mortality, unseating the parent's from the throne of invincibility was, then, for Simon, a crime beyond measure. The penalty he paid for it was exposure. It tore the cocoon away, leaving him in a state of raw vulnerability.

CHAPTER NINE

Friends

Monday morning Joanne saw Simon in the playground when she arrived at school. He stood against the red brick wall on the far side of the yard, leaning against the high iron palings which surmounted it and which separated the yard from the main road. He was on his own. She wandered over to him.

"How's it going?" she asked.

He shrugged. "She's not said anything," he said. He paused, then he added, "I wish she would."

Joanne looked at him in silence. "Well, maybe that's it then," she said at last.

Simon shrugged again.

They had not seen each other since Saturday. Joanne's family had been out visiting relatives in Oxfordshire all day Sunday. It was quite a drive, so by the time they got back it had been too late to go out. Simon had spent most of the day in his room reading comic books and making an Airfix plane to distract himself. He had got a headache from the glue by the time Philip had called round in the late afternoon. They played Monopoly in the sitting room and Simon's mother gave them lemonade and biscuits. It had all felt very ordinary.

Joanne frowned. "Buck up," she said.

Simon pulled a face. He didn't know what he wanted, but something felt very incomplete. He felt restless in his head, but his mood was heavy and slow.

"I'll see you tonight," Joanne pulled back. The school yard was filling up, and she did not want to be seen talking to Simon for too long. At the same time she felt drawn to linger with him a bit longer. Perhaps it was the inconclusiveness of his mood. Perhaps it was her own uncertainty over the weekend's events. Being close to him felt unusually comforting.

****

Wendy was standing by the entrance door. After she had left Simon, Joanne went over to speak to her. She wanted the ordinariness of conversation.

"Hiya," she said when she came within range. "How are you doing?"

Wendy put her head on one side and squinted at the sky. She had spent Saturday in the shop with her mum. Yesterday had just kind of disappeared hanging round the house, watching her sisters with their make-up and hair-styling, reading their magazines and listening to Radio Luxemburg. Looking back, it was hard to know where the time had gone. It all felt a bit of a haze. She wrinkled her nose.

"It was a bit boring this weekend," she said. "Sometimes I'm glad to get back to school."

Joanne was taken aback. Wendy's response had shocked her. Did people really think like that? How could school be the high point of one's week? It was not as if Wendy seemed particularly happy there. She wasn't very popular at school and just seemed to tag along with Sarah all the time. If this was better than home, home couldn't be very good. Suddenly Joanne felt sorry for Wendy, and for a moment almost guilty for never having invited her over to her house at weekends. She had always imagined that Sarah was Wendy's real friend, so it had never occurred to her that Wendy might be lonely. Now she felt less sure.

"Don't you see Sarah?"

"Not often," Wendy shuffled her feet as she spoke, "She doesn't go out much."

Joanne hesitated. She felt an impulse to reach out, but in the same moment felt a contrary one. A voice inside her urged caution. Wendy looked down at her feet. Her shoes were black patent with ankle straps. Joanne noticed that they were a bit scuffed on the toes. "You could come to my place next weekend," she said suddenly. Then she added, "But do wear some old shoes."

Wendy's face brightened. "Oh, yes please," she said.

"You can come round on Saturday after breakfast. You know where I live, don't you."

"Oh, I'll try," Wendy flushed, "I don't know what Mum will say. I usually help out in the shop Saturdays. I'll let you know tomorrow."

Joanne shrugged. Well, at least she had tried.

At that moment, Sarah came up. She was hot and red faced from running.

"Goodness, I overslept!" she gasped, mopping her brow with a theatrical sweep. "I was reading so late last night. David Copperfield. Just couldn't put it down."

Neither Joanne nor Wendy answered.

Mr Rodway, their class teacher was standing in the doorway behind them, looking out across the yard. In his hand was the large brass bell which was to mark the start of another week. Children scattered randomly across the tarmac: lines of older boys sweeping towards each other in a game of tag; a football bouncing forlornly in a corner, its owner puffing over to retrieve it; small children, bundled in gabardine raincoats and long woollen stockings, running excitedly to greet one another, tripping over shoes laces and tumbling on bare knees. Now as the bell sounded out, all of them paused, frozen suddenly to attention as they awaited the familiar instruction to line up. Huddles of girls lifted their heads from whispered conversations. Tea-cards were bundled away into jacket pockets to avoid confiscation. Shrieks and cat calls stopped. The moving ant hill of children fell still and silent. The bell sounded again. Slowly the mass of children assembled itself into lines that stretched out from the wall beside the door way, back into the yard. There was silence.

Mr Rodway paused, resting in the all-embracing quietude, savouring the morning air. He felt the power that his position bestowed. Then he spoke. "Class One girls!"

Obediently the line of girls filed into the cloakroom. Joanne, Wendy and Sarah were at the front of the queue. They hung their coats on the cast iron pegs without saying anything. Mrs Marsh was on duty and stood sentinel in the doorway. She looked across the rows of metal coat racks, checking for anyone dallying unnecessarily at their peg. Only the clatter of footsteps of younger children broke the silence. It was an ordinary Monday morning.

****

The following Saturday Wendy rang the bell on Joanne's front door.

The week had been uneventful. Another storm had blown in on Monday and the weather had been wet and blustery all week, so the gang had been mostly kept indoors. On Tuesday after school the rain had slowed to scarcely more than a drizzle. Michael and Ian were at cubs that evening, so they had gone straight home, and Simon wouldn't go to the scrap yard, as he didn't want to disobey his mother, so Joanne had called in with Philip on the way back from school. Simon stood in the lane, shouting a conversation to them through the fence for a while, but eventually the rain had come on again and he had gone off home. That had left Joanne and Philip sitting under the tarpaulin. They watched the drips forming along the edge of the canvas for a while and drank sweet tea from tin mugs with Alf and Ray, but Joanne didn't find Philip much company.

The men had been a bit glum that night too. Two days of working in the chilly rain had put them in a bad mood. Nor did things improve. The rest of the week the rain was even heavier, with winds battering the driving shafts against the windows of the classroom. Classes grew restless as wet weather comic books and games became boring and youngsters cooped up all day vented their frustrated energies in quarrels and unruliness.

Once or twice Joanne waved to the men as she hurried past the fence of the yard on her way to or from school, huddled in her thick anorak, with the hood pulled hard over her head against the stinging rain. Mostly, though, they did not seem to be around. Perhaps they were in the shed, she thought.

On Saturday the sky was clear at last. Bright sunshine streamed through Joanne's bedroom curtains. The air from the open window smelt fresh with that particular sharpness it has after rain.

Wendy's knock was timid, but Joanne was expecting her, so she was ready to run down the stairs and open the door. Wendy stood on the doorstep, head slightly on one side, looking nervous. She was wearing dark red corduroy trousers and a brown knitted sweater and had white plimsolls on her feet. She bobbed up and down nervously as she waited. Joanne felt some relief when she saw her. At least she wasn't wearing a dress.

Opening the door, Joanne suddenly realised that she hadn't given any thought to what they were going to do. She had invited Wendy over on a whim, but she didn't really know what sort of thing Wendy would be willing to join in. What was she expecting? Wendy hadn't been to Joanne's house before. Joanne was not sure that she would fit in with the rest of the gang. At the same time, being with the gang was so much part of her usual routine that she didn't know what else they would do on a Saturday.

She could hear her mother washing up the breakfast things in the kitchen. One thing she was sure of was that she was keen to avoid being organized into some activity by her.

"Come upstairs," she said.

Wendy followed. Up in her bedroom, Joanne got out the collection of old annuals which she had acquired the previous weekend from an Oxfordshire cousin. The battered volumes filled the gap, giving something they could do which moderated the need for conversation for a bit. Wendy seemed appreciative. Joanne's confidence was restored. Soon the girls were sitting side by side on the bed reading comic strips.

It was mid-morning when Simon called round. Joanne heard his bark in the road outside but did not answer. In front of Wendy, making a bark in reply would have seemed silly. The gate clicked and Joanne ran downstairs to answer the door before Simon had time to ring the bell. She wanted to catch him before her mother heard them.

"Is that you, Joanne?" her mother called from the kitchen.

"Yes."

"If you're going out, be home lunch time. Is Wendy staying?"

Joanne's mother always seemed to know who was visiting. Joanne was perplexed by it. No matter how quietly they slipped into the house, her mother always seemed to know what was going on. In one sense it was no problem. She was always welcoming and accommodating of Joanne's friends. At the same time, Joanne felt uncomfortable. It irritated her. If she had been able to pin down her feelings, Joanne might have said that when her mother watched her friends in this way, she felt compromised, her privacy invaded, her life laid open to scrutiny, but she did not have the words to frame this for herself. Also, as a child on the brink of adolescence, she had no expectation that adults would respect her integrity. So, shrugging off her irritation, she answered her mother with a quick glance over her shoulder.

"May she?"

"Yes, but she'd better phone her mother to ask if it's all right with her."

"OK."

Joanne turned the door knob cautiously. Simon was standing on the step under the porch. She indicated silence to him. It was a habit, trying to outwit her mother, whilst knowing at the same time the futility of doing so. She beckoned him in with a gesture, ushering him straight upstairs to her room.

"I'll just get Wendy to ring then," she called through to her mother, loudly enough to cover his footfalls on the wooden stair treads.

With Simon and Wendy in her room, Joanne felt a strange curiosity and some awkwardness. Of course they knew one another a bit already. Being in the same school year, they saw each other in the classroom during some of the lessons which the two classes shared and they passed each other in playground and corridor at other times, but that didn't mean they *really* knew each other.

Joanne looked around her room. It was a small box bedroom with mauve curtains and pale spotted wallpaper. There was a turquoise blue rough weave bedcover and a green striped mat. She had chosen the furnishings herself. Now, suddenly, it felt very small. This was a new scenario. Wendy didn't know about Joanne's friendship with Simon or about the gang. They were part of Joanne's home life. At school, except in occasional encounters, she and the rest of the gang acted as if they were strangers. Now Wendy would get to know all about them. Joanne didn't know if she could really trust her in that way. She suddenly felt uncomfortable. Wendy's gaze threw the ordinary aspects of her home life into new relief.

At the same time Joanne felt even more self-conscious relating to Wendy under Simon's scrutiny than she had before. She didn't know how to be Wendy's friend, and the added complication of his presence made her acutely aware of every move and gesture. With the two of them present in one space, Joanne realized that there were things about her that she actually didn't want either of them to see. Standing uncomfortably beside the bed, Joanne knew immediately that she didn't want to spend all morning reading comics. She felt suddenly claustrophobic.

Yet having Simon there also helped. He would back her up and help draw Wendy into doing something outdoors. That would feel much more comfortable. With him, going out and hanging round the Amazon and the scrap yard would be normal. Wendy would have to join in. That way they would get over this embarrassing hiatus.

"Are we going out then?" Joanne asked, confident that Simon would agree.

There was silence. Joanne looked at Simon. He didn't answer.

"Where are we going?" he asked eventually.

"The scrap yard I guess," now Joanne felt cross. He was supposed to support her, not quibble about details in front of Wendy.

"But my mother..." his voice tailed off.

"I thought your mother said it was all alright. I thought that was what you were so upset about." Joanne hissed back at him.

Simon flinched. Her words cut through him. It was a betrayal. He had tried to tell her how he felt, but she had just thrown it back at him. But he didn't have an answer.

"OK," he said at last.

When they reached the scrap yard, the three younger members of the gang were already there. Michael and Ian were just coming out of the gate, hauling a long metal pole behind them. Philip followed, jeering at them as it caught against first the gate and then some brambles.

"What on earth are you doing with that?" Joanne asked, scowling at her brothers in a mix of curiosity and disapproval.

"We're going to build a new camp. This is for the roof," Ian huffed, stumbling slightly as he spoke, as the weight of the pole pulled him off track.

"But how are you going to stop it falling on your heads?" Joanne asked, still disbelieving.

"Stop fussing, big sister," Michael taunted, "We can do it."

Joanne shrugged her shoulders and cast her eyes to heaven affectedly. She was not going to argue. Alf, who stood by the gate watching, laughed.

"Bring it back when you've finished with it," he called after them, then turning, he walked back into the yard.

So the gang divided for the morning. The three youngest, out in the waste ground beside the Amazon, struggled to wedge their pole between some wizened elders and a couple of wooden crates. The three older ones sat on the old sofa beneath the tarpaulin.

The sofa smelled damp, and the springs were uneven. Joanne noticed how Wendy dusted the seat cushion before she sat down. She noticed how she perched on the edge instead of flopping back into it as she and Simon did. Simon was watching her too. He was still smarting from the earlier conversation, but he knew Joanne was right. To have not gone back to the scrap yard would have meant cutting himself off from everything. It would have been suicide. He had to be able to be with the gang to survive, he thought, he would just have to make sure his mother never found out again.

There was an awkward silence and Joanne wondered what they usually talked about when they sat there in the yard.

"Make us some tea," Alf called across.

Joanne was relieved to get up. She opened the door of the shed. Inside was the stove, standing on the formica top of the old kitchen cupboard. She took it out onto the concrete slab under the tarpaulin. She had lit it before, but not often. She felt a little nervous. The meths was in an old lemonade bottle. She poured it carefully into the well. There was the familiar sharp smell. Carefully she struck the match against the rough side of the block then dropped it into the well of purple liquid. A blue flame crept across the surface and miraculously the smell disappeared. Joanne filled the little kettle at the tap at the side of the hut and put it onto the stove.

While the kettle was boiling, Joanne went back into the hut to get the mugs and tea bags. It was the third time she had been into the hut that morning. Each time had brought a strange feeling of hot anxiety into her stomach. She felt her cheeks flushing. Making the tea broke the intensity of having to be with Wendy and Simon together, but in the shed she felt unsettled, conscious that her eyes wanted to look in the dark space under the table. She struggled to avoid looking but she could not help wanting to see if the magazines were still there. They were.

The pile had been rearranged. A different magazine was on the top. Would this new magazine be like the others? Joanne's fingers seemed irresistibly pulled towards the volume. She felt an overwhelming need to know what was inside this new edition. Crouching beside the table, she quickly flipped the pages open. Images of bare flesh, pink and smooth, sprawled across the pages. There were different themes, one woman blonde and shy looking, lying on pink shiny sheets and fluffy ostrich feather cushions, another dark and fierce looking standing against a background of black and red. Each page turn increased both her anxiety and her need to see more.

She could only have spent a minute or so skimming the pages, yet in that minute time seemed to stand still. Her ears were attentive, ready to spur her into activity at the slightest sound. Then, suddenly afraid that the kettle might be boiling, she shoved the magazine back onto the heap. She brushed her hands down the sides of her jeans as if to clean them, then, threading her fingers through the handles of the mugs, she took them outside to make the tea. Her cheeks were burning. She bent over the stove to hide them, willing the colour to subside. Simon and Wendy were still sitting in silence. He looked bored and sulky, she awkward.

Joanne called to Ray and Alf to let them know tea was ready. Perhaps they would help to ease the tension. The men ambled over and sat down.

"Who's this then?" Alf grinned, looking at Wendy.

Wendy looked shy, but smiled tentatively as Joanne introduced her.

"Get the cards." Alf said, perhaps sensing a need for direction, "I'll give you all a game of cheat."

Joanne went back into the hut. She took the dog-eared pack from the ledge. The cards were well thumbed and bound together by an elastic band. Sometimes the men used them to gamble for shillings when the rain got too hard. With the kids they played games like cheat or knock-out whist. The pack felt comfortable and slightly greasy in Joanne's hand. As she took them, she glanced back at the magazines one last time, checking that she had left the pile straight as before, then she went out to join the others.

Soon they were all playing. It was a lively game. Alf loved cheat, but they always managed to catch him out. Ray won as usual, his rather dour features giving nothing away till they broke into a grin as he placed his last cards on the pile.

****

Negotiating friendship is a complex mix of altruism and the satisfaction of personal needs. How far do our friendships reflect a real concern for the other, and how much a bolstering of our sense of self or an exchange of reciprocal benefits? Joanne had given only scant attention to her friendship with Wendy prior to that weekend. Indeed whether Wendy could really have been called a friend at all was an open question.

The convenience of spending time with Wendy and Sarah seemed simply a social requirement. If one were cynical, one might say that their company provided some way of passing time and meant that Joanne avoided the stigma of being friendless. Joanne seemed just as content to spend her time lugging milk crates round the school as in being in conversation with her class mates. Yet to dismiss the relationships as purely ones of convenience would be too simplistic.

Joanne had been fascinated by Sarah. Something in her bookish enthusiasm resonated with Joanne's own imaginative life. Sarah sought solace in the worlds that she entered through the pages that she read and those on which she wrote. Joanne escaped from her pressures into her imagination and in her games, particularly in her explorations of the Amazon.

Wary, yet admiring, each sensed in the other something which was both exciting and dangerous in the school yard community. Each held an edge of reserve with the other, but nevertheless felt an alliance as they were both different from the mainstream. Each observing the other's way of operating in the world felt confirmation and enrichment of their own way. This fascination had, however, run its course for Joanne. Her changing emotions left her craving a different kind of friendship.

So that Monday morning it was Wendy who caught Joanne's attention. When Joanne had been confident in her home life, school life had been just a pale interlude in the day to be endured. She had no real need for close friendships at school because her place within the gang was central and secure. It met those needs.

Her family too provided stability and support for her. Taking after her mother, she had learned to use her sensible authority to take command of situations and relate to others as an organiser or a carer. Her father's easy going liberalism had freed her from the worst excesses of conscience, and given her a free-wheeling attitude to life. In addition, in their slightly old fashioned attitudes, her parents set an example of being somewhat removed from the forefront of social trends. They would make little comments about others that distanced them from acquaintances. Although they were socially active in the community, at a personal level, they kept themselves to themselves. They did for others, but did not like gossip or entertain casual friendships.

For Joanne, with the discovery of the magazines, an emotional storm had entered a previously ordered world. In the past the exploits of the gang had always provided space for expressing her imaginative energy and, no doubt, through this play, the children had explored the emotional themes of their lives. Danger and death, inspiration and ambition flowed naturally into the fabric of their games. The problem was that this new threat, arising from her encounter with adult sexuality, could not be dealt with in the same way. Feeling vulnerable, she could no longer find comfort in her position of strength in the gang or in the games they played. She looked for ways that she could perhaps be supported by others. This shift in her desire for relationships was not something she could have described, but instinctively she started to gravitate to those people in her circle who might offer such friendship.

In her state of vulnerability, Joanne saw Wendy in a new light. Previously almost invisible, Joanne had seen Wendy simply as an appendage to Sarah. Now Joanne felt intuitively a greater need for the kind of reassurance which a friendship with another girl might bring. Wendy seemed to offer this.

****

Although Joanne's initial impulse towards Wendy on that Monday morning was simply a desire to find company, their conversation brought feelings of surprising affinity. Joanne saw in Wendy a neediness which seemed to echo her own. In her shyness, she saw her recent feelings of social ineptitude magnified. She felt sorry for Wendy, struggling with loneliness and an unspoken feeling of difference. Whether the sympathy that rose in her was really for Wendy, or for her own reflection mirrored in Wendy's uncertain response, it softened Joanne's view and led her to reach out and make an invitation.

With new insight into Wendy's personal world Joanne's first response is an expression of caring. She reaches out, but then, with the anticipation of the social implications of taking Wendy into her home life and introducing her to the gang, she is plunged into new anxiety. She fears how others will perceive her. She does not know if Wendy will fit into the gang's culture. She becomes anxious and uncertain how to behave, losing her usually confident façade. Her response becomes ambivalent. She invites

Wendy to join in, but at the same time holds back from really welcoming her.

It is often so. In our vulnerability, layers of defence are shed. Self-satisfaction crumbles and with in may go barriers which we have created between us and the sufferings of the people around us. A space is created where real empathy for the plight of our companions grows. The pain of loss or hurt feelings helps us appreciate others. So it is that those in distress are sometimes better able to offer others support, but not always. Pain also makes us more self-absorbed. It pulls us back into self-protective strategies. We reach out and we draw back. We open to others and we close emotional doors in their faces. Pain makes us unreliable. Perhaps this is why Joanne is so unsympathetic to Simon.

Joanne's relationship with Simon has changed a great deal over the past week. In some ways her experiences seem to have deepened her bond with him. Their exchanges the previous weekend had been quite sensitive, and a new understanding seemed to have grown up between them. Since then, new elements have come into their conversation, both enticing and scary.

It is against this backdrop that Joanne turns on Simon. Beset by conflicted emotions, and a general level of anxiety, she insists that he come to the scrap yard. As if she cannot bear to show sensitivity towards him in front of Wendy, she cuts across his feelings in a way that is quite shocking and cavalier. Yet he accepts her rebuff, relieved to have the decision made for him.

So Joanne wavers; one moment caring, the next withdrawing. First concerned for Simon, but then retreating into practicality, and even cruelty. She becomes unwilling or unable to understand his unease or tolerate his hesitation. She does not appreciate the distress his mother's reaction caused him, and wants the issue to be over, consigned to history. She cannot engage with his turmoil when her own is so pressing. Yet also she craves Simon's company with a new fervour. She longs to deepen their intimacy. She longs to share her churning thoughts. She softens towards him, reaches out, but in the end, dismisses his feelings, her irritation burning in her words. So Joanne is caught, craving and fearing intimacy with an intensity that springs from the rawness of pre-adolescence.

****

Friendships reflect our identities in two ways.

Firstly, to ourselves, our chosen friends reflect the different facets of who we are. They confirm our identity. Some of those we are close to offer a mirror in which we see ourselves reflected. Others, conversely, being different from us, provide a contrast against which we differentiate ourselves. Good friendships are complex. Part like, part different, within their territory we find both walls and mirrors, discover a rich variety of capacities reflected and yet maintain a sense of psychological boundaries.

Secondly, to others, our friends display our nature. They reflect our image, our characteristics, how we would be seen. Birds of a feather flock together. Some choose their friends like wallpaper, an attractive backdrop. They seek out those who mirror a preferred social face. They find companionship with those they would emulate, hoping to be seen as alike. We stand alongside people who are popular, seek out the attractive and the bright, so that we can bask in their reflected glory. We are energised by lively wits, dazzled by the glamorous.

Other times people choose contrasting company. The plump girl finds a fatter friend to accompany her at the party. Beside her, she becomes thin and attractive, slipping between the canapés. The would-be intellectual meanwhile enjoys the company of those who can only listen in admiration. Pontificating loudly, he finds appreciation.

How embarrassed and regretful we feel when friends act in

ways that invite public disapproval or rejection. Tarred with the same brush, we cringe beside them at the unfashionable clothes, the ill-chosen joke, or the naïve comment.

Thus our concern for others mingles with layers of self-concern. We sympathise. There but for the grace of God, it could be me standing in your shoes. We praise our friends, delighted as we receive the added credit that comes from their success. We advise, hoping that in doing so our friends will make improvements in their lives that suit our needs as well as theirs.

And yet, in spite of all this, sometimes we offer our friends straightforward love. In spite of ourselves we are social animals and genuinely care for one another.

Joanne brings Wendy into her home world. She opens the door of a space that previously she has kept private. She introduces her to the gang and to the men at the scrap yard. It is a risky moment. Crossing social boundaries is always so. Lives are complex. Each environment has different ways, different identities. The friend, who crosses from one context to another, risks finding inconsistencies. Joanne at school, Joanne at home, Joanne in the Amazon are all different. Bringing together people from different areas of our lives may be exciting, welcome, or daunting. It is an exercise which has uncertain outcomes.

So Joanne negotiates her changing world. She manages her friendships and seeks new comforts in the storm of feelings. And in between it all, her curiosity and unknown passions drive her to look again. Despite her feelings of anxiety and revulsion, the magazines have a magnetic pull for her. They draw her back, tempting her.

CHAPTER TEN

Secrets

It was two weeks later. Wendy and Simon were once again sitting in Joanne's bedroom. The rain slashed down outside, making cold hollow drum beats against the window pane. There was a dark chill in the air, the sodden dishumour that comes from days on end of rain, which did not invite outdoor play.

Since her first visit, Wendy had been over several times. They had been at the scrap yard the previous weekend, helping Ray and Alf to lift a pile of old copper piping onto the lorry to go to the dealer. Then they had played cards and read comic books. They had also walked across the factory site. Joanne had pointed out the Amazon and various other features of the landscape and places which had been their camps in the past, realizing as she did so that the names did not slip quite so easily off the tongue as usual. Wendy's arrival seemed to have shifted something.

Her arrival had changed the dynamics of the group too. The three younger boys did not spend much time with the older ones. They spent most of the time off across the waste ground, playing their own games. Joanne could hear the whoops and shouts that suggested Red Indian battles. The boys had also been working on their new camp and on Sunday afternoon they arrived at the scrap yard. They stood shoulder to shoulder with serious expressions on their faces, and invited the three older ones to visit it.

Ian led the way. The new camp was hidden behind some thick furze bushes, and they only saw it right at the last moment as they pushed through between the prickles. Joanne was impressed. The boys had cleared quite a big area, which was circled by a paling of milk crates and planks. The metal pole which they had salvaged the week before was propped firmly between the forks of two elder trees, some eight or ten feet apart, and branches and planks were laid against it to create a roof on one side, which was interwoven with branches and pieces of torn plastic sheeting. Under this shelter some old coal sacks made a carpet on which the three boys could sit quite comfortably. Outside this covered area, under a milk crate, were the ashes of a fire. Pieces of sawn log were spaced around this for seating.

"It didn't get wet through the week." Michael told them proudly.

Philip grinned, "We did it all ourselves."

Joanne looked round, hands on hips, then she sat down on one of the wooden stumps. "That's super," she said unreservedly.

Simon and Wendy, who had been hovering behind, came into the centre of the clearing and Simon sat down too.

"Yeah," he said admiringly.

"We've got a new war cry too," went on Philip. His red hair was ruffled and his eyes looked a bit wild.

"Uhu?" Joanne's reply was consideredly non-committal.

The three younger ones looked at one another, their faces explosions of excitement, then Philip counted them in.

"One, Two, Three," his hand gesticulated, "Hey! Willie, willie, willie, willie, willie, willie, Whoop!" With the last syllable the three boys leapt in the air, waving arms wildly, then they collapsed giggling.

"You're not supposed to laugh," protested Michael. "It's supposed to be frightening."

Joanne and Simon were laughing too. Wendy looked puzzled.

"You boys are always on about willies," said Joanne, regaining her calm, "about time you grew up."

This weekend, the rain was back. It was a very wet spring. Even sitting under the tarpaulin lost its attraction. So it was that they were indoors.

Simon sat on the floor, his knees up in front of him, his back wedged against the door. Joanne and Wendy sat on the bed, dangling their legs.

"What shall we do?" asked Simon.

"Let's play deadliest secrets," said Joanne.

"How do you do that?" asked Wendy.

"We each have to think of our deadliest secret and then the others have to ask all the questions they can think of till they guess what it is," said Joanne.

"What if we don't guess?" asked Simon, looking a bit doubtful.

"Then you have to tell anyway, or it wouldn't be fair," said Joanne.

"But I haven't got a secret," said Simon.

"You must have. You just have to think of it," said Joanne.

There were a few minutes of silence. Simon continued to look confused, but then he blushed. "OK," he said.

Wendy had been silent up till now. Her mind was running in circles. Thoughts and images crowded in. Why had Joanne suggested the game? What could she say? Part of her wanted to share something, but what was her secret? What was it that was true and that was safe to tell? Did it really have to be your deadliest secret, or just the one you were willing to share?

"You can start then," said Joanne, responding to Simon.

"Are we all going to do this?" he asked warily.

"Of course, but we have to take turns," said Joanne.

"OK." Simon braced himself.

The questions came. Had it happened at home or at school? Had other people been involved? Had he done something bad? Had he been found out? Was it embarrassing? Did it involve taking clothes off?

As he answered, it became apparent that Simon's secret had indeed happened at school, that he had done something bad, and that it had affected someone else but he had not been found out. The questions went on but didn't seem to get them any further.

"OK, what is it?" asked Joanne, getting frustrated.

"I'm not telling you till we've done your questions," said

Simon. "That's only fair. You didn't guess."

"OK, it's Wendy's turn then," said Joanne.

Wendy's secret was equally elusive. They found out that it happened at home, most days when she was in bed. She wasn't sure if it was bad or not, or if it affected anyone else. The questions continued and Wendy looked increasingly uncomfortable. They couldn't guess what it was and she was not sure if she wanted to tell her secret.

Then it was Joanne's turn. Simon and Wendy tried to find new questions, but the same thoughts kept coming into their heads. They weren't as good at this game as Joanne was, or maybe they just weren't as interested.

"I don't know," said Simon after a little while, "I give up. We'll never guess it. We haven't guessed any of them. Let's all tell our secrets and get it over with."

"OK, you go first," said Joanne.

"No, it was your idea, you spill the beans," said Simon. He was getting a bit cross with the whole thing.

"But that's not fair," said Joanne. "You went first."

"I know," said Wendy, "Why don't we all write our secrets down. That way we can show them all at once."

The others looked at her. Her suggestion made perfect sense.

Joanne tore up strips of paper from the scrap pile on her table and gave them out, one for each of them, and a pencil. The three children wrote seriously for a few minutes, guarding their papers from view with curled arms and hunched backs.

"OK, now show them."

There was an awful pause. Each child looked at the others, clutched their own paper out of view, dared the others to reveal first what was written.

"Go on," Joanne insisted.

She flung her paper onto the ground as she spoke, sliding off the bed to sit on the rug as she did so. It lay, crumpled but defiant between them. She looked at Simon and Wendy. They each put their paper down in front of them. Wendy also moved onto the floor.

Joanne looked first at Simon's. I DELIBERATELY SPILT INK ON JOHN CARTER'S BOOK it said.

Joanne looked puzzled. The word "Deliberately" had been added as an after-thought, stuck above the rest of the line, with an inverted "v" shaped omission mark below. John Carter was the class swot and teachers pet in Simon's class. Joanne knew him by sight and reputation.

"When did you do that?" she asked, feeling new admiration for Simon.

Simon blushed again. "It was last year. I was plant monitor, so I could stay in at break to water all the plants in the classroom. I was really mad at John that day because he had been showing off about beating me in the test. Miss Thornton left the pile of books on her desk, so I just went through and found John's book and poured a lot of ink all over his work."

"Didn't you get caught? Surely she must have realized it was you!" Joanne frowned.

"No, Miss Thornton always left the books for days before she marked them. She didn't find it till three days later. By then lots of people could have done it." Simon grinned. "Anyway, she thought I was a good boy."

"There was a heck of a row though," he added. "She shouted at us all and told us someone had to own up or we'd all be kept in, but nobody did and in the end she had to just let us go."

As he told the story, Simon found himself feeling less embarrassed and even a little proud of what he had done. As a secret, the incident had eaten away at his conscience. After the first euphoric excitement that had overwhelmed him as he saw the ink trickle irrevocably across the page, no, even as he poured it from the little china ink well that he'd taken from his desk, a sick feeling had risen in his gut. The impulse had been a moment of craziness. It had been the kind of thing you think of, but never do. On this

144

occasion his anger at John, his smarting indignation at the boy's smug certainty, had clouded his mind like a fog, drawing him into a trance in which one could act as one dared not act. Transported into a world that usually belonged to comic books and television programmes, anything suddenly became possible. Once it was done, however, like a cold draft when a door is flung open, the knowledge of what had happened hit him like a cricket bat. He had certainly expected to be discovered and crept around the classroom in great fear. The next days unfolded slowly and painfully. Somehow he had hidden his guilt through all the recriminations, hiding behind his quiet reputation, allowing others who might more easily stand accused to take the full brunt of the inquiry.

Now, however, his audience allowed the story to be re-told, even embroidered, in a space that was safely distant from the threat of discovery. He was his own author and could at last become the story's hero. As Simon sat back against the door, a smile of relief spread across his face.

Joanne turned to Wendy. Her paper was crumpled and hard to read. Joanne smoothed it out. I CRY AT NIGHT TIME it said.

Joanne looked at Wendy. What on earth did that mean? She felt something approaching disgust rising in her. What kind of a secret was that? What a sissy thing to admit to.

"Why?" she asked in a voice that didn't hide her disbelief.

Wendy looked down at her hands. She wished that she could run away.

"I don't know," she said. "Sharon was horrible to me. She said things about my mother."

Joanne looked at her steadily. She hadn't heard Sharon say anything to Wendy all year. What Wendy was saying didn't really add up. Yet she also felt something of the pity she had felt a couple of weeks earlier when she heard Wendy say that she had been looking forward to coming back to school. There was something about Wendy she did not understand, something that hinted at a loneliness and unhappiness which she couldn't fathom. The thought of it embarrassed her.

Simon broke out of his reverie. "I cry at night sometimes," he said.

Wendy looked at him. Her face brightened up suddenly. "What do you cry about?" she asked.

Simon hesitated a minute. "Losing my anorak," he said, "and not knowing my spellings for the test."

"I only cry when I'm angry," said Joanne sharply.

"What have you written?" Simon scowled at Joanne's paper.

Joanne snatched the paper up. "I'm not sharing mine. Its more secret than all of yours," she blurted out.

"You can't do that, it's not fair," protested Simon, then he lunged at Joanne, wrestling her back against the bed and grasping her hand to uncurl the fingers. Joanne fought back. Her feet kicked the air and elbows flailed as she protested through gritted teeth. Simon was on top of her, forcing her hand out and calling to Wendy to prise open her grip and get the paper. To Joanne's surprise, with this invitation, Wendy joined in.

Joanne was strong, but between them, Simon and Wendy managed to get the paper from between her fingers. It was ragged and torn into several pieces.

Defeated Joanne stopped struggling and as Simon moved back to unfold the fragments, she sat up and dusted herself off. Simon and Wendy spread out the pieces. THERE IS A PILE OF PLAYBOY MAGAZINES IN THE HUT AT THE SCRAP YARD they read.

If Joanne had thought her secret more serious, Simon and Wendy were not convinced. They both sat looking at her.

Eventually Simon spoke. "Well, that's not your secret, that's Ray and Alf's," he said. Then he added, "and it doesn't even sound like much of a secret. Any of us can go in and see them if they are just in the hut."

Wendy looked embarrassed.

It was now Joanne who sat silenced. Of course, Simon was

right. She had not really told what was secret about the magazines. Indeed, she was not sure she could have said what the secret bit was. It wasn't a thing; more of a feeling, the feeling that made her keep wanting to look again and again and again.

"Where are they?" Simon asked, "Have you read them?"

"They're under the table," said Joanne, "and, yes, I've looked at them. There are lots of pictures of naked ladies."

She tried to sound casual. Now that she had shared the secret, she felt the power that it gave her. She sensed Simon's curiosity. She sensed that he would like to see the images too, but that he too would feel the turmoil they had brought in her mind. She wanted to share the burden of that conflicted emotion. In bringing him into the secret, she regained her equilibrium, once more took the upper hand.

****

So secrets weave their mysterious trails around the darker areas of the mind; some shameful, hidden, lurking like dangerous creatures ready to mutilate and scar us if they are discovered; others deliciously private, indulged and pampered in quiet moments, then dangled in the twilight of innuendo for others to crave.

Some secrets hide our feelings of guilt from the world: things we have done but wish were otherwise, that which we would score out if we but had the chance, things that cannot be undone, or even forgotten, that wake us in the early hours with sweating palms and beating heart. They speak of those things which we have said and ways that we have acted which, if known, would dash to fragments our reputations, crush our comfortable identities. Such guilty secrecy is laced with pride, but more than that, a desperation to survive. Such secrets hold the key to our destruction.

Other secrets are the opposite. Things which we hardly dare to be, words that we hardly dare to say, they hint at bolder identities. These secrets we are all too keen to let slip, to accidentally reveal. Our cautious side hides in the shadows, guarding the anonymity of ambiguity, but whilst we hold the secret for propriety's sake, the devil in us wants it out, and longs for notoriety.

And many secrets hold the middle ground. The act of sharing casts a die which may fall either way – in throwing it we do not know the outcome. We fear, we hope, but as it falls we do not know. Sometimes our fortune turns and in the sharing comes recognition that we are less vulnerable than we believed. Sometimes like Simon's story, in their unspoken state the secrets conjure images of fear and retribution, but in the event, their revelation brings not just relief, but also status. Other times, though, our worst fears unfold in dreadful predictability. As Wendy expects rejection, so Joanne's cold incomprehension simply reflects that anticipation.

So secrets may become the mirror of our expectations. The act of secrecy reflects our view of both ourselves and of others. The image of the self which is most disliked, the self which we most want to disguise from others, so shameful, lies cowering behind the edifice of dissemblance. The image that we cling to of those around us, the ones from whom we hide our weeping sores, reveals our nightmare fears about the world in our reluctance to give voice to sensitivities.

Disguising the under fabric of our lives, we show our expectations, our fear of judgement and recrimination. Our expectations may be accurate. They may be based on hard won experience of criticism and punishment. But they may also be out of date; a hang-over from an earlier time, now past, whose shadow has not yet faded.

Of course, not all secrets are our own to share. They may have been trusted to us by another. This creates a special responsibility. The privileged knowledge holds us in a pledge of honour. The power of secrecy binds us. Its weight pulls us into the intimacy of shared information. Sometimes a welcome binding of the souls, other times the unasked for secret becomes the uneasy burden that we are forced to carry. It all depends. One secret cements a friendship, forms a bond which forges links that endure for decades. Another creates a debt which festers. The confidante taunts, dripping subtle revelations into conversations, uses it in underhand coercion. In worst scenarios, the secret shared, fuels blackmail or treachery.

But for the children, secrecy with all its tantalising edges becomes a game. Just as they toy with risks, enjoy the thrill of playing *chicken* or climbing heights, the emotional risk of telling secrets pushes the boundaries of the mundane. The edge of fear adds spice to a rainy morning that would otherwise be dull. Secrets flirt with forbidden territories, the undefined areas of danger, embarrassment, wrong doing and sexuality. Inviting the search for secrets, their questioning probes the unspoken, eludes the censorship, reaches beyond everyday conversations, and pushes back the frontiers of what is allowed to be said.

Joanne suggests the game. The burden of her feelings, tumbling uncontrollably in mind and body, dominate her thoughts. Overwhelmed, anxious yet excited, she is uncertain, her reactions ill-defined. Part of her longs to share, to normalise with ordinary conversations, yet she cannot even name the extent of these responses to herself. The magazines are one thing, but her reaction, with extremes of revulsion and fascination, troubles her in ways she cannot explain. She wants to tell the others, include them in her discovery, but has no pretext on which to talk about her preoccupation.

In the end it is by slight of hand that she encourages them to literally wring from her grasp the knowledge. Only when they are fighting to uncover her secret can she honourably reveal it. But still she fears making the revelation. She half retracts her will to share, tries to halt the process that she has started, but it is all too late.

She is ambivalent. The game feels out of hand. She feels her secret different to those of the others. In some ways it is. Their secrets, though in some respects more personal, more private, linger in the childhood spaces. They involve childhood feelings. They speak of naughtiness and fearfulness, loneliness and night-time terrors, humiliating not least because they are caught up in childish preoccupations.

This no doubt fuels the reticence with which they are shared. Simon blushes. Wendy dissimilates. Each feels smaller, shameful, as they speak their truths, but they are not in the same territory as Joanne. Her secret is of the future, a glimpse through the crack in a door into the realm of adult passions.

For Simon, sharing brings surprise. Having told his story, his mood changes dramatically. Once too awful to confess, the account of his revenge now evokes interest, even admiration. He steps into the role of victor, rewrites the script. The secret told becomes a source of energy and positive identity. He is uplifted, buoyant.

But still, essentially, Simon's secret rings of childhood affairs; his stage, the school room and his tale of children's conflicts. For Wendy too, the secret is of childhood things. Sunk in the loneliness of unpopularity, she shares the pain of classroom bullying. Her account speaks of the isolation and misery which such ostracism brings.

Yet, despite their childish themes, both stories are timeless in their unhappiness. In sharing their painful secrets, Simon and Wendy find connection, offering consolation to one another, and excluding Joanne, who already feels distanced. For Joanne's secret is different. Dabbling in new and frightening adult concerns, delicious as they are dismaying, it drives a wedge between the three. She feels the different nature of her knowledge. She becomes an exile. And so Joanne protests. Her secret is more secret than those of the others. She senses its ramifications, fears how the sensual temptations she has touched will inevitably decimate the world of childhood that the three inhabit. And yet the feeling eats at her, and so, ambivalently, she longs to convey it.

Of course at a practical level, Simon is right. The secret is not hers at all. The secret part is still unvoiced, even in Joanne's own mind, yet its rising energy, its fascination, has already taken hold of her. All she can name are the facts, the magazines. All she can hope is for to share the knowledge she inadvertently acquired and in doing so, unburden herself of her solitary struggle.

****

Play rehearses many important lessons. Through games the child extends creatively into new territory, learns to face danger and to handle relationships, to solve problems and to think imaginatively. The game becomes an arena in which life is sampled.

Playing *deadliest secrets* meets deep felt needs. Firstly it creates an opportunity for the three to share their preoccupations without the responsibility of taking first initiative to speak. Joanne suggests the game, driven to play by the burdensome feelings which haunt her mind. In doing so she creates a context in which the flow of events will impel her to reveal her discovery.

Secondly the game creates a bond. The dynamics of the gang are changing. New relationships are forming and, in that process of formation, the game cements new friendships with important shared experiences. Like an initiation, crossing the painful barrier of honesty creates shared scars which bring the three eldest members of the gang together. The fire of embarrassment forges the new alliance.

Thirdly the game brings intimacy. Even as they struggle on the edges of childhood, the three youngsters are drawn into growing interest in one another. The game becomes a tantalising dance of hide and seek. They play. They reveal personal thoughts, then coyly retract them, teasing each other with hints of information.

They struggle to overcome Joanne's resistance and capture her piece of paper, locked in physical proximity. Both childhood romp and intimate encounter, the unvoiced changes creep stealthily into innocent play.

The game is urgent. Simon leans protectively against the door, their henchman, guarding their privacy. Joanne hopes her mother will not hear. Neither sees the implication, yet each feels sheepish descending the stairs after the event under the parent's gaze. The secret is secret even to the holders.

Mostly the choice to speak or not is ours, consciously made, at least in part. Our secrets are our own, the balance of breaking them our choice. Sometimes it is wise, courageous, honourable to speak, but other times the honourable way is to hold silence.

Other times we guard another's story. The confessor guards his tongue. The protector says nothing of her hidden refugees. In such cases personal comfort is not the deciding factor. The impulse to tell, if it comes at all, may be for the others' benefit, but sometimes it comes from the aching of a heavy heart, from the pressure of knowing another's burden. Mostly, when trusted, keeping thoughts and feelings, knowledge and actions to ourselves is best. There is no benefit in plunging yet others into the same confusion or anguish as ourselves to no avail, and, secrets may be better kept. The role of confidante is heavy, for the secret is not our own to share.

Sharing often brings relief. Telling the secret silences the inner critic, as Simon found. Voicing the tale we invite mercy. Others rarely condemn us as harshly as we do ourselves. And as we speak we can subtly mould, adjust the tenor, polish the details, and then cement them in our minds through reiteration. We may dilute the story, add a twist that subtly transforms our actions, so, even to our own surprise, we seem vindicated.

Other times, sharing is painful, its consequences uncertain. Sometimes the secret hides our guilt. We guard our reputation with pretence, knowing the impression we give is false. So here, confession may be the nobler route, a route to peace and reconciliation with our conscience. It draws a line, finishes the matter, defines perhaps our punishment, and releases us from the ongoing fear of discovery. The mind tormented by our actions runs in endless circles, trying to make amends, to change, undo, retract, when none of these are possible. Discovery brings relief. At such times, going beyond the pride which hides the truth may be the noblest way.

As humans, our impulses are never clean, but always complex, muddied and driven by different needs. For all these reasons, we are drawn to speak.

CHAPTER ELEVEN

Changes

Sarah was already in the yard when Joanne arrived. She was leaning against the door post, looking pensive, a notebook and pencil in her hands.

"Hiya," Joanne called as she approached.

Sarah looked startled. "Sorry, I was just thinking." She said.

"What are you writing?" asked Joanne, half interested.

"Oh, I'm making notes for my latest book," replied Sarah, "its all about a little beggar girl in Victorian times who runs away from her cruel uncle."

"What happens to her?"

"She has lots of adventures in the slums in London then she gets a job as a maid in a big house. I've not decided what happens next. Perhaps she will marry the son of the house."

"What are you writing about now?" Joanne nodded to the notebook.

"Oh, I'm collecting people. Daddy says that if you are going to write you have to observe people carefully and make notes."

Joanne looked around the yard. It didn't look much like Victorian London. Children were running round nosily, playing tag or football or huddled in little groups, trading tea cards or just talking. A little boy was running round, arms spread wide, making noises clearly meant to be an aeroplane. A bunch of girls were skipping arm in arm singing Beatles songs.

"I thought they all played with hoops and spinning tops then," she said rather vaguely, images of pastel coloured dresses and poke bonnets floating before her mind.

"Maybe," said Sarah in an offhand way, then after thinking a moment or two she added, "I don't think they had toys much in the slums."

The conversation broke off as Sarah looked up and saw Wendy approaching. Joanne turned too and greeted her.

"Hiya," she said again.

Wendy grinned. Her face looked quite different, Joanne thought. She hadn't got her usual timid, evasive glance. She looked happy.

Sarah looked at Wendy, then at Joanne. "I went to the theatre on Saturday. Daddy took me to see *A Midsummer Nights Dream*. What did you do?" She asked.

"Oh, we spent most of the weekend at the...." Wendy's voice tailed off. She looked at Joanne, then at Sarah. Neither of the others spoke.

"You saw each other at the weekend?" Sarah's voice was a bit hesitant.

Wendy looked at the floor, her smile evaporating. She sensed Sarah's discomfort.

Joanne looked straight at Wendy. She willed her to stop, not to say more. She did not want Sarah to know about the scrap yard or the Amazon. For an instant she felt vulnerable, uncertain whether Wendy shared her sense of the divide between home and school life, recognizing even as she stood there how important that distance was to her. But Wendy did not say more. Outfaced by the disapproving gaze of her two companions, she muttered, "Yes, we spent Saturday at Joanne's house."

This was only half true. They had spent Saturday morning at Joanne's house, but by the afternoon the rain had nearly stopped and the three of them had been over to the scrap yard. She and Simon had been eager to find out if what Joanne had said about the magazines was true. They had arrived at the yard as the men were tidying up. They were sorting out various piles of scrap and putting things away, so it had been hard to creep into the hut unseen, but she had seen the pile of magazines just as Joanne had described, under the table. She hadn't had time to look properly, because Simon was hissing at the door for her to hurry up in case the men came back, but she knew they were there. He had seen them too whilst she stood guard.

Sarah shuffled her feet and pushed her notebook into her school bag. She exhaled loudly. Wendy had always been her friend. She would have liked to glare at Joanne, but as soon as she caught her eye she thought better of it.

"I'll see if Daddy can get extra tickets next time we go to see a play so that you can come with me," she said to Wendy.

Joanne was all too aware that she was not included.

There was an awkward silence, then Miss Forster, who was on duty that week, appeared in the doorway, bell in hand. The school day was about to begin. Unsettled, the three girls filed into the cloakroom.

Relations continued to be uncomfortable at playtime. Sarah wanted to create a play based on the story she was writing. Initially Joanne and Wendy were willing enough to join in, but when it became apparent that Sarah wanted to play her own heroine and that all the other parts involved either walking past and ignoring her or talking to each other admiringly of her virtues, Joanne lost interest.

"That's boring," she protested. "Can't we play something where we are all running away together?"

"No." said Sarah firmly. "The whole point of the story is that Martha is completely alone and misunderstood in the world."

"OK," said Joanne, "then we'll be part of a robber gang whom she meets."

She swept Wendy into a corner of the yard to plot, leaving Sarah standing dramatically alone. After a couple of minutes, Sarah approached them.

"Oh, robbers, can you shelter a poor maiden who has fallen on hard times?" she asked, her voice quaking with feigned emotion.

"No. It is your destiny to be on your own. We are too busy hiding from the policemen who are trying to catch us and throw us into jail," Joanne returned.

"Perhaps you could become bad and join us?" Wendy asked tentatively.

But Sarah was not willing to give up her virtue so easily. She stomped off to the other side of the playground, narrowly missing a stray football. "Alas, alas," she cried loudly, oblivious to the amused looks that Miss Forster, who was patrolling the yard, coffee cup clasped tightly to her breast, was giving her.

Wendy turned to Joanne. "What are we going to do?" she asked.

"If we are going to carry off this bank robbery, we'd better plan it carefully," returned Joanne. "Maybe we could crawl across that roof top and look in at the sky-light to spy on the people in the bank."

So Joanne, with Wendy following, sidled along the narrow space between the two painted lines on the playground which edged the netball court. She paused and glanced in both directions, searching the vicinity for possible assailants, then darted across the remaining distance to the safety of the perimeter fence. Coming to the railings, she threw herself against the low brick wall, creeping cautiously along, hugging it as closely as she could. This was a high building and one misplaced step could send them toppling to certain death on the paving slabs below. Besides they needed to stay hidden from searching eyes on the ground. She clung on against an imagined high wind, feeling her clothes tugged around her as she struggled against its buffeting force.

"There," Joanne breathed hoarsely. She had come to the place where an upright in the fence was missing. This had often been an important feature in the mapping of their games. Today it was the window they had been trying to reach. "Look, we can just squeeze our heads through this sky-light and see what is going on in the bank."

She pushed her face against the railings. "There! Can you see?

Look. They are going to operate the safe. Now we need to watch them when they use the code to open the safe and memorise it."

"Five, nine, six, one," Wendy squinted at the imagined safe obediently.

"Now we can climb down at night and get in," said Joanne

A noise made them stop.

"What are you doing?" Sarah stood behind them, hands on hips.

"We're going to break into that safe," said Joanne.

"But there aren't any safes or banks in this part of London." Sarah protested.

"How do you know?" Joanne turned on her.

"Because I wrote the story," Sarah was close to tears.

"You wrote your story," Joanne corrected. "We are playing bank robbers."

Wendy stood back, looking on silently during this exchange. She hovered behind Joanne, waiting to see what would happen. She didn't like arguments.

Sarah said nothing. Her face was very red. She looked first at Joanne, and then at Wendy, then she turned and walked across the yard and stood by the door to the cloakroom. There were still ten minutes before it would be time to go in. Wendy looked at her watch. She looked at Joanne. Joanne said nothing.

Wendy walked over to where Sarah was standing. "Don't be upset," she said.

Sarah turned her back on her. She folded her arms and did not speak.

Wendy shrugged her shoulders and walked back to Joanne. "Come on then, let's get on," she said.

"I'm fed up with the game," Joanne said. She leant back against the railings and surveyed the yard. It was nearly the Easter holidays. Just four more days of school, then nearly three weeks off. Then it would just be one more term till she went to the grammar school. She felt very old and a little weary of this world of childhood.

On the other side of the yard she could see Simon deep in conversation with a boy from his own class called Andy. She wondered if Simon had told Andy about their discovery, and hoped he had not. She did not think it likely he had broken the secret because she trusted Simon, but still the fact that he and Wendy now knew about the magazines nagged at her uncomfortably. But Andy didn't look as if he had just been told about something as important as that. She sighed. It was probably all right for now.

"Did you go back to the scrap yard on Sunday?" Wendy asked, breaking into her thoughts.

"No," said Joanne. "They're closed on Sunday. Simon and Philip and I went over on the factory site and made a fire."

"Can I come over some days in the holidays?" Wendy asked.

"I expect so," Joanne replied, absently.

Her attention had left Simon and she was watching Sarah, who was still standing beside the door with her arms firmly folded and a scowl on her face. How had she ever thought of Sarah as a friend? Looking at her now, she felt no connection, no sympathy. It was her own fault if no one wanted to play with her.

"Come on," she turned to Wendy, "let's go for a gallop."

So saying, she set off, hand held up, clasping imagined reins, in front of her, feet taking on the movement of hooves across the tarmac. Wendy followed, letting out a whinny as she did so.

****

The ten or eleven year old sits awkwardly at the bridge between childhood and adult concerns. Sometimes immersed in the world of play, other times watching, uncertain; caught by new possibilities. Play, the rehearsal of life, sometimes explores worlds yet unfound. Other times it reiterates the known and the familiar, digesting experience in packages of dramatic enactment. Play, the source of refuge and solace from the confusion of childhood, exorcises the ghosts of experience. Play, the creative canvas of possibilities in which anything can be and the mundane is alchemically transformed into the magical, becomes the crucible of imagination.

Sarah explores her isolation. She writes her script, literally creating a play into which she invites her friends' participation. Her story is elaborated through the metaphor of poverty. She dances with her loneliness and in doing so reinforces its hold.

She offers parts in the drama to her companions, forges them into the bit players of her story, reduces them to shadows. And so, becoming wraiths they offer no support. She makes her isolation, and thus creates her misery but also her protection. We all do so. Supported by her father's patronage, her dramatic persona enjoys its richly written domain. In historical romance and noble impoverishment, she seeks approval in the certainty of values of a previous age.

Meanwhile, Joanne, edges uneasily towards more adult concerns. She flirts with the expansive energy of Sarah's drama, shares the drive to inhabit parallel worlds of play, and finds confirmation in her friend's uninhibited enjoyment of imaginative space. But even this is faded. The vibrancy of that other world is dulled by the seeping realisation of adulthood. In Sarah, Joanne sees the unreality of the game reflected, the image broken. No longer wholly able to immerse herself, she strays across the divide. Her play becomes self-conscious.

So in the same conversation, side by side, worlds lie contiguous. The playground with London slums, high buildings hovering on the markings of the tarmac court. Childhood and adolescence tied in conflicted union. The game unfolds in uneasy fragmentation whilst the girls jostle for first priority in each other's favour. Sarah feels sorely her exclusion.

Lost in her own story, Sarah has trusted Wendy's loyalty. Expecting unchanging friendship, she has lulled herself into complacency. Companionable history, based in common loneliness, has led her to rely on Wendy's presence as an ever willing supporting actor. The discovery that Wendy and Joanne were capable of a functioning friendship without her orchestration burst the balloon of her world view. She was excluded.

Strangely, the reality of isolation hit harder than one might expect, given its central location in Sarah's drama. For, whilst the persona plays the tragic heroine, whistling in the wind, it secretly guards the opposite dream of popularity. It waits expectantly, the plain-Jane wall flower, knowing that one day her turn will come for the handsome hero to arrive, take off her heavy rimmed spectacles and shake out her tightly coiled tresses, announce her beautiful and sweep her off her feet. Girls' annuals of the sixties were full of such discoveries.

So Sarah both believes and disbelieves her fate, her solitary destiny. She plays it, and in doing so creates the insurance against its reality. She scripts the story, a happy ending far beyond her immediate horizon, dutifully discovered after much tribulation. But in her dismay discovers the complexity of the tale.

Whilst the script tells wistfully of isolation, in the human drama she secretly longs for companionship. Resenting their newfound friendship, her attempts to re-establish her supremacy, to dominate the others, fall on united opposition. Her previous strategy, the influence she holds over Wendy, fails. Retreating, Sarah seeks sympathy through her emotional outburst. She throws her hurt feelings into stubborn sulkiness.

Joanne, also changed, looks on. Recent experience has not only left a legacy of unease, but also torn open the childish seclusion, the safety of the play-world. Defiantly she re-treads the familiar territory, perhaps to annoy Sarah, but the magic is lost. The scaffolding of pretence is revealed. Like the façade of a film set, the power of the drama no longer completely captivates her energy.

With altered perception, she looks again at Sarah's world and sees that it is small. The friendship, never strong, feels hollow, as she surveys this display of over-sized emotion.

Meanwhile, Wendy, her life opening up under the benevolent warmth of her recent experiences of companionship with Joanne and Simon, feels a debt of loyalty to Sarah. She reaches out, attempts to mend the rift, but repeatedly receives rebuffs. Uncertainly she hovers, tries to hold the middle ground, but in the end follows Joanne's lead.

Perhaps the conflict will resolve. Such ebbs and flows of friendship create the tapestry of childhood. But with the prospect of the move to secondary school that summer, changes in friendships are already imminent. There is less pressure to mend broken ties. Another term in animosity or isolation is not so daunting. Pride costs dear, but if it means the preservation of our identity, sometimes the price is worth it.

Joanne anticipates from strong ground. Her future at the grammar school is yet uncharted, but her home-life is secure. Its certainty provides a bridge, a vantage point, a quay from which to launch the new adventure and to which she can return.

Perhaps she is hard on Sarah. Perhaps Sarah deserves it, invites it even. At what cost could she have entered Sarah's game on Sarah's terms? Might the exercise have smoothed her ruffled feathers? Or would it simply have compounded the inauthenticity? Did Sarah need to discover the limits of others' willingness, the boundaries of her own control, like the far younger child, impaling her ego on the shards of adult proscriptions, paring down her grandiosity? Or did she need love, compliance, friendship?

Perhaps too, Joanne needs to understand the pain her actions cause. Perhaps in her security, and in her troubled thoughts, she too is wrapped in a constructed world in which the other's needs are not sufficiently apparent. Only the water drip of such encounters wears away the rock solid confidence of youth and mellows our perceptions, makes us wiser – sometimes.

****

Simon was standing in the middle of the playground when Andy came out. He and Andy had been friends since the infants, though they saw more of each other in school than out of it. Andy, like Wendy, lived in the semis across the main road, so they only met up out of school when one of their mothers was willing to take them to the other's house. As he approached, Andy looked excited.

"Guess what," he began. "I've joined the scouts. Not cubs, proper scouts. It's fantastic. I went on Friday for the first time. We're going camping at Easter, at a place in Surrey. We had to practice putting up a tent on Saturday in captain's garden. I held the poles. I'm in the Eagles patrol."

"Wow!" Simon responded.

He knew about the Scouts. You had to be eleven to join. A couple of the older boys in the class had been going since Christmas. He hadn't really given it a lot of thought himself because it was still ages till his eleventh birthday. He and Andy had tried the cubs a few years earlier but they had dropped out after six months because it was boring. The word camping, however, caught his interest. He wished he were older.

"I'm too young to join," he muttered, kicking at the tarmac as he spoke.

"Yes," Andy said, "But maybe you could go camping. It's the week-end after next, Easter weekend. A few of the older cubs are coming. I could ask Captain."

For a moment Simon felt hope rise in him, then he felt a surge of disappointment. Easter week-end they would be at Grandma's again. They were going for the whole week. Even the thought of it made him gloomy. The idea of spending another week in Cornwall whilst Andy was happily pitching tents and singing round campfires under the stars was almost unbearable. He sighed.

"I'll ask. I'll see if I can ring Jonathan our patrol leader. He might know," said Andy. "He's fifteen and his voice has broken."

"Oh, yes. Please do." Simon didn't know what would happen if Jonathan said yes, but he had to find out.

****

That evening, Simon was preoccupied with thoughts of the coming holiday as he sat down at the tea table.

"Did you have a good day at school, dear?" his mother asked. She had a concerned expression on her face. She knew when Simon was unhappy in the way that only the mother of a single boy could.

"Do I have to come to Grandma's at Easter?" Simon asked.

His mother looked surprised, "Why, whatever else would you do? You know we're all going." She said. She felt a little hurt.

"Andy's going camping with the Scouts. Can I go?" Simon heard his words echoing in the silence. Sometimes talking was like pegging your underwear on a washing line, he thought. The words just sort of hung there, embarrassing you. He knew Andy wouldn't have asked if he could go yet, but he felt impatient. He had to know. Would they let him go if he were allowed to go to the camp even though he wasn't a Scout yet?

"But you're not a Scout, dear," his mother smiled. "Perhaps you can go with them next year."

Simon sank into his chair. Next year seemed a long way away.

"What makes you think you could go, son?" his father paused, his tea cup in his hand, and looked from Simon to his mother and back again.

"Some of the older cubs are going and Andy was going to ask if I could join them. It's only a weekend."

"Only a weekend? But we're going to be away for a week." Simon's mother shook her head, "No, next year's soon enough. We can't change all our arrangements at this short notice."

"Well, why don't you go and ring Andy now and find out what the answer really is before we go any further," his father intervened.

Simon looked at him in disbelief. He still had bread and jam on the plate, hardly touched. His parents were both still eating.

"Go on," his father encouraged.

As Simon went out into the hall to the phone, he heard his father's voice again, this time hushed, addressing his mother.

"Don't say it," he said, "give the lad a chance. It may not happen, but don't spoil it without knowing. He can't spend all his holidays with your mother."

Simon grinned to himself and picked up the receiver.

Andy sounded surprised when Simon got through.

"I've not rung him yet," he said, "give us a chance. I've only been home half an hour." Then he added, "I'll do it now if Mum will let me use the phone, and then I'll ring you right back."

In the event, Simon had finished his tea and been playing in his room for quite a while when Andy phoned back. He had checked it out with Jonathan, but Jonathan had told him to ring Captain. He had had to try a couple of times before getting through, but the news was good. If Simon came to a meeting at the Scout hut that week, he would be allowed to go to camp. He would need his mother or father to fill in a form, but it would be OK.

"Dad," Simon shouted as soon as he put the phone down, "It's OK, I can go."

So Simon found himself facing the Easter holidays with new prospects opening up. The trip to Cornwall which he so dreaded postponed at least on this occasion, he was instead to go to scout camp.

As anticipated, this eventuality had not been without its problems. His mother and father had already arranged to spend the week in Cornwall. The bed and breakfast was booked and Grandma was expecting them. The camp was only going to be for three nights. This left the rest of the week.

Fortunately Andy had already told his mother of the situation and, with his persuasion, she had kindly invited Simon to stay the remaining nights at their house. Simon's mother had shaken her head at the idea at first. She didn't like being beholden to people she didn't know, and she hardly knew Andy's family, but Simon's father had been adamant that if they did not accept this arrangement, he himself would drive back early from Cornwall to look after Simon, leaving her to get back by train.

****

So life began to change for Simon. The move to secondary school would soon be upon him, but even in anticipation of it, he sensed possibilities shifting. The prospect of Scout camp had seemed at first a distant dream, something that other people did which was beyond his reach. Suddenly the dream became possible.

Of course his father's intervention made a difference. No doubt the unhappy half-term visit had left him all too aware that Simon needed a different kind of holiday. He was getting too old to be always fitting into family agendas.

More than this, though, Simon needed to spend more time with other boys of his own age. The gang had perhaps served its purpose for him and, though it would continue to be part of his life for a while yet, the prospect of real camping was far more exciting than the make believe camps that he and the others built on the waste ground.

With this transition, Simon stepped from the world in which he had been the oldest boy, into a new world where he would be the youngest. His role models became the likes of Jonathan, maturing lads already well into their teens, who could take responsibility and manage their patrols of youngsters with authority. To Simon, such people seemed almost adult, nearly old enough to join the army or to get married; old enough to have left school and be going out to work.

Between himself and these impressive figures an open vista of time stretched uninterrupted. It was hard to imagine that he, but for a matter of time, would one day be like Jonathan, tall, strong, with a slight haze of bristle on his lip and a strange, deep voice, yet here was the prospect. Beside the patrol, with lads whose ages ranged from close to his own to fifteen, the gang seemed young and childish. Burrowed in his sleeping bag next to Andy in the big canvas tent, he heard the older boys' whispered conversations about grown up things. They talked of motor bikes and races, football teams and paper rounds, and even girls. One day he overheard two of the patrol leaders talking about beer.

In some ways it was a relief. Being the youngest, nothing was expected of you. The big lads did all the heavy work, the fetching water and carrying wood for the fires, though sometimes they expected him to run errands. Other things were irritating, like not being allowed to be the one who lit the fire, even when he had been making fires for years. He felt cross when Jonathan pocketed the matches with his little superior grin. But mostly Simon admired Jonathan. He looked forward to the time when he could properly become a scout and hoped that he could be in Jonathan's patrol.

That would be after the summer. He would be at the secondary school then. From where he stood that prospect, though close, seemed as far away as the other bank of the Thames.

CHAPTER TWELVE

Being Bad

So, change was coming to the gang. The prospect of new schools hastened the natural processes of growing up, and both Joanne and Simon found themselves making new friendships even as they foresaw the move creating inevitable breaks in their social spheres. In the uncertain prospect of such changes, almost instinctively both children found themselves cementing their links with children of their own gender.

The younger children noticed the difference. Wendy was now frequently joining them when they went to the scrap yard. They weren't sure if they liked her. She didn't talk with them like Joanne did and they sensed she was Joanne's friend and not really part of the gang. Sometimes they called her names behind her back, but they were careful not to let Joanne hear them.

While Simon was away, the two girls spent even more time together. Sometimes they went to the scrap yard, but even when they went there, it was often without the younger ones. Other times they played in Joanne's bedroom or went round to Wendy's house. Now that Joanne was allowed to cross the main road by herself, getting together was easier.

Michael and Ian carried on playing out with Philip. They would go to the factory site where they continued to work on their latest camp, but it was not the same. Without Joanne to encourage them, their games became thin and often descended into brawling. They became bored with one another and quarrelsome. They missed the excitement of the imaginative games which Joanne had so often initiated. The Easter holidays had become a drag. So it was that on the Tuesday after Easter, Michael muttered across the dinner table at his sister.

"You're never around these days," he said, "You and Wendy don't want to be with us lot any more."

Joanne was taken aback. It was true that she had drifted into doing other things, but she hadn't realised that Michael minded. That morning she and Wendy had been in her bedroom making flipper books. You stapled lots of small bits of paper together, then drew cartoon figures on each page, each one slightly different from the one before, so that you could make them run or jump or dance or whatever you wanted.

"Joanne's growing up." said her mother, "Next year she'll have too much homework to be playing out with you all the time. You boys will have to find your own friends."

Joanne cringed. She didn't like the idea of growing up or of being too busy with homework. Suddenly she felt nostalgic for the Amazon and the scrap yard. It was only a couple of days since she had been there, but her mother's comment had given her a sense that it could all change soon. Besides, she felt sorry for Ray and Alf. Would they feel abandoned if she didn't come so often?

When she thought of the yard an image of the shed came into her head. Recently, when she had been there she had found herself making excuses to be in the hut so that she could go back and look again at the magazines. When she was there, something kept pulling her back time and again to look at the pictures. It left her feeling uneasy, but she couldn't stop the impulse except by staying away. Now she realised that had hardly spoken to the men all week. That felt bad.

That afternoon Joanne decided she would go to the scrap yard on her own. Wendy had gone home before dinner, and the younger boys were playing in their camp. In the light of Michael's complaint, she had promised them that she would join them later, but for now her mind was more on seeing Ray and Alf.

As she pushed open the metal gate, Joanne suddenly felt a bit strange. She was not used to visiting the men on her own and now that she was there, she felt a bit shy. Ray was stacking old radiators on the far side of the yard. They were heavy cast iron things, like the ones in the class room at school. They looked awkward to handle. It was a warm day and his jacket hung on a fence post where he had discarded it and his dark hairy forearms and hands were smudged with dirt and grease. He whistled as he worked.

Alf stood nearby, hands on his hips, cigarette held between his teeth. He wore a grubby vest that was partly tucked into his trouser tops, but which hung in folds over his right hip. Every now and then he would shout an instruction to Ray.

"Left a bit. No, not there. Try the other side."

Eventually Ray turned to him. "Don't just stand there telling me what to do, do it yourself," he retorted.

Alf shrugged and turned. He saw Joanne standing by the gate.

"Hey, Jo. Good to see you. You on your own this time?" He grinned, "Where's your pretty mate then?"

Joanne hesitated for a minute. She had never thought of Wendy as pretty and didn't realize at first who Alf was talking about.

"Yes," she replied, "she had to go home."

"Go and stick the kettle on, will you. We're gasping for a cup of tea." Alf said.

Joanne felt strangely grown up making the tea. It felt responsible. She liked the feeling of being trusted. Also, making the tea gave her an excuse to be in the shed.

She filled the kettle from the stand pipe in the yard then she got out the stove. The stove had to go outside on the concrete block, but she could go back into the hut whilst it came to the boil because it always took at least five minutes. While she waited she could get out the other things ready on the table top.

Joanne swilled out the greasy tea stained mugs and put a tea bag in each of them from the jam jar on the shelf. Then, taking the tea-stained Tate and Lyle bag, she covered each tea bag with a couple of spoons of sugar. Finally she sniffed the milk bottle to check that it had not gone off, and poured some into each mug.

The water still had not boiled. She could hear the kettle was only just beginning to splutter. It would be ages until it got to the boil and it had to be well boiling before you made tea. There was time to have a quick peep at one of the magazines.

She crouched beside the table. Her back was to the door. She had realized some time ago that if she did this, the page she was reading would be hidden from immediate view should anyone come in. She was always ready to bundle the evidence back onto the pile and pick up the old maths book which she kept there tucked under the table for just that purpose.

Her ears were always on the alert for footsteps coming across the yard, but as long as she heard the clanging and banging of metal as the radiators were lifted and stacked and the grunted conversation of the men, she knew they would not disturb her.

Joanne was half way through reading a *reader's letter* when the door opened. In the split second after she heard the click of the catch, she realized that the story had caught her attention so strongly that she had lost track of time.

Alf's shadow blocked the light. She turned, her face reddening from pink to scarlet as she reached too late for the maths book. Aghast she realized that in front of her, beside the *readers' letters*, on the open page of the magazine, a naked woman was reclining on a sofa, showing her body to the world in full colour pink fleshiness.

Time stood still. It was one of those moments that you just wished the floor would swallow you up, or that just thinking could teleport you to the other side of the galaxy. She could hear the kettle boiling furiously outside, and through the doorway, behind Alf, she could see clouds of steam billowing up under the tarpaulin roof.

Alf grinned widely.

"Well. Sure caught you at it. You randy little...."

He tailed off. She blushed. What had he called her? She didn't know what the word meant, but somehow, in her gut, she knew it was something she shouldn't be called.

He carried on grinning. Then he leant forward and looked over her shoulder. The woman looked back from the page, eyes lowered slightly, provocative, inviting, and a little sulky. She was pretty and wore heavy mascara which made her lashes thick and dark.

"Corr, she's a looker," said Alf. "Bet you'd like to be like her...." he grunted "...when you grow up, that is."

Joanne said nothing. Her voice had vanished. Her throat was dry and she knew if she tried to speak only whistles and crackles would come out. Her tongue stuck to the roof of her mouth.

"They get a lot of money for that, you know."

Alf carried on cheerfully. He spoke fast, blustering a bit.

"Models, they are. Models." She could feel him breathing on the back of her neck as he lowered his voice. "Would you like to be a model? When you grow up I mean..."

Joanne looked at the picture. She felt desperately uncomfortable. She wanted to close the magazine but she couldn't quite bring herself to do so when Alf was looking at it. The woman looked happy. She looked confident. No one would take advantage of her. She was a model, after all, almost a film star. Joanne felt silly.

"It's all right, you know. I'm not going to tell anyone." Alf grinned at her. "We all like.... err, looking at pretty pictures, don't we?"

Embarrassed, Joanne half smiled back at him. She didn't know what to do. She knew she shouldn't be there. She should never have come into the yard in the first place. She shouldn't be talking with the men. She shouldn't be making them tea on an old meths stove. She shouldn't be looking at the magazine.

"You're growing up aren't you," Alf continued, "been coming here a while now."

She lowered her eyes, trying not to see the picture in her lap.

"Come on, we're old mates aren't we. How's the tea going?"

Alf turned and went out of the door to take the kettle off the stove. Joanne stuffed the magazine back onto the top of the pile as fast as she could before he reappeared in the doorway. A huge cloud of steam accompanied him as he brought the kettle back into the shed. Alf looked at the three mugs with their tea bags ready, all neatly lined up, and smiled.

"You going to pour them then?" he asked, holding the kettle out to her.

It was difficult to take the kettle from him because the handle was so hot. He had gripped it with an oily rag. His hand was so big that it took up most of the hand hold. Beside it, hers seemed very small. She noticed his smell of sweat and tobacco smoke and the brush of his bare arm against hers as she took it. She recoiled slightly.

Pouring the water into the mugs, Joanne relaxed a little. The smell of tea was strong and familiar. Perhaps it was alright. Alf was her friend. They'd known each other at least two months and that seemed like forever. Now they were sharing grown up things. Soon Ray would join them and it would all be ordinary again.

"Hey, Joey."

Alf's voice sounded soft and even a bit hesitant, but it was kindly. That was what he called her when they were specially friends; when she had talked to him about her plans to join the army special service when she grew up, or the time she told him about how she had got into a fight with one of the boys a school and won, or when she asked him if he had kids, or a wife at home, and he just answered with a little laugh.

"Hey Joey, how's about you come back on Sunday? This place is closed. We could meet up just the two of us. You could try being a model... sort of try it out, you know. We could take some photos. Just for fun like. I'd pay you. You have to be paid if you are a model."

He thought for a minute. "Five shillings. Is that a good fee?"

Joanne did not have time to reply. Ray was already crossing the yard. She could see him coming over Alf's shoulder. Alf heard his footsteps.

"Now, don't say anything. It's our little secret." He said quickly, "but think on it."

★★★★

The next few days seemed to pass very slowly. Joanne ran over and over in her mind what had happened. What should she do? Should she tell someone? She doubted it. She wasn't in the habit of telling people things like that, and anyway telling an adult would mean telling all about going to the scrap yard and everything, but what should she do? Should she go on Sunday as Alf had suggested?

She knew it would be wrong to go. But then, it had been wrong to trespass on the scrap yard in the first place. It had been wrong to hang around with the men without telling her parents and wrong to cook on the stove without their approval. It had been wrong to be unkind to Sarah and to encourage Wendy to stop being her friend. It had been wrong to keep looking at the magazines. Most of the things she enjoyed doing were wrong, so was this really worse? Now Alf wanted her to take her clothes off and practice being a model, was that much more wrong? Five shillings was a lot of money. It was five weeks' pocket money.

In some ways she felt tempted. Taking your clothes off was hardly a big deal. At the same time, she could not put aside the uncomfortable feeling which came over her whenever she remembered the feeling of being in the hut with Alf. Try as she might, she couldn't stop feeling sick and hot when she remembered the sound of his voice or the smell of his breath. It was like when she had first found the magazines only ten times worse. But she had got used to that. Each time she had looked at them it had all seemed a bit less scary and a bit more normal. Since she had told the others, the feeling had disappeared altogether. Reading the magazines had become like anything else she shouldn't do. She avoided being caught, but she didn't think much about it otherwise.

****

On Thursday Joanne went round to Wendy's house. Wendy's sisters were both there because their school was on holiday too. Maureen would not be going back after the break. As she wasn't taking any exams, she was allowed to get a job. She was going to work in Woolworths and learn hairdressing at night-school till she was qualified to help her mother out full time. For now there wasn't enough work and their mother needed the extra money.

"Let me do your hair," Maureen said as the girls sat at the kitchen table drinking tea.

Wendy turned to Joanne, "Go on, let her. She's good."

Joanne felt doubtful. She found the endless prattle of fashion talk boring, and couldn't really understand why Wendy put up with it.

"You've got lovely hair, I'd love to style it," went on Maureen, looking at her this way and that.

Kerrie giggled. She had often had her own hair styled by Maureen. It was fun seeing someone else getting the treatment.

"Go on," Wendy encouraged again.

Doubtfully Joanne agreed. At least she wouldn't have to carry on the conversation.

"I think one of the new bobs would suit you," Maureen continued. She looked at Kerrie.

Kerrie looked at Joanne for a minute, head on one side. "Yes, you're right. Do it!"

Soon Joanne was sitting on a beige vinyl covered stool in front of the basin in the bathroom. It had been recently modernised and had a large, plain mirror which covered most of the wall behind the pale blue wash basin. Her hair was already shampooed and wet and a big white towel was draped round her shoulders. No one had ever cut Joanne's hair wet before. When she was small she had been to the hair dresser once or twice for a short trim, but since she had been in the juniors she had grown her hair long. Her mother cut the split ends off from time to time herself, but otherwise it took little care beyond being tied into bunches or a pony tail in the mornings.

Thinking of her mother, Joanne wondered what she was going to say. When she had agreed to have her hair styled it had not occurred to her that Maureen would do anything that could not be set right afterwards. Now as she stood behind her, scissors in hand, Joanne felt anxious.

"Are you going to cut my hair much?" Joanne asked in panic.

"Oh no, just a bit of styling," Maureen replied cheerfully.

Wendy, sitting on the edge of the bath, grinned encouragingly.

So saying, Maureen picked up a comb from the shelf in front of the mirror and began to comb through the wet hair. Drips fell on Joanne's shoulders and hands. Sometimes the comb caught on a tangle and Maureen tugged at it. She was not as rough as Joanne's mother though. Then, taking the scissors, she began to cut.

One by one, strands of hair were lifted, straightened, and snipped. Joanne watched mesmerised. The process was so smooth, so satisfying. Curls of fair hair tumbled onto the lino tiles around her stool, where they gradually unfurled as they dried into clumps of blonde hair.

"Don't cut too much off!" Joanne gasped as Maureen moved from behind her to one side. It was too late though. The back was already cropped to just below her collar, some four inches shorter than it had been.

"Oh, it's going to look so nice," Maureen exclaimed.

Wendy nodded enthusiastically, "She's good you know."

Kerrie, leaning on the door post said nothing, but smirked

quietly to herself.

Maureen moved round to the other side of Joanne. "It's terribly fashionable like this!" she said. Joanne was not sure she wanted to look terribly fashionable. She was not sure what her mother would say either. She was wishing she had said no to Maureen in the first place.

Eventually the cutting was over and Maureen led her into the bedroom so that they could use the hair dryer. As Maureen brushed it into shape, Joanne was horrified to see that, with a round under-curl, her hair hung even shorter than she had imagined. She gasped as she looked in the mirror.

At the same time, once she got used to the reflection, Joanne was surprised by how attractive it looked. That's not me, she thought. The girl in the reflection was older than her. She looked confident, the sort of person you might see on a bus or a train and think they were nearly grown up. She looked almost as if she might be someone with a job; something glamorous; a secretary, an air hostess, or even a model. Joanne had never wanted to be grown up or glamorous, but now she watched the reflection with fascination.

"You look great!" said Wendy, enviously, "I wish I had straight hair."

Joanne looked once more at her reflection.

"Whatever is Mum going to say?" she muttered.

"I'll come with you," Wendy said cheerfully. "I'm sure she'll love it."

Joanne was not so sure, but she was glad Wendy was going to be there to see what happened. Wendy had changed over the last few weeks since she and Joanne had become friends. She seemed happier, more confident, sometimes even outspoken. She was always taking Joanne by surprise. Or perhaps it was just that Joanne had got to know her. Perhaps she had always been more interesting than she had seemed when she was Sarah's friend.

Joanne was glad that Wendy's mother was not around.

Mothers were unpredictable and could want to interfere in all sorts of unhelpful ways. She wanted to get home before there was any risk of her mother hearing about the hair cut through other means.

Joanne's mother was in the kitchen preparing tea when they got in. She was buttering a slice of bread when they opened the door. When she saw Joanne she froze, knife in hand.

"Oh my goodness! What on earth..." her voice trailed off.

"My sister did it. She's good isn't she?" Wendy said brightly.

Neither Joanne nor her mother spoke. Joanne looked at Wendy in amazement. Did she not understand that her mother was likely to be furious about the hair cut? How could she take it so lightly?

There was a long pause. Then eventually Joanne's mother laughed. "Yes, you're quite right Wendy, she's very good. But goodness, you do look different Joanne. This is going to take some getting used to."

She paused. "But I like it," she said.

****

Friday morning was bright and sunny. Wendy called for Joanne after breakfast.

"Oh dear, you have messed your hair up," she complained, frowning as she surveyed Joanne.

Joanne frowned back. She didn't like being scrutinized like this. She felt as if the haircut had made her into Wendy's doll or something. She had also not slept very well. It was the tossing and turning that had crunched her hair into knots and tangles and made bits of it point in all directions.

"Come on I'll tidy you up before we go out."

Reluctantly Joanne led her to the bedroom where Wendy got out a brush and, with the aid of a tooth-mug of water managed to smooth out the worst of the night's damage. It was like having her mother with her only worse.

"Not that you need it to go down the scrap yard," Wendy laughed.

Joanne pulled on her jumper. She didn't really want to go back to the scrap yard. She felt strange about it, but she also didn't want to tell Wendy what had happened yet. She was still undecided what to make of the incident, or indeed what to do about it. The thought of seeing Alf again made her anxious, but she was used to out-facing her anxieties and didn't want to chicken out this time. The fact that Wendy would be with her gave her courage. Nothing could happen to her if she wasn't on her own.

They went downstairs.

Catching a glimpse of herself in the hall mirror, she once more saw the strange, nearly adult girl. A second glance gave Joanne the uncanny sensation of inhabiting someone else's body. Who was this young woman? What did she do? What could she get away with?

Her mother had not been cross about the haircut. Despite Joanne's trepidation, once she got over that first shocking impression she had actually liked the new style. Wendy had been right. Perhaps expectations were not always to be trusted. Perhaps sometimes one's instincts about right and wrong were wrong.

Wendy was putting on her shoes which she had left on the doorstep. They had lots of laces and it was taking her forever to get them tied. Turning, Joanne smiled at the girl in the mirror. She nodded her head up and down, watching the reflection with interest. Then she laughed. The girl had the same old crooked teeth that she had always had. Those hadn't changed.

Yet still, the illusion of being someone else stayed with her. Whether it was the sleepless night or the new hair style, the things Alf had said in the shed or the prospect of the new school, Joanne still felt as if she was living a different story. It was like being in a film where the script has not yet been written she thought. That thought made her feel powerful.

"Come on!" Wendy stood up and hustled her out of the door.

The two girls made their way round the corner. The flowering cherries were over now, their bronzed leaves glistening new and fresh where the pink pompom blossoms had been. The sky was blue and the sun already warm.

As they turned into the alley way beside the Amazon, Joanne felt suddenly anxious. Her legs felt like jelly and she didn't know how she was going to take another step. Be the girl in the mirror, she said to herself. Pulling herself up tall, she carried on walking. Wendy had not noticed. She chattered on as if nothing had happened.

Wendy was in front when they got to the gate. She heaved it open, swinging it on the big hinges. Ray and Alf were unloading the lorry in the forecourt. When he saw the two girls, Alf stopped and let out a loud wolf-whistle.

"Hey, that was for you with your new hairstyle. I wish men would do the same for me when I'm on my own," exclaimed Wendy.

PART TWO

CHAPTER THIRTEEN

Return

Jo looked out across the playground. Most of the children had already left, but a few still hovered by the gate, distinctive in their royal blue sweat shirts. Several clutched plastic lunch boxes in bright primary colours. The sky was still deep blue, though the sun had mellowed and seemed to cast a more amber light as it caught the first yellowing leaves on the poplars in the park beyond.

Strange to have finally secured a proper teaching job after all these years. Luckily she had been able to finish her probationary year before she went abroad, cobbling together a maternity leave cover with a couple of supply posts, but the promised bonanza of jobs had never materialised and six years abroad had filled the time with a variety of tutoring contracts, casual jobs and English language classes.

Of course travelling had been fun at first. Paul had been keen to see the Far East so she had followed him dutifully to Thailand, Burma and Nepal, then headed further East through Hong Kong to Japan. New Zealand had been easier, since she had been able to find work as a play leader, but Australia had worked best, where she had joined the staff of the language school. That had given her two years of uninterrupted security.

Now she was back, by an even stranger quirk of fate not half a mile from the primary school where she herself had been a pupil twenty years or so earlier.

Perhaps it was not so coincidental. Coming back to England on her own after an eight year relationship, the familiar address had leapt off the page of the Times Educational Supplement. It had almost dared her to apply. There was a kind of strange relief in coming home.

Of course it wasn't home. Her parents had moved away several years ago, retiring to the Oxfordshire village where her mother had grown up. Her brothers too had moved on. Michael was now a junior doctor, working in a large teaching hospital in the Midlands. Ian had drifted into the travel industry through a series of holiday jobs and now took groups of middle-aged adventurers on safaris across Africa in jeeps. She had seen him briefly when she got back to England, bronzed and fairer than before, his hair bleached by the sun. She thought he was doing all right for himself despite their father's doubts.

It was good of the school to take her with her rather unorthodox work history, but, she supposed, there were more jobs around than there had been when she had left, and inner city posts in London were notoriously hard to fill.

The bad side was finding somewhere to live that she could afford. Even with London weighting, her salary was not going to stretch very well. She was grateful to her parents for paying the first month's rent on the bed-sit in advance.

Turning to the empty classroom, Jo started to tidy up. Her first week was over. She felt some small satisfaction as she scanned the ordered groups of tables with their little wood and metal chairs standing on top of them for the cleaner. The cardboard boxes of wax crayons were neatly stacked at the centre of the tables and workbooks were in the children's trays in the unit under the window. On her desk was a pile of new red exercise books, the children's diaries, which she had to take home. Beside it the maths worksheets she had marked in the lunch hour. As she walked between the tables, she picked up the debris of the day. There was not much; a wooden ruler, a couple of pencils, and a crumpled piece of paper with writing on it and a lot of crossing out. She smiled as she recognized the handwriting. Picking it up, she threw it in the bin.

The books were heavy to carry, but she wedged them into her

bag which she could carry on her shoulder. Then picking up her jacket, she left.

****

Saturday morning the library was open, so Jo took the opportunity to join. The library was a good source of materials and she had already discovered that it held a collection of museum items that could be loaned to schools. Besides this though, living on her own, Jo wanted to join so she could get books and tapes for her own use. The weekend seemed to stretch out ahead like a gaunt empty chasm after her busy week and she wondered if she was going to like living alone.

Her bed-sit was in one of the roads behind the library, but once she had found a couple of books she fancied, Jo decided to go for a walk. She started to wander along the row of shops. Of course they were familiar. Several had changed ownership in the twelve years since she had left home. The newsagent was still there, but had been taken over by a Cypriot family. She had discovered this when she called in to buy a newspaper earlier in the week. The electrical shop had closed down and had a big *To Let* sign in its dusty front window alongside a few scraps of dirty plastic, a couple of faded instruction books and some odd ends of wire. The Co-op was still there, much as it had always been, and the greengrocer looked busy. His wares, which spread onto the pavement, included new vegetables; yams and okra, water melons and long white radish, reflecting the different cultures of the people he served.

Almost at the end of the row of shops was the hairdresser's. This had been Wendy's mother's business. As she approached, Jo suddenly remembered Wendy and wondered if it was still there. She and Wendy had pretty much lost touch after she went to the grammar school. They saw each other occasionally on the street, and had once met at a party of a mutual friend when they were much older, but somehow once they were at different schools the link between them had become tenuous. Wendy must have done quite well for herself, for that last occasion when they met she had been at the new sixth form college, but what had happened after that, Jo did not know.

Jo had made new friends at the grammar school. Being a forty minute bus ride away, they had not seen each other much during the week, but they had got together most weekends. Now that she was back in London, Jo thought she might try to trace some of the people she had known then, though she already knew that most of her close friends were scattered across the country. University was a big transition. Once you moved away, few came back.

The hairdresser's looked as if it was doing well. The sign board above the door was new and the window was decorated in black and silver with large stylised flowers. On impulse, Jo peeped in. The shop was busy. The chairs in front of the row of basins were all full and a couple of women were sitting under the large dryer hoods, some with coffee cups in hand, others flipping through glossy magazines. More women sat in front of the row of mirrors opposite. Between these, assistants moved swiftly. Stylists preened their customers, chatting enthusiastically as they teased out sections of hair and clipped them with a sharp sweep of the scissors. Juniors carried cups of coffee or cleared up the cuttings with long handled dustpans and brushes.

Just inside the door was a booking table where a middle aged woman sat, making notes in the big diary which almost covered the table top. As Jo looked in the woman looked up. She was somewhat plump and dressed in a tight black dress. Her hair was coloured a deep plum red and she was well made up. Jo recognized her immediately.

"Did you want to make an appointment?" the woman asked, "I'm afraid we can't possibly fit you in today."

"It's OK," Jo answered, "I was just passing. I don't expect you remember me, but I was a friend of Wendy's from primary school."

The woman looked at her. Her look did not register recognition.

"I've just moved back to the area, and when I saw the shop...." Jo's voice tailed off.

"Wendy still lives here. She's back at home now. If you want to see her, why not give her a ring?" The woman seemed a little impatient.

She took one of the little appointment cards off the pile on the table and scribbled a number on it with her pencil. She held it out to Jo. Jo took it. She thanked the woman and put it in her pocket. She would ring Wendy, but she needed a bit of time to think first. Perhaps she had to get used to the idea. The impulse to check out the shop had been spontaneous, a moment of nostalgia and a thought of finding something of her old life still in tact, but now she was faced with actually phoning Wendy, she was not sure if there would be much to say. How much did they have in common? In all those years when she was at grammar school they had hardly seen each other, so what made her think there would be anything new to say now?

The shops gave way to houses. There were a couple of large semi-detached houses actually on the main road. These were larger than the rest of the houses in the roads behind, probably built earlier. They had big bay fronts with diamond leaded windows. The rest of the semis were in streets that stretched back away from the main road. More modest houses, they had small gardens front and back and garages in between, with concrete drives onto the road. It would be just a short walk up there to Wendy's house.

Jo turned the other way, however, and crossed the main road. There was a pelican crossing now where the lollipop lady always stood. It let out insistent beeps as the light flashed for her to cross. The two school buildings were in front of her. They looked big and forbidding compared with the more modern building where she was teaching. She walked round them to the front. The site was not as big as she had remembered, and the secondary modern hardly seemed to have any yard at all. They had turned it into a teachers' centre. She had been there a couple of weeks ago to attend an induction day. The secondary children all went to the big comprehensive now, unless they opted out and were sent to one of the independent schools.

Her old primary school was much as she remembered it. It felt strange to be looking at her old school now that she was herself a primary teacher. It was as if she saw the scene from two viewpoints simultaneously. Of course, being the weekend, the buildings were all locked up. As she skirted the site, she peered through darkened classroom windows and caught glimpses of bright displays. They looked much like any of the classrooms she had seen on teaching practice or now in the school where she was based. There was children's art work and pieces of writing, neatly mounted on contrasting coloured paper; big displays on topics that the class would be exploring, that owed more to the teacher's ingenuity than to the children's efforts. Some boards were still blank. It was, after all, only the first week of term.

The infant classrooms had been expanded with new pre-fabricated buildings that had encroached on the playground area. The windows were brightly painted with big flowers and trees and a rather incongruous snail. Numbers were going up. The post-war baby boom was repeating itself as that generation produced its own offspring. Every school in the area was full to capacity.

Immigration played its part too. As she turned towards the terraced streets, Jo saw a woman in a sari leaning against her doorway, her gaze on a group of dark skinned lads who were playing football. A couple of little girls in headscarves squatted against the wall, playing with some small toys on the ground between them.

Caught by the pull of the past, Jo started to retrace the familiar walk home. The terraced houses seemed rather neater than she remembered them. Many had been freshly painted and some of the net curtains had been replaced by slatted blinds. The population was clearly more mixed than it had been, but there were still a number of older people on the street who looked as if they had always lived there. The corner shop was still there too. Jo remembered children from her class calling there for sweets on the way home from school. Once someone had stolen a Mars bar and the shop keeper had come to speak to them in assembly about honesty. She had only been seven at the time and had felt desperately guilty, even though she had never set foot in the shop herself.

The park was as inconsequential as it had always been. A small expanse of grass between the houses and the road, with crisp bags and newspaper caught in its iron railings. It looked uninviting. As teenagers her brothers had sometimes hung out there in the evenings drinking illicit cans of beer with other lads, but she had never joined in. A couple of swings and a small climbing frame had been installed at one end, but these were unoccupied. One of the swings hung awkwardly. It looked broken.

At the far side of the park, where the ditch they had called the Amazon came out, was the alley way. It was pretty over-grown and didn't look as if it were used now. Jo would have liked to go that way, but the brambles put her off, so she took the road instead.

Here the biggest change hit her. As she walked round the corner towards the cul-de-sac, yet another new housing development faced her. The factory site had gradually been built over during her teens; neo-Georgian houses set in neat green turf on absurdly named roads which seemed to wander in aimless curves without ever going anywhere. With them came more families, and the population of the area changed so that her brothers made new friends with the sons of young doctors and bank employees, social workers and teachers.

The newest houses were more traditional in appearance, built in brick with fake stone lintels, sash windows, and red tiled roofs. They completed the estate, adding an air of sobriety.

The cul-de-sac looked very small. The eight houses, earliest in the new development, were showing their age, and several had peeling paint on the white boarding, revealing rotten wood behind. Some of the boarding on her parents' house had been replaced before they moved, and in consequence it looked rather smarter than some of the others.

Jo wondered if any of the families whom she had known in childhood were still there. Simon's family had moved out to the country while she was still living at home. He had transferred to a school in Surrey and they had lost touch years ago. Philip's parents had bought one of the new larger houses. She knew that because her mother still kept in touch with them, and gave the family news of what Philip was doing. Last Christmas when the round-robin arrived he had been working as an administrator for a packaging company in the Midlands, but was thinking of going back to college if family commitments would allow.

Jo looked up at her old bedroom window. It had flowery pink curtains and a fluffy pink bird hung on a spring in the middle of it. There was also a sticker advertising the local radio station. She stood looking for a few minutes, then, because there was nothing else to do, she turned to go. The visit seemed inconsequential, but she was not sure what she had been looking for.

Walking on towards the flats, Jo felt empty. She suddenly missed her family and felt an urge to go and visit her parents. It would be easy to catch a bus or train to Oxford and she was sure they would meet her from there in the car. She wanted connection, for something from the past to still be alive. She wanted to know that these empty ghosts of memories were not all that remained.

The flats ahead of her were gaunt, the concrete just as unattractive as ever. Jo had no desire to revisit them. She was beginning to feel unsafe in the area. Instead she turned back towards the main road.

It was as she walked back along the main road that Jo thought about the scrap yard. Its entrance was between two of the shops, a cobbled alley way, just big enough to take the small truck. This was not the way they had gone as children, for the gates could also be reached from the over-grown footpath where they had played, but from the main road it was easier to get to. Jo looked down the passageway.

The big gates were still there. The chicken wire was now rusty and there was a big padlock and chain looped through the upright supports. It did not look as if it had been opened for a long time. Going up to the gate, Jo peered through. The rustiness mingled with the smell of damp decay. It was the smell of disuse.

The yard was still half full of piles of scrap metal. The shed was shut. It looked in poor condition, with its roof-felt breaking away in places. Beside it the remains of an old tarpaulin flapped against a pole to which it was tied. It had large rips in it where the fabric had rotted through, and the fallen portion draped across the old sofa. That was still the same one that she remembered, but now its covers were completely rotted, exposing the springs and clods of cotton waste stuffing. Beside it was the concrete block on which they used to stand the stove. Someone had had a fire in one corner of the yard, away from the hut, and there were some crumpled cans and food wrappers nearby, but these were old, the writing on the wrappings faded by exposure to the sun. The yard had clearly been abandoned for some time.

As she looked, Joanne felt a chill come over her. She did not know what she had expected. Perhaps she had hoped that this too would be swept away with the other changes that time had brought. Perhaps she imagined the site re-developed, its memories concreted over by some new super-market or housing. Or maybe she imagined Ray and Alf still there, but older, characters from her childhood whose troublesome faces could be rehabilitated into new adult understanding. But none of these happened. Only the rusting hulk of the familiar space remained.

****

The landscape of the past lives in our memories. Re-treading its geography in our minds, we imagine we can return. We look for familiar places, points to which we can attach our recollections, but the search is often frustrating. Sometimes we stumble upon a fragment; a view, a building, an encounter that opens before us into our histories. We find our memory jogged by the recognition. Small details matter; the flag stones of a pavement where in childhood we played hop-scotch or ran to escape the bears; the marked wooden counter of the sweet shop, with its dark, wax filled grain, where old pennies could gouge out fresh channels as we waited to be served; the iron supports of the climbing frame, polished with use, that chilled the hand and left little pinch marks on the palm if you swung too fast on it.

Returning is risky. The past more easily settles into the pockets of memory if left to its own devices.

Yet, tantalising, old places beckon. The childhood story embeds our present, giving it moorings which, for most of us, are comfortably familiar. Untainted by new development, our memories are oases where we can venture, selecting the nostalgic and the pleasant to bolster our sense of who we are. In this, our minds go back and longingly seek the security of parental certainty. We recall those times when we were loved, searching out evidence that once, for a while at least, we were held by the warm nest of the family.

Of course, this is not the whole story. Other memories are painful, seek resolution, or are helplessly suppressed. Some bring embarrassment or shame, the galling knowledge that what was done cannot be changed, ever. The past recedes but will not disappear or re-write itself. Hurts can burn as raw as twenty years before. Injustices can be seen more clearly with advancing years.

But still we cling to stories from the past, retrace our steps, seek out the pillars on which we have built our identities.

So Jo returned. Her life had moved on since leaving home. The days of the gang, over-laid with other scripts. The grammar school, university, her teacher training course, and all the experiences which come from years of travel; all these had brought new aspects to her current self, but like the salmon following its birth river to the source, in the hiatus which her lonely return to England brings, the call of childhood draws her back. With the ending of her eight year long relationship with Paul, the recent keel of her life had gone and, with it, aspects of her identity had been dismantled, a new uncertainty arising. Instinctively she retraces her steps; seeks footholds in her history from which to recommence her life.

Of course her work as a teacher colours her memories. The children mirror her own childhood, evoking with their interests and concerns, their games and friendships, echoes in her own store of recollections. It is not surprising. The store is vast, an archive rarely tapped, from which we draw such stories. Yet she is now different. No longer the taught, but rather the teacher, she watches them across the insuperable ridge of having grown up. She is the guardian, the source of authority, the knowledgeable and the representation of the rules. No longer the rebel, she must set the example of propriety. It is she who tidies, who sets the tasks, who serves the process.

But in her wanderings, her thoughts are drawn to revisit the past. Her need of anchorage tempts her back into the well known places of her childhood. Curiosity brings her back along old tracks. The row of shops, little changed, hovers in that strange half space of being known from other contexts. So often when we revisit places, that quality of walking in a half remembered dream juxtaposes the present. I am here now, and I have been here before; the deja-vu all the more disturbing for its reality.

Discovering that Wendy's family are still in the area comes as a shock. It is as if the trance is broken by this interpolation of reality. Jo is not ready to meet Wendy. Still in the childhood trance, she does not want to break through to forging new adult friendships. She keeps that opening for a later time.

Her instinct is torn; whether to continue to explore this place, once so familiar, now decayed, transmuted into new elements by the alchemy of time, or whether to retreat to the other familiarity of parents and the warm welcome of their homely embrace. The place is barren, yet it holds within it memories which current relationships skate over. Solitary, she is confronted by the reality of loss, encapsulated in the little details of change, but also by surprising happy recollections. The place is bitter-sweet, redolent with the smells and textures of childhood.

Much of the past is gone. The factory site is long developed. Some of this she witnessed in the latter years of childhood. The slow encroachment of bulldozers and diggers, roads muddied with heavy clods of clay from lorry wheels, rising walls of breize-block and brick; the new houses took shape, were landscaped and occupied, as gradually the old features of the gang's territory were eroded. By then it hardly mattered. New interests had come in and the old camps were already abandoned. Her brothers welcomed the company the new houses brought, new mates with whom to hang out in the twilight world of adolescence. They found new gangs among the disaffected youth of in-coming families.

And the scrap yard remains, an almost forgotten reminder, locked and deserted, the remnants of its former usage decaying behind the wire mesh fencing. The old darkness of half forgotten incidents invades Jo's body even before her mind has grasped their memories. The smell of rust ingrained into her hands as she leans against the gate, grasps the lock and chain, to better see, lingers like the aftermath of those childhood days as she walks back towards her room.

CHAPTER FOURTEEN

Remembering

Jo sat in her bed-sit that evening. There were seven bed-sits in the house and hers was on the attic floor at the back. It was quite a nice room, bigger than many, and interestingly shaped with sloping ceilings and a little pointed window that looked out over the yards of the shops and the gardens of adjacent houses. It even had its own little bathroom with a shower and toilet, which many bed-sits did not have. She had a Belling for cooking on, and some cupboards and a strip of worktop in the kitchen area, which was in one corner of the room. There was a sink for washing up outside on the landing, which she shared with the couple in the room opposite.

She had not met many of the other people in the house. The couple opposite were students and she heard them coming in late at night sometimes. They tended to leave the sink full of dirty washing up, but Jo was used to sharing houses, so it didn't bother her much. She just put the crockery and pans on the floor and got on with her own dishes.

She knew that one of the women on the floor below was a nurse because she had met her coming in one morning after night shift, and she had spoken with a man from Malawi who had taken one of the ground floor rooms. He was studying at the university on some exchange programme. His English wasn't very good and it had occurred to Jo that she might help him, but she thought better of it. These things could get complicated, especially if you were living in the same house.

The room felt very empty. Through the week this had been quite welcome. After a day in the classroom, a quiet space to prepare lessons, catch up on marking, and then watch some television before bed time was just what she needed, though part of her resented the predictability of it. Now, however, she suddenly felt like the only young person in London who was at home on her own on a Saturday night.

Of course, she thought wryly, she wasn't really so young any more. At thirty one you could hardly think of yourself as a teenager. Many people her age were at home, settled in comfortable domesticity with husbands or wives and families. Both her closest friends from the grammar school were married. One had two children and the other was expecting her first baby any time. This thought left her feeling sad. She had at one point thought that she and Paul might settle down, but it hadn't turned out that way. Time had passed and here she was, on her own again, living in rented accommodation with students and other young single people. It was like being twenty again. She felt as if she had stepped into a time warp. How ever was she going to kick-start her social life?

She thought of going out, but what could one do on one's own? The cinema seemed unappealing and she didn't feel she had the courage to go to a bar alone. No doubt there were things she could do. Maybe she could find friends among the other young teachers in her area. She resolved to be more active in seeking out companionship. There might be classes, or clubs. She could try the library. That was what she always advised other people to do if they seemed isolated or lonely.

Standing by the window, Jo could see lights coming on in the flats above the shops; so many people, living ordinary lives, each person with their own story, their own happiness and frustrations. Why was it so hard to meet other people? In the city it seemed even harder. Travelling it was easy. When you stayed in a back-packer hostel you just had to go into the kitchen or lounge and people would talk to you. Everyone had something to say. Everyone had their advice and their horror stories; they were often on their own and glad to make friends even if it was just for the evening. They were all in the same boat.

That world was timeless. You met people who had been travelling for years, working a bit here and there, living out of a back-pack. There were older people too; people who had done it all the wrong way round, who had done the marriage and children bit and in their forties or fifties had thrown it all up to pursue a dream. Jo liked meeting them. Often they were women. They had a zest for adventure and a confidence that came from having seen a bit of life. But sometimes they could be frightened too. Sometimes they were new to the travelling thing and looked to the youngsters with their brash confidence and naïve optimism for support and advice. At one point when things had ended with Paul, Jo had been tempted to head off on her own too, but a sensible voice, which was probably her mother's, told her it was time to get a proper job and stop whittling her life away on the road.

She thought back over the day. It had not been so bad. The afternoon had passed quickly. After she had got back from her morning walk, Jo had read the new books for a while, and then she had been out to the shops again to get in food for the week ahead. Later she had walked down to the swimming baths and done some lengths. Swimming had been her favourite way of relaxing while she had been in Australia, though she had to admit, she thought with a little smile, that the local baths were not quite the same as the Pacific Ocean. Even so, it would have been good exercise, but the pool had been crowded with children, so she had not enjoyed it as much as she had expected. It was a bit of a busman's holiday.

She still half wondered about going to see her parents. Oxford was so close you could even go for the day. It wasn't difficult for her parents to pick her up from the station, as they went into town all the time to attend some of the many concerts and theatrical events that went on there. Her mother would often say to friends, and to Jo on half the occasions when she phoned home, that they had the best of both worlds, living deep in the country, but with easy access to some of the finest culture in England. Somehow, though, the idea of going home now felt like chickening out. It would be taking an easy solution when what she really needed to do was to find a life for herself on her own in London.

Jo frowned. "I'm not going to achieve anything sitting here moping," she said out loud. Then she felt self-conscious. "Now I'm talking to myself," she muttered. She laughed, "Things must be getting bad."

She stood up. There was nothing for it but to get out and do something. For a fourth time that day she put on her jacket and, with her key and purse in her pocket, left the bed-sit.

The sun had gone down, but there was still a pale light in the sky to the west. Jo walked up to the main road. She stood looking up and down the street. She was not sure where she was going, but she felt the need to walk. At least she could do that on her own.

After a few moments hesitation, she turned and walked along in front of the shops. Some of them were still open. She enjoyed the bright light and the smell of fruit and vegetables and spices. They reminded her of street markets in the East. Then she crossed the main road and cut down through the new houses towards the river. There was a landscaped park there, running right up to the river bank, newly created when the houses were built. It had seats on which you could sit and look out across the water. You could see the warehouses and flats on the far bank and watch the boats going up and down.

It was still mild enough to sit out. No longer the fierce heat of August, the September air was nevertheless still warm and pleasant. People were strolling along the riverside path, walking dogs, couples arm in arm, youths on bikes. It was a beautiful evening. Jo looked up. The first stars were just appearing overhead as the last of the light faded. She felt at peace.

****

Humans are social animals. Our sense of well being often depends upon our connections with others. An important aspect of the way we see ourselves is linked to our social networks, our ability to form friendships, and the type of people we associate with. Our confidence mirrors the faith that others put in us. Whilst we feel socially well connected, our sense of our own merit is high.

The axis of judgement is human. We are not subject to divine retribution, but to the criticism or ostracism of our peers. Others enjoy our company, so for the most part we assume we are likeable people. If others reject us, we take it upon ourselves and assume that there is something blameworthy in our nature. Of course, this is not universally the case. The confident or arrogant person may hold onto their sense of righteousness far more tenaciously than the person who is naturally more diffident. Conversely, the unconfident may be hard to convince of their capabilities.

By and large, though, we feel enhanced by others' appreciation and shrink under their disfavour. We assume the time we spend in others' company to be confirmation of their approval and so feel diminished by their absence. Our social standing contributes to our sense of our own worth.

Being with others affects our mood in other ways. Partly this happens through the natural process whereby we are distracted from our own thoughts by our interactions with others. It's simple. As herd animals, we are designed to be with others and we grow lonely on our own.

When we are in company, our minds are drawn into conversation and engagement. We are occupied by the relationship. We do not have time to dwell in the malaise of our habitual preoccupations. If we have a depressive tendency, we are lifted out of it by good humoured connection, or by empathizing with the troubles of others. If we tend towards the grandiose, we are brought down to size by the measure of others' responses. We hear new ideas and new ways of interpreting experience. Other possibilities open up and we become obliged to look more closely at our assumptions. In particular, we have to adjust from simply reiterating our world view to taking on board other perspectives.

Of course company does not always work this way. Groups of people share prejudices, and often we seek out friends whose views match our own. Then company may simply reinforce our habitual perspectives. Groups can be punitive and the loneliness of the isolate within the crowd can be far more bitter than that of the solitary person. Besides this, aloneness has its attractions, and, when sought, can be a space where experience crystallises in new clarity, a source of great appreciation and pleasure. To be alone need not be lonely.

Isolation that comes upon one uninvited is often different. The breaking of the familiar patterns of relationship cuts deep dykes across our lives, which drain away our energy, leaving us exposed and vulnerable.

When important relationships founder, our social capacity is hurt in two ways. Firstly, in the loss of the loved one, we lose our strongest connection with the world. This has its pragmatic side. If we lose a life companion, whether through death or separation, we can lose our main source of social support. We become emotionally isolated, no longer have an easy way to share our thoughts and ideas. We become locked in our own misery at just the time when we most need to talk and share our thoughts. Bereavement can be like this. Secondly, in losing our closest loved ones, we are separated from those who tell us who we are; those who have previously been a support to our identity. We are no longer part of a couple, no longer the mother or child, no longer the trusted friend. Not only do we lose our source of solace, but also we have to find new structures in our life. We have to forge a new identity. It is not easy.

Commonly such experiences can become a source of shame. Where our sense of worth is based on popularity and social accolades, to sit at home alone and friendless takes on a flavour of social condemnation. Whatever its cause, the state of being alone feels like evidence of failure. The social pressure to be happy, popular, and successful creates a sense of obligation which compounds our unhappiness.

In particular, the young adult struggles with coupledom. Although by the eighties, many chose to be single, enjoying, sometimes, the freedom of changing partners, still the pressure to be in relationship was strong. It still is now. The comfort of knowing that somebody cared, mirroring the social expectations to set up home and settle down, created a climate where having a partner was often seen as a sign of success. Marriage was no longer as important as in previous decades, but having someone with whom to shop and cook and set up home, to holiday with, to visit restaurants or cinemas, to share a bed; all these were still expected.

Such norms were challenged. Women asserted the value of friendships with women. Increasingly they met the needs for company and companionship with one another. In one way it had always been so, but now, with stronger voices, they refused to relegate their friendships to a lower status. Yet still the need for social connection remained.

The life of the bed-sit is transitory. For the young it is an exciting necessity, a first step to independence perhaps. A personal space, it may give respite from other shared accommodation. The Yale-locked door providing privacy and control, an improvement on the sleazy mess of student flats. Pragmatic, it is a staging post between home and the first flat; a twilight area where occupants pass one another on the stairs but need not talk a common language. But as a temporary abode, the pressure is always towards moving on.

The fear of permanence hovers in the background, menacing

and dark. To get caught in this eddy of society can be to enter a glowering cloud of ignobility. The middle-aged occupant desensitised to his own feelings of failure, taking each day as one more faltering step towards the pension, shuffles the familiar route to the benefit office, the corner shop and back again. And so, inevitably, time moving on becomes a theme.

The biological clock is not amenable to negotiation. Whilst fashions and social politics come and go, the young woman knows that time is limited. Implicit decisions about children are made in the forming and dissolution of relationships. And in this matter head and body may not agree. In her early thirties already, Jo's time is limited. Already in decline, her fertility will not outlast many more aborted relationships.

Our reproductive processes are not our own. Our children, not simply our prerogative, are also concerns of our parents and of wider society. Governments worry about declining birth rates and aging populations. Statistics are collected and scrutinised. Manipulations of taxation and propaganda infiltrate our decision making, mostly unseen. Parents worry about grandchildren who do not come, about inheritances, but more, about the continuance of their blood-line, their genetic seed. Each generation straddles the line between past and future generations, holds the responsibility for its preservation.

And still Madonnas smile from aging canvases, clasping their buxom babies to the breast, the smug satisfaction of motherhood. Woman fulfilled, the fruits of the womb displayed in rich autumnal light. And in the shopping malls and streets, the coach-built prams are proudly trawled, their occupants, swaddled in soft pastel wool, admired by passing strangers. The childless bear the shame of their decision, or, if the choice was not their own, of their inadequacy. So guilt falls, penetrating as November drizzle, upon the single childless woman.

In the face of such pressures, the urge to regress may be strong. Nostalgia for childhood with its different pressures, or the longing to start again, to make those first steps into adulthood differently, can tempt one back into the family fold.

For the young person, recently emerging from the family home, there is on the one hand a sense of needing to prove his or her independence; to show that it is possible to survive alone. Also, though, there is a pull back towards the comfortable, or perhaps the uneasy, support of the family. At least, even in all its restrictions and conflicts, with Mum and Dad there is always someone there.

****

Jo walked back slowly in the darkness. She still felt uneasy. Sitting by the river had interrupted her thoughts, but now as she cut through the neatly winding roads of the estate she found her mind once more going back to the scrap yard. There had been something so poignant about the sight of it, all shut up and neglected, as if part of her childhood had been ripped away. She suddenly felt terribly bereft. She wanted for a moment to see the others, to track down Simon or Philip and say to them "Don't you remember?"

The old sofa where they had spent so much time playing cards or just being silly had still been there. It had looked so pathetic, rotting and abandoned. It had been strange to see the fence, still overgrown and even more tangled with brambles than before, where they had stood, peering through into the forbidden territory, or shouting insults that first time when Ray and Alf invited them in.

Strange to see the hut which had been so exciting, such a resource, full of all those mysterious objects which the scrap men hoarded. She had so enjoyed making tea there, playing at being domestic in its warm dark interior. And with memories of the hut, she remembered finding the pile of magazines. She laughed for a moment as she thought of how many times she had crept into the hut to look at those pictures, how exciting and shocking they were, and how grown up it made her feel showing them to Simon and Wendy. What a big deal things like that seemed when you were young. She thought of those nights, tossing and turning, worrying what to do after she had first discovered them, and then the gradual settling of emotion into normality as she got used to the lurid illustrations.

Then there was Alf. That memory still roused some discomfort. What *had* happened that afternoon when he had caught her with the magazines? The main thing she remembered was the embarrassment, the shame. It was the worst thing she could have imagined, getting caught looking at those pictures. Of course, looking back, it was bound to happen sooner or later. They had been sneaking into the hut more and more, and since Wendy and Simon had been doing it too, someone was bound to catch one of them. It was probably only fair that it was her.

She thought about what Alf had said about taking photos. Somehow that bit had got confused over the years with her feelings of guilt at being caught, but now as she thought back, she saw that it stood on its own. Looking back, the whole conversation felt very creepy. Yet it was also true that she had been quite tempted to go along on the Sunday and find out whether he really meant what he had said. In some ways the idea of being photographed had sounded exciting. After all, she wasn't the sort of kid to chicken out of something just because it sounded wrong.

What a struggle with her conscience it had been. All that week she had debated with herself whether to go. The money had been tempting too. She didn't get as much pocket money as other children in her class and she was always on the look out for ways to top it up by doing odd jobs. Her parents encouraged this and often created ways for the children to earn extra pocket money by doing a bit of housework. Five shillings was a lot in those days. Also the money sort of made it OK. It made it more grown up. The women in the magazines were paid. Were they bad? They didn't look it. They were models. Alf had said so. Being a model was alright. In fact it was a glamorous thing to do. Models were like film stars. Everyone wanted to be one if they could when they grew up, but you could only get to be one if you were beautiful enough.

Then there had been the part of her that kept telling herself that it wouldn't do any harm to go. She would have to take her clothes off. So what? She did that every night when she went to bed. Her mother often came in when she was undressing. She even got undressed on the beach sometimes. What was the big deal? After all she was only a girl still. It was not as if she had anything to hide yet.

It was the haircut that nearly did it. When she looked into the mirror at Wendy's house and saw someone who looked like a model looking back, she just had to know if she could do it. Up till that point she had always thought of herself as a tomboy. She hadn't wanted to be pretty or fuss about her appearance. She had despised the girls at school who spent all their time talking about make-up and clothes. Seeing the reflection in the mirror, something had changed. The young woman in the mirror was fashionable and beautiful. It wasn't her, so it didn't matter. That young woman could do anything. Jo remembered how she had wandered round in a haze of excitement, peeping at herself in any mirror she passed and feeling suddenly grown up.

Besides, there had been the fact that her mother had liked the new hairstyle. She had expected to get into trouble. Arriving home looking so different was just asking for it. She had been completely astounded at her mother's reaction.

For once something that she had expected would get her into trouble had turned out well. She was used to having to justify herself, to make excuses, to conceal the truth, or, where she couldn't, to manipulate it so that it sounded different from what it was. In a funny kind of way her mother's approval had made her doubt her own judgement and feel that perhaps, all this time, she had been too cautious.

By Friday she had more or less decided to go. She imagined herself slipping down to the yard on Sunday. It would be easy enough. Her brothers were used to her going off on her own so they wouldn't say anything. No one would ask what she was up to. It wouldn't take long. She would just have to pose for a few photos then she could come home. She imagined herself, glamorous and languishing like the women in the pictures. It would be the first step to being a film star or something.

Then she and Wendy had gone down to the scrap yard. Once she was there, it all started to feel more real, and, in doing so, it started to feel a bit different. The hut was cold and draughty. It was so full of junk it seemed like you could hardly turn round, and it looked very dirty and untidy. She couldn't imagine looking glamorous in there. Also, Alf seemed different. He seemed a bit preoccupied. She couldn't imagine taking her clothes off in front of him and anyway she felt very embarrassed about what had happened on Tuesday. She had begun to feel very uncomfortable about the whole idea. Above all though, she knew that to go would be wrong.

She was a bit hazy about what happened next. She knew she hadn't gone. She remembered that she had spent Sunday morning in her bedroom making a comic book. Occasionally she had looked out of the window. It was quite a chilly day and the trees were blowing around. She was glad she was safe and warm at home. She wasn't sure what had happened to Alf though. Had he ever said anything? She didn't think so.

After that things had gradually got back to normal. She had not gone to the scrap yard on her own again. That felt a bit scary. She preferred to go with the others, and began to encourage the younger children to join them once more. Simon came back from scout camp and his stay with Andy, enthusiastic about cooking on fires and putting up tents. His presence gave her a feeling of ordinariness. They sat on the sofa and chatted while the men worked. Alf seemed to get back to normal too. He joked and cursed at the children as he always had and it was easy to imagine nothing had happened. The pile of magazines was still under the table, but she had not looked at them again. When she did see them she still felt slightly queasy, so she hadn't gone into the shed more than she could help.

And so that last summer before grammar school had unfolded. Her hair had gradually grown out and became lank and untidy as the sun bleached it several shades lighter. Maureen offered to style it again, but she shook her head. She and Wendy and Simon hung out together quite a bit, but they also included the younger ones sometimes. In August her family took a cottage in the Lake District.

As Jo walked, she had been completely absorbed in running over the events in her mind. She suddenly realised that she was actually standing at the entrance to the cul-de-sac, not a hundred yards from where it had all happened. The alley way behind the houses was dark and spooky. The brambles had completely overgrown the path at this end too. In any case, it was not somewhere you would walk at night. She peered into the darkness and wondered how long it would be before this area too was redeveloped.

****

So, with the distance of time, perspectives change. Some things clarify, others become more confused. Memory can be deceptive as it is revealing. New vantage points colour interpretation.

Across the years, we are often kinder to ourselves than we were at the time when events first unfolded. The humiliation of being caught with the magazines becomes a source of adult amusement. The youngsters' trespassing becomes a source of adult pride. 'I got up to all sorts of pranks in my youth,' we think.

Those things which seemed frightening or dangerous at the time when we did them become stories which we enjoy recounting. Having got into trouble loses its sting, and punishments are remembered with amusement or indignation. But the adult's view-point also sees the dangers, the potential troubles which were only just avoided. Remembering what nearly happened, imagining consequences, we feel anxiety for what might have been. Perhaps we judge the child, working out its own logic, justifying actions it knows to be wrong, but without comprehending the full import. We feel alarmed at our past stupidity, angry at our stubborn disregard of good advice. Or perhaps we feel protective of the child and blame the adults. Why were the parents not more aware of what was going on? Why did they not ask questions? Surely they guessed what the children were up to? We demonise: Alf, the manipulative perpetrator, Alf, the danger to society, Alf, the callous opportunist. We think of retribution. Is he still at large? Could he be tracked down and even now brought to justice? Is he a danger to other children?

Such thoughts stand in their own place, but they do not change the fact that what happened, happened. Nor do they change the flow of thoughts and impulses, wise and not so wise with which, as a child, Jo struggled. They do not change the fact that, in the end, she made a choice. They do not change the fact that in the end her conscience stopped her from going to the scrap yard. They do not change the fact that, given a slight change of circumstances she might have gone.

CHAPTER FIFTEEN

Starvation

It was Wednesday when Jo put her hand into her jacket pocket and found the appointment card with Wendy's phone number on it. She was just putting her coat on at the end of the day, about to head home from school. The week was half gone already and she had not yet got round to calling in at the library to look into classes or societies. Somehow she was always just too busy.

On Sunday she had gone to visit her parents after all. She had justified the visit to herself by the fact that she wanted to collect some of the materials she had created when she was on teaching practice years before. They would be useful for the project that the class was doing. It had been comfortable to visit, even though the house was not her house any more. She had never lived there. Her things were stored in the loft in boxes so were difficult to get at. Yet her parents' presence made it home of sorts.

"You'll have to get a proper place of your own soon so that you can take them all away," her mother had said, eyeing the cardboard cartons.

Her father had collected her from the station. He was genial as always, full of enthusiasm for life in retirement. He had enjoyed teaching, but he had been quite ready to move on by the time retirement came, he said. Things were changing and even in an independent school you couldn't just teach the way you used to. It was all forms and paperwork. He wished her well with it. For him all sorts of new things had taken over: the local history society, a luncheon club for retired professionals, the bowls club, for which he was treasurer, and the parish council. Her mother, of course, had found herself another Guide troop, he added. She liked hearing him talk even though he had said much the same on her last visit.

The house was small and old fashioned. It was much cosier than the house in the cul-de-sac had been. After lunch, Jo curled up on the chintz window-seat and finished preparing her lessons for the coming week. Papers and work cards spread around her as she worked. Outside, the garden was falling into that dishevelled end of summer state where all the flowers had flopped on their over-grown stalks and seed heads were still drying untidily on the poppies and lupins.

"I can't wait to get out there to tidy it all up!" said her mother, following her gaze.

Jo smiled. It was good to be home.

Back in the bed-sit that evening, Jo had felt good about being on her own again. On reflection, the visit had been just what she had needed; a bit of ordinariness in the middle of the chaos of starting a new job and finding one's way round a new locality. It *was* new, she thought, despite her history with the area. There was nothing of her childhood experience left that was of any use to the present. If anything the memories got in the way. London was tough. It was hard to relax. Oxfordshire had felt almost decadent by comparison.

Now finding the card, Jo was suddenly back, lost in childhood memories. Should she phone? What would Wendy be like? What was to say that they would have anything in common? She remembered the last time she had seen Wendy at the party. She had been tall and quite stunning looking in a full-length white and gold cheesecloth dress with cream crocheted lace trimming. Her hair had grown into a full dark mass, framing her face. She had seemed older than Jo, perhaps because she was at college, whereas Jo was still at school. They had chatted briefly, but Wendy had been with a group of lads and had gone back to dancing with one of them. Jo watched her, fascinated by her languid, snaking arms and swaying hips. It was hard to believe that this was the same girl who she had been friends with six years earlier, who had been so shy and diffident. How much more change would another fifteen years have brought?

There was a phone box on the corner which Jo used when she wanted to call home. It was a new one, but it still smelt of urine. Jo took out the card and a couple of coins.

The voice that answered was that of a young woman.

"Is Wendy there?" Jo asked.

"Hold on a minute, I'll just go and see."

Jo supposed that it must have been one of Wendy's sisters. The receiver was put down and she heard footsteps retreating a little way, then a voice calling Wendy's name. Eventually the woman came back. "She's just coming." She said.

"Hello."

Jo didn't recognise the voice, which had a flat London accent.

"Hello, it's Jo, Joanne. Did your mother tell you? I'm back living in the area and I saw her at the shop the other day."

There was a pause, then Wendy exclaimed, "Hey Joanne! Yes, she did say. What fun. Where are you?"

Discovering that Joanne was just around the corner, Wendy was immediately keen to meet up.

"Hey, are you doing anything this evening?" she asked, "How about going for a pizza?"

Jo felt relieved. Going for a pizza seemed so ordinary, so comfortable. It was what you did with friends.

"Great. I need to take my things home first and get sorted out, but suppose we meet up..." she hesitated, "how about seven o'clock outside your mum's shop?"

****

Wendy was standing in the doorway of the hairdressers when Jo approached. She was tall and slim as Jo remembered her, looking very elegant in a loose black shirt and a straight dark grey skirt. She had on leather brogues with low heels and over her shoulder slung a brown leather bag. Her hair was still full, although not quite as much so as it had been the previous time Jo had seen her.

There was an Italian restaurant in the next block of shops. Wendy knew it well, and it was only five minutes walk away. As they walked, the two women started to talk. Conversation came easily for there was much to catch up on.

Jo told Wendy about her travels. She talked about how she and Paul had met as students and about the struggles they had had with deciding what to do. She told Wendy all about the different places they had been and the work she had done in New Zealand and Australia. She told her about her teaching, and how she had managed to get the job in spite of everything. Wendy listened attentively.

Entering the restaurant, they found a little table by the window. It was in a quiet corner, away from the door. The restaurant was almost empty as it was still early. A young waiter with a heavy Mediterranean accent put large glossy menu cards in front of them on the round marble table. While they chose their pizzas, he lit the candle in the Chianti bottle. Wendy ordered a half carafe of house red to go with the pizzas and Jo asked for a jug of water.

"What do you do?" asked Jo, looking at Wendy when the waiter had left.

"Oh, I'm a receptionist for a community project." Wendy replied. She smiled.

"Sounds interesting," said Jo. "How did you get into that?"

"Oh, it's a long story." Wendy leant back in her chair and looked out of the window.

"Tell me," said Jo.

Wendy looked back at her and took a deep breath. "Well, I sort of got involved there a few years ago and when this job came up I took it. Before then I was a volunteer."

"And you still live at home?"

"Yes," Wendy hesitated again, "I went through a bad patch a

few years ago. I moved back in with Mum then."

"...A bad patch?" Jo echoed.

The conversation felt stilted. She was suddenly aware of how readily she had shared so many details of her own life and how uncomfortable it was now getting Wendy to talk at all about what she had been doing.

"I was anorexic." Wendy spoke in a calm, even tone. She looked straight at Jo as she talked.

Jo said nothing. What could you say? You could ask crass questions like 'how thin did you get?' or 'were you in hospital?' or you could ask 'are you better now?' but none of these really seemed to help.

"I'm over it now," went on Wendy, seeming to read Jo's mind. "...mostly," she added and laughed.

Jo looked at her thin wrist on the table. Wendy was playing with the carnation which sat next to the candle in the little china vase as she spoke.

"When did it start?" Jo asked.

"Oh, when do these things start? I don't know." Wendy looked distracted, "I guess it crept up gradually. Kerrie was really into dieting too. I think she was a bit the same way. We both used to count calories all the time when I was at home."

Jo remembered Wendy at the party, tall and willowy. At the time that was how everyone wanted to look. She had felt envious.

"It wasn't really a problem then." Wendy continued, "It was only when I went to university that it got worse. There was no one to stop me, so I just stopped eating." Wendy's voice tailed off. "I collapsed in the corridor one day. The girl in the next room called the warden. I think she had been worried about me for a while."

The waiter brought the pizzas. They were big ones, falling over the edges of the plates. He ground the pepper onto them from the oversized mill, giving it a little flourish as he moved it from one plate to the other.

"There you are, ladies, enjoy yourselves," he said, smiling broadly and giving them a half wink.

Jo looked at Wendy, then at the pizza.

"Don't worry, I eat well enough now," Wendy responded.

She must have to justify herself all the time, Jo thought. She felt sorry for Wendy. She wanted to know more, but she didn't want to push her. Jo had had a classmate at the grammar school who had become anorexic. The weight had dropped off her alarmingly during their "O" level year. The girl had been sent to a psychiatrist, but it hadn't seemed to help her much. Eventually she had left to go to a private school for the sixth form. Jo had always wondered how things had worked out for her. But that girl had never got thin enough to collapse, Jo thought.

Wendy poured wine into their glasses. "Well, good health," she said.

The rest of Wendy's story came out gradually over the meal. She had been admitted to hospital on something called a section. That meant she couldn't go home again till she had gained weight. It had felt like being a prisoner. There were other young women there in the same position. They were all terrified of gaining weight. Sometimes if they got too thin, they would be put on a drip. That was the worst thing because you just got bigger and bigger like a balloon but there was nothing you could do about it. Mostly they were just obliged to eat specially prepared meals.

"They used to give us Mars bars and crisps, can you imagine? Anything with lots of calories in it. And Build Up. How I got to hate Build Up!"

Jo looked puzzled.

"It's a drink they make for invalids. It's just packed with calories." Wendy shook her head. "It was terrible."

"Of course we learned tricks," she continued. "We would drink loads of water before we were weighed or hide anything heavy we could find in our clothes. They'd frisk us before they weighed us. It was a real battle of wills. In the end, though, you had to give in or you wouldn't get let out, but once you were out, the whole thing started all over again."

Jo watched Wendy eating. She seemed to be tucking into her pizza like anyone else.

"How did you get over it?" she asked.

"I think in the end it just burned itself out. It did what it had to do." Wendy made a face and shrugged, "who knows. I had some counselling too. I think that helped."

Jo had the impression there were other things she wasn't saying.

Wendy drained her glass and poured a second. Jo watched her thoughtfully. Her own glass was still half full. She picked it up and held it between finger and thumb. She didn't want to drink too much because of school tomorrow. Nevertheless, she took another mouthful and felt the warm rush of alcohol flow through her. Since she and Paul had split up she hadn't drunk much. There wasn't the opportunity to, unless she was going to drink alone. She could feel the wine was affecting her more than usual.

"I'm really glad I called you," she said.

She didn't really know why she had said it, but she knew it was true. Something about how Wendy was seemed to be just what she needed, like a breath of fresh air. Despite everything, all the troubles she had been through, something about her seemed to have got itself together in a new and exciting way. She was alive in a way that most of the people Jo mixed with were not.

"Me too," said Wendy. "You don't think I'm mad do you?" she hesitated, looking at Jo anxiously.

"No!" Nothing was further from Jo's thoughts. She smiled, "not at all."

They both laughed.

"It's five years since I was last in hospital," Wendy carried on, "you never really get over it completely, eating problems I mean, it's a bit like being an alcoholic. But it's not a problem now."

So saying, she cut a last sliver off the pizza on her plate and put her knife and fork down beside the remains. About a quarter of the original, mostly the crust, still lay uneaten.

"They do very big pizzas here," she grinned.

****

Anorexia: the battle of mind and will, of body and soul. Food is so basic to our existence, not only in the obvious ways, in supporting our physical well being, but also to so many of our dealings as human beings. From our earliest days, food has been the way that love is communicated and denied. It has been the stuff of celebration and ceremony, of indulgence and imposition. We have used food to communicate caring or control; solemnity or joy.

Even our religious life holds food in a position of importance. Food occupies the centre place in ceremonial and is the stuff of offerings, the Eucharist and the Passover meal, the tribal feast and the alms round bowl. Fasting too has its place in many traditions. It is the route to holiness and purity, to enlightenment and salvation. It heightens mind states and exemplifies self-denial. Refusing food is a potent symbol, the route to redemption and to the purging of sin.

From what sin, then, does the anorexic hide? In denying the most basic sustenance to herself, what archetypal penitence is she undertaking? That quest for purity, a haunting mirror to the saintly traditions, grips deeply on the soul. Fasting in earnest, young women strive to starve the passions into submission. Wraith-like, with skin translucent, skeletal and frail, they cling to virtue, extending the possibilities of self-control into an art. Though deeply pained, the hollow eyes reflect determination.

What guilt can underlie such suffering? For what, is this punishment meted? Only the heart of she who is afflicted knows the struggle in its particulars, uniquely painful for each of those affected. Only the secret place of understanding, buried deeply in the layers of history and imagination of the anorexic knows the meaning of the offering.

Refusing food is a strong act. The child refuses and the parent weeps. A potent rejection of the proffered love, to see one's offspring choose starvation rather than accept nourishment wounds deeply. Yet naturally small children assert their independence. Naturally they learn rejection as a means to strength. Naturally they take control, declaring their separate existence and their right to choose.

So Wendy fought her battles. Enmeshed in the ferocious compulsion of self-starvation, she expressed the pain of her life through denial of food. Was this expression one of guilt? Or is it yet some battle of wills, cursing at an unknown god?

She might have reason to be angry; deserted by her father at her birth, scorned by school mates on many occasions, placated by her mother and sisters. The list is endless, and when grievance starts to get a hold it is all too easy to find ways to multiply it. And likewise guilt, her legacy; a childhood founded on her mother's imprudent infidelity left its mark. Anger, guilt, the two are simply opposite sides of the same coin. Self blame, other blame, it's all the same. Anorexia and guilt are anger turned inward or the quest for perfection turned outward.

Anorexia came easily in a home where three sisters vied for pride of place through cultivating their attractiveness. The fashion of the time brought accolades to the thin, intoxicating admiration heaped upon those who hovered on the brink of pathology. But this alone was rarely enough to tip girls over. Other, darker factors played their part.

A paradox, the means to such attraction turning sour, creating from itself the ugly form that only brings revulsion: stark bones, emaciated skin, hardly to be admired. But in that paradox, perhaps a clue, the woman now reduced to half her size reverts to a pre-pubescent childhood state, a semblance of innocence. Deserting her adult form, her body returns to immaturity. Menstruation stops. Breasts disappear. Asexual, the new child-woman finds tranquillity in cessation.

****

Back home, Wendy sat on the floor in front of the gas fire thinking. Her mother had gone to bed and Kerrie was still out working. She worked in a small nightclub as manager and was often out till the small hours. The house was quiet. Meeting Jo had reminded her of a lot of things. Despite the wine, she still felt stirred up by images of the past.

"Don't push them down," she thought.

She had learned that from her counsellor. Now she told it to other people. But could she take her own advice? So many things, pushed down over the years. Things she blamed herself for, things she would rather forget.

"It's not your fault, you were only a child. How could you have done anything else?"

Wendy knew that with some things this was true. How could it be her fault if her mother had had an affair? Looking back, she was now sure that this was what must have happened, though she had yet to challenge her mother directly about it.

How could it be her fault if she looked different from her sisters? That had to be her mother's fault too. Was she to blame if she was teased or criticized as a result? Of course she shouldn't have to feel guilty for things like that, but still she felt the shame of being the little girl who didn't understand. She felt she ought to get over this.

Other things though, she was not so sure about. There were things she had done which she felt guilty about which she had chosen to do. Some of them were little things, like stealing people's pencils at school. Others were big. Were these really not her fault? Her counsellor said not. The theory she read in self-help books said not. They said it was just because she had been an unhappy little girl that she had done them, but somehow this didn't ring true. She didn't want to argue because everyone around her thought that way, but she felt in her bones that there were some things she had done wrong. This made her feel anxious.

"Stop thinking. Change the subject," she thought.

An image of the hospital unit came back to her. They were in the day room. There were four of them: herself, Debbie, Charlotte and the new girl, Anne. Anne was sat in the corner, knees hunched up to her chin, staring out of the window in sullen reflection. It was her first time in the unit. They all remembered how that felt. Debbie was sporting a large fluffy white lint bandage on her arm. She had cut herself the previous evening and as usual wanted everyone to know about it. Charlotte had been cooing over it all afternoon, but Wendy was fed up with Debbie's self harming.

"When are you going to grow up?" she had snapped accusingly.

"I need to do it to express my pain," Debbie had whined, "My therapist says so."

Wendy glared at her. "You're the pain round here," she retorted. She knew as soon as she said it that it was a cruel thing to say. No one could really want to cut themselves for fun, could they?

At that point Julie, one of the student nurses on the unit, came in. She had come to do bloods.

"OK let's have your arms," she said, "Yours first." She turned to Wendy.

Wendy offered her arm, sleeve rolled up. Julie drew out a sample with the syringe and put it into the little bottle on her tray.

"Now I need some from you, Debbie."

"Haven't we had enough blood out of her recently?" Wendy had jibed. She didn't really know why she had said it. It was gratuitously unkind, but it did make her feel better.

Julie looked taken aback. "Don't be horrible to her," she

scolded.

"You tell her," joined in Charlotte.

Debbie held out her good arm and sniffed. Julie took it. It looked thin.

"Have you been throwing up again?" she asked. "I thought I smelt something in the bathroom." Then she added, "Well, we'll soon find out when we get these processed." She deftly slid the needle into Debbie's arm.

Debbie fell silent, her mouth in a pout. Wendy had suddenly wondered what she was thinking. It was strange how you could live so closely with people and know so many personal facts about them without ever understanding how they thought. But then again, it was the same with herself. She had no idea what compelled her to keep starving herself.

Why had she remembered that incident, Wendy wondered? It had been just another tiny fragment of conversation in the dreary day to day interactions of ward life. Then she felt cross with herself. There you are, she thought, you're just trying to make yourself feel guilty again. She sank back into the chair, feeling defeated.

****

And so guilt becomes the taboo. Wendy's counsellor admonishes her for feeling guilty. It was not your fault. You are not to blame. Of course she is right. How could a child be guilty of their choice of parents? How could the child be responsible for the colour of her skin or for the responses of other adults and children? How could a child be responsible for choices made out of naïve rebellion or attention seeking, out of the voicing of unexpressed needs or the build up of frustration that impossible family circumstances created? Yet Wendy struggles. She knows that some of what she has been told is true, but some of it, she doubts.

The idea that the client is never guilty is problematic. What are the implications? First, she struggles with the powerlessness of her own position. If she has never been guilty, she has never acted of her own volition. Any choices she has made would simply be a sham, a deluded sense of her own power. If she has not been responsible, she has not been capable of independent action either.

Second, suppose what she is told is not true and she is indeed guilty? Suppose she has merely tricked the counsellor into thinking she is innocent? Perhaps really she is beyond the pale, unlovable and ugly as she has feared. Perhaps if her counsellor really knew the truth she would not care for her. Perhaps her counsellor's approval depends upon her being guiltless. Perhaps if she admitted what was really true, that conditional regard would evaporate.

Third, such guiltlessness depends on blaming others. It is not her fault. It was her mother, her teacher, the other girls. One day Wendy will have to confront her mother with the results of her actions. It is part of the healing process. Already she senses that her counsellor sees her mother as the one responsible for so many of Wendy's problems.

So does the cycle turn. Wendy feels guilty at her inability to shift her sense of guilt. She feels guilty for her disloyalty to her counsellor and to her mother, and the impossibility of pleasing both. Such is the problem. Guilt is not so easily vanquished.

Of course not all counsellors want to dismiss guilt. Not every counsellor wants to attribute blame to everyone except the client. Back in the eighties, though, many did equate unconditional positive regard with a position in which the client could never be seen as guilty. From such a place, how could honest exploration of our truth happen? How could we embrace our past and present in all their multifaceted qualities?

****

The strange thing about the incident in the day room, Wendy thought, was that after that things got better. She had been dozing in her chair. Her thoughts were scrambling and re-forming; the memory, her frustration, images of the other girls' faces all floated in her mind.

She had been unashamedly horrible to Debbie and had really hurt her. She had felt awful about it afterwards. But then they had talked, really talked. Debbie had told her about her father who had done all sorts of nasty things to her. She had told Wendy how she had started to cut herself to stop the awful feelings. That had been ages ago when she was still at school. Now she didn't know why she cut herself. It had just got out of hand, like the eating and starving.

Wendy had felt sorry for Debbie. It was the first time she had felt sorry for anyone in a long time. It wasn't just sentimentality. It was about understanding her and really caring. They became friends. Debbie didn't cut herself again for ages. She became less dramatic altogether in her behaviour and began to want to get better.

Now that she was on the other side, so to speak, Wendy sometimes tried to make sense of what had happened with Debbie. What was it in the incident that had changed her? Perhaps she needed someone to tell her to stop. Like a small child in a tantrum, perhaps she needed someone to tell her enough was enough. Or perhaps it was something about the ordinariness of the interaction. The two of them had squabbled like girls at school used to. Perhaps they had needed to bump heads a bit and get something out of their system, as her mother used to say. Or maybe she had felt listened to by Wendy in a way that she hadn't other times when she had talked to people about her father.

Whatever it was, something had made a difference.

CHAPTER SIXTEEN

Guilt

On Friday evening Wendy came round to Jo's bed-sit. It had been Jo's suggestion that they spend the evening together. She had invited Wendy almost as an afterthought as they had parted on Wednesday when Wendy turned off the main road towards her house. Friday was a good night because school would be finished for the week and they could relax and catch up some more.

Jo had ordered a take-away from the Chinese round the corner, so they both walked down together to pick it up. As they stood in the little steamy shop, with its white plastic display boards and artificial wood panelling, Jo looked across the road. She saw the bus stop where she used to catch the bus to the grammar school. Next to it the optician's was still there, and a new sandwich shop had opened. The shop that sold woollies and underwear had gone, but the ironmongers' was there. Further along she could see the dark gap between the buildings where the alley way was that led to the scrap yard. Behind these facades too was the cul-de-sac. How strange it was seeing them from this angle, as if her old life was being presented right there before her. This area had all seemed so big then, but actually it was small, tiny.

Wendy had brought a bottle of wine and they opened it with the meal. They ate sitting on the floor, Jo's back against the wall by the little cast iron fireplace, Wendy leaning against the arm chair.

"It's strange coming back," Jo's mind was still with her earlier thoughts.

"It must be," Wendy said. "I guess you see the changes. You don't notice if you've been here all the time."

It was true, she had hardly been away; a couple of terms at University, the times in the hospital. Always this place had been her base, the place she thought of as home. Compared with Jo's travels, her life seemed narrow and restricted. As she thought this, she felt the old familiar feeling coming up in her. Just for that moment, once again, she envied Jo.

But then, other things had happened for her. She didn't really regret it, even though it had been hard. In her mind she had travelled light years. She had been to the end of the universe and back.

Jo put her empty plate on the floor. "I'm glad we met up. It's hard coming back," she said.

"I know what that feels like."

Wendy thought of the times coming out of hospital; that first moment, standing on the doorstep, after you had walked through the locked door and out past the big reception desk, looking out into the bright sunlight, blinking like a pit-pony.

Of course it must have been an illusion. There were outdoor spaces in the hospital grounds where you could walk, but somehow it had always felt as if she had been in the dark, or rather in artificial light maybe, whilst she had been inside.

Outside it was all bright, so bright. The air was so fresh, and every branch on every little shrub along the path seemed edged with colour so vibrant it elated her. Little birds, perky and bright-eyed watching her, squirrels, playful, busy, excited, running across the grass and up the trees, across the branches like little roller-coasters; it was as if layers of dullness had been peeled off her senses and every nerve was raw and painfully alive.

Then there was that awful adjustment back to ordinariness; trying to cram your mind back into the familiar grooves of family life, as if with a shoe-horn, when it had grown wide and flaccid with months of introspection; facing the conversations and the questions, the inconsequentiality of living on benefit, and the monotony. Oh, how monotonous it had all been at home. No job, no friends, nothing to do but try not to think. She had watched daytime television, read chat magazines, anything to fill those long tedious days.

Even that had been easy beside the pit of her own mind. She had had to face it in the end, square on. The behavioural programmes had changed things for a while, each time, giving her respite, but they had not touched the dark places. Those dark places had always brought her back. Back? Back into the world, back into the pit, the cycling wheel of memories, half buried, and the finger-nail struggle to get out up the slippery mud slope of her thoughts, again and again and again.

Those three years of counselling had brought her to an uneasy truce with the past. They had brought some relief. They had started to build some tentative, tiny bridges between that bright, bright world outside and the inner darkness.

Since then her thoughts had mellowed. She didn't know how. Something had lifted. Perhaps it was her work at the crisis centre, first as a volunteer, and now in the office, meeting other women and hearing their stories. They put it all in perspective.

Wendy poured some more wine into her glass. She was drinking more than Jo again, she noticed.

"It's strange walking round the places we used to know," Jo said. "I went down to the river the other day. Those new houses are nice. It's strange to think that was all derelict land when we were kids."

Derelict land. Yes, that was what it had been. The Amazon, the camps, the great open spaces on which they had played, it had all just been derelict land, waiting for redevelopment. Worlds within worlds, like windows into other universes, how those great expanses had opened up! Who was to say the adult reality was more real, brought down to the level of the mundane, the dull, the practical?

"It was amazing then. We used to play such amazing games, so imaginative. I'm sure children now don't get half the freedom we had," she said.

"You used to," Wendy smiled, "I wasn't there for most of it. But I remember being amazed by all those camps and making fires and things you all did when you invited me over. I never did anything like that."

"Yes, we only really got to know each other that last few months at primary school," Jo continued, thoughtfully. "Whatever happened to Sarah?"

"No idea, we lost touch when I went to sixth form. She's probably either on the stage or doing something really boring. There were no half measures with Sarah," Wendy laughed. "Do you keep in touch with anyone?"

"Oh, just a couple of friends from secondary school. My mother is still friends with Philip's mother too, so I hear what he's up to. He's married with two children, would you believe it. They live in Nottingham. I've not seen him for years though."

"How about Simon?"

"I don't know. I never really had any contact with him after he moved away. I'd love to know where he ended up."

Jo's voice tailed off. For a moment she felt a bit wistful, as if she had touched a thread that went back to something a very long time ago; something that had been tender, fragile, precious. Then she laughed, "I expect he's a professor somewhere in some dusty old university. He was awfully serious."

They both laughed.

"I saw the scrap yard when I was walking round the other day," Jo said, "It felt really sad seeing it all rusted up like that. Do you know what happened to it? What became of Ray and Alf in the end? Are they still around?"

There was a long silence. Wendy looked at her. Her face had changed. The lightness that had been there a moment earlier in their shared laughter had gone. Jo wondered what she had said.

Eventually Wendy said, "Do you really want to know?"

"Why? What happened?" Jo was searching, struggling to catch

up with Wendy's mood. "Do you know something?"

Wendy continued to watch her. Her eyes looked cold and sharp. "No," she said, "and I don't want to know." Her voice was steady. She spoke very deliberately as if trying to keep feelings down.

Now Jo was silent. She did not know what Wendy was talking about, but she sensed that something terrible had happened. She felt that sick feeling in her stomach. Part of her knew what that meant, but she didn't want to listen to it.

"What happened?" she asked. Her voice was faint and yet seemed to echo in the silence.

"I went," Wendy said, "When you told me about being a model, I went."

"What?" now Jo was astounded, "I told you?" her voice trailed off.

Suddenly she remembered. It was the bit of the story she had tried to forget, the bit she couldn't remember the other day when she had walked past the old scrap yard. In some ways it was unimportant. She hadn't really done anything bad. Nothing kids didn't do all the time.

It had been after that time when they went to the scrap yard on their own, that Friday, after she had had her hair cut. She had been so full of herself, thinking she looked like a model and everything. Then Alf had wolf-whistled at her. Wendy had been jealous. It all came flooding back. She hadn't been able to resist telling Wendy about the modelling, that she was going to be a star and everything. She had enjoyed watching Wendy's face, and how envious she was.

By the time they left the scrap yard on Friday she had decided she wasn't going to go, but she was enjoying Wendy's reaction, so she'd carried on, pretending to be really cool about it all. Taking your clothes off was just part of being a model, she had said. It was what you had to do. Wendy had been shocked by that bit. Jo remembered her face: mouth open, eyes wide. She had enjoyed the feeling of superiority it gave her. She had carried on winding her up, commenting that you had to be quite grown up to do it.

Then on Saturday, Wendy had started asking her about it again. They had been sitting in Wendy's bedroom, making crepe paper flowers to decorate their summer flip flops. Jo had got fed up with baiting Wendy, so she had told her that she'd changed her mind about going. She had said it casually, just dropped it into the conversation.

"But what about Alf?" Wendy had asked. "He'll be waiting."

"Oh, he'll find out," she had said jauntily.

That had been it. Now she realized with sickening clarity that Wendy must have gone in her place.

"What happened?" Jo asked, not sure if she wanted to hear the reply.

"I went," said Wendy, "I took my clothes off for him so I could be a model, just like you said."

Wendy went on to tell the story. The actual thing had been over in no time. She remembered walking up to the gates on her own. That was when she knew that what Joanne had said was true and it was really going to happen, for they weren't locked.

On a Sunday the padlock and chain were always there. She had hesitated. It was her last chance to run away. But she felt sure she didn't want to. Alf was all right. He was Joanne's friend. She knew him well. He wouldn't make her do something that was bad. He was just going to make her into a model, to teach her how to do it, if she could persuade him to photograph her instead of Joanne.

Pushing open the wire mesh gate, the hinges squealed loudly. She had never noticed how noisy they were before. She opened it just enough so that she could get through, then pushed it shut again. There was no sign of Alf.

Again she stopped. Perhaps it was a mistake. Perhaps he wasn't here after all. But then she realized he must be waiting in the hut. How silly of her, of course that was where he was going to take the photographs.

Sure enough, when she pulled open the shed door, Alf was sitting by the desk. He had cleared up some of the clutter and was seated on the old wooden kitchen chair. For a minute she thought he was reading one of the magazines, but he wasn't. He was just sitting there, waiting. He had a shirt on today. She had never seen him in a shirt before. He looked smart.

He had looked surprised to see her, almost startled.

"Jo didn't want to come." She said, shyly, "I've come instead."

He paused for a minute, and then he grinned. Now looking back she couldn't think of that grin without seeing it as menacing, but at the time she didn't remember thinking that anything was wrong.

Maybe they talked for a bit first. She didn't remember. The next thing she remembered was taking her clothes off. Then she was standing against the wall while Alf took photos with his old Kodak camera. It was all a bit squashed. The hut wasn't very big and the door was shut. He had had to use flash cubes.

She remembered there had been one picture where she had turned her back and looked over her shoulder at him, just like a film star. Then there had been another when she had had to lean back against the rough wood of the shed and frown. The boards had prickled her back. She remembered thinking that she must look just like the models in the pictures. Thinking that, she had felt a bit smug.

The next thing she remembered was putting on her clothes. It was quite chilly and suddenly she seemed to be fumbling with all the fastenings. Alf had given her the five shillings before they started. There were two half crowns. She had stuffed them into her trouser pocket. One of the coins had rolled out onto the floor as she struggled to get the trousers back on. She had bent down to pick it up and just caught it before it rolled into the heap of bric-a-brac.

How she had got away, she wasn't sure, but she remembered that once she was out of the gate again she had just run and run.

She had hardly looked as she crossed the main road. She had to get home as fast as she could. She could remember lying on her bed, her heart beating and her face hot, trying to make sense of it all. Was it wrong? What had she done? What would happen now?

In that moment she vowed she would never tell anyone what had happened. She felt deeply ashamed and it just felt like the worst thing in the world would happen if anyone ever found out.

"The trouble was," Wendy went on, "Once it had started, it was difficult to stop."

"You went again?" Jo was shocked.

"Yes, lots of times. It went on for years." Wendy paused, "It's all right. I'm used to talking about it now." She hesitated again, "That's why I work for the Rape Crisis Centre."

Jo nodded slowly. The facts were spinning in her head. Gradually it all fell into place: the bits she hadn't remembered, Alf behaving as if nothing had happened, the way she and Wendy had drifted apart when they went to different schools, Wendy's anorexia. More though, she could see her part in the whole thing, how her own arrogance, her anxiety, her enjoying making Wendy jealous, had been the conditions for Wendy's suffering over all these years. She shuddered. Then another thought came to her. It could so easily have been her.

Jo felt a lump rising in her throat and her eyes stinging.

"God, I feel so guilty." She said. Her throat felt tight, her voice croaky.

Wendy said nothing.

"If I hadn't told you…" She hesitated, "I think I just needed someone to know."

Wendy nodded. "You were just a kid," she said.

It was true. The whole thing had been so difficult, so confusing. There had been so many things she hadn't understood, or had only half understood. It had felt dangerous, but she hadn't been able to see enough to know why. Like old bits of iron that stuck out of the mud flats of the river at low tide. She had felt small and grown up all at the same time. Yet somewhere in it all, too, she had known it was wrong. She had known it was wrong to do what Alf had asked, and she knew it was wrong to tease Wendy.

"But I feel terrible," she continued. "If I'd never said anything, none of this would ever have happened. It was all my fault. I should have known."

Again, her voice petered out. There was nothing else to say.

Wendy gave a little smile, "Well you don't have the monopoly on guilt," she said.

"I went because I chose to. No one made me. I didn't have to. He hadn't even asked me. I did it because I was jealous of you. I was jealous of everything about you, your life, your friends, your house, your family being a proper family..." She paused.

"I felt ugly, hideous. I wanted to be beautiful like you, and for people to admire me. That's why I did it. I thought perhaps one day someone would see one of the photographs and I would be discovered. That's why I carried on. It made me feel special. Like somebody cared. I could have stopped any time."

Jo looked at her. It was hard to believe now that Wendy had felt so ugly. She looked so attractive, her long legs stretched out on the floor in front of her in her natural linen summer trousers, her silky top skimming her brown shoulders, her smooth, even features and striking hair. A rush of emotion came over her.

Wendy saw it and moved towards her. The two women hugged one another.

****

So the complexity unfolded; two stories, inter-twining, yet separate, isolated from one another by differences of circumstance, of personality and of fortune. Secrets and forgotten details, hidden truth and misunderstanding; all confound the process of communication, but more than this, the truth falls, clattering its way out of the crevices of details.

The truth in this case is ugly. Despite the previous sharing, Jo is not prepared for what she hears. Somehow her mind has already censored the vital clue. Even as she explored, reminisced, retraced her childhood steps, that vital bit was still omitted. Jo has somehow laid aside her memory of teasing Wendy.

Although she did not know the consequence, even her own part in the events has been suppressed. Memory is a strange phenomenon, capable of all kinds of tricks of this kind and worse. Protecting itself, our ego clings to details and distortions which occlude the truth or else creates a fiction to explain the unforgivable.

The jaws of guilt close tighter, each woman knowing her part, her deliberate actions, as well as those which came about through misadventure, innocence and inexperience. A fine balance; the child caught in a web of adult preoccupations, playing with fire whilst never realising the danger. Mis-read cues, the trust that Wendy puts in Alf because she thinks of him as Joanne's friend, her need for appreciation, all contribute to the situation.

The conversation ebbs and flows, one minute accusations, the next confession. The finger points this way and that, the pain spills over. Who takes responsibility? Who is not to blame? What mitigating circumstances existed? Do they constitute enough to make excuses? Beyond it all, each holds their own part of the truth, each is willing to share only by degrees.

Jealousy plays its part. Strangely symmetrical, Jo watches Wendy, admiring her elegance and that dignity embodied in her thoughtful sharing, despite all that she has gone through. Perhaps she too longs for the resolution Wendy seems to have found. Perhaps it is some guilty residue, some ironic reflection of the envy which as a child Jo cultivated in her friend. Jo feels herself a little out-shadowed.

For Wendy, envy has played a bitter part. She has suffered at Joanne's hands. Wendy was already jealous of the admiration

Joanne was attracting. She was all too ready to fall into the trap, a willing victim of the game in which her friend deliberately cultivated that emotion, spinning out the tale of stardom to tantalize her.

Envy, though, had already been an ongoing force in Wendy's life. The retaliation of the impoverished, it had held her in its power a long time and made her vulnerable. She watched and learned to crave what others had from her youngest days, seeing her older sisters with their attractive, fair skinned looks, creating successful, beautiful lives for themselves. Or at least this is how it looked to a young child. Out of her loneliness and unconfident misery, Wendy the child was ripe for Joanne's ploys, ready to be exploited in return for crumbs of hope. It is a not uncommon situation for vulnerable children to be so exploited.

In the end though, whilst envy and the search for status has forced the two women apart over the years, it is the recognition and owning of their personal guilt which brings them back together.

Their understanding is embedded in the humanity of their sharing. The deep acknowledgement of fallibility makes space for fellow feeling to emerge. The women embrace, understanding their common bond of ordinariness. They discover the ability to empathise with one another in sharing the murky mix of emotions and motivations which drive their actions, as indeed, they drive most human process.

Until such sharing happens, the real depths of people's lives are so often hidden beneath a façade. People try to preserve the illusion of their virtue, of their superiority. Only by breaking through the façade and really communicating with one another, warts and all, do we come to appreciate one another in our full human worth and love each other in any meaningful way.

****

The evening had been an emotional roller-coaster. Jo felt she had never got to know anyone quite so fast in such a short space of time, and yet of course they had known each other for years. It was a strange paradox. How much was Wendy or Jo still the same person as they had been as children? Only the common stock of memories, a few short months of shared experience, twenty years earlier, seemed to weld their friendship, yet the glue was powerful. Even without knowing it, their lives had been shaped by the same forces, by experiences which came from a common root.

It was late by the time Wendy stood up to go. They had talked and cried and talked some more, sharing the stories from different angles in different ways. Both were tired and yet reluctant to say goodbye, for having found one another, they had each found a source of confirmation for a part of them which had been desperately alone.

"It's funny," Wendy said, "In a way I don't regret what happened. Of course I hate him for what he did, but it's made me who I am. I'm much stronger than I might have been. Who knows, if it hadn't happened I might have just joined Mum in the business like Maureen, or done something equally ordinary. As it is I'm doing lots of exciting things. I've had to look at my life and make it into something. I've got to prove I can be somebody. I've been studying again, and I've just got onto a counselling course. I'm going to turn my experience round so that I can help other people."

Jo nodded. She sensed Wendy's strength, strength which she herself did not have, which only came from having turned your mind inside out and faced every ghoul it contained. She hugged Wendy one last time and watched her go down the stairs.

CHAPTER SEVENTEEN

Light

That night, after Wendy had left, Jo lay in her bed struggling with her emotions. Although her initial feelings of guilt had been allayed somewhat by Wendy's response, now that she was on her own, the hot flood of remorse once more came upon her. If only it were possible to turn the clock back, to go back with all the knowledge of her adult self into that turmoil of childish emotion. If only.

Of course she couldn't, but the impetus, the aching longing to reverse what had inevitably, intractably been so, was still there, a tension in her body, a hunger for action. Memories raced around her head, phantoms that would not be exorcised. If only. Again and again the voice of regret, going over and over those few days, struggled to remember details, now twenty years embedded in memory, tried vainly to re-write history.

One thought that haunted her was the realisation that had come to her as Wendy spoke that the whole thing could so easily have happened to her. She had been within a hair's breadth of deciding to go and meet with Alf. She had only decided against it at the very last minute on that almost chance intuition that had come when they had gone down to the yard on the Friday. If they hadn't gone, or if Alf had been different, or if any one of a number of things had configured differently it would have been her and not Wendy who would have been in that hut, shivering in front of the camera.

Her mind wriggled and twisted, trying to find reasons why it would not have been so. There were so many different possibilities, different potential outcomes. Working out which would have happened, especially after such a passage of time, was like trying to predict the throw of a die. It was completely arbitrary. It really could have gone so many ways.

And if she had gone, what then? Would she have gone again, and again and again, like Wendy had? Would she have become intoxicated by the flattery, or would it have been the money? Or would it have become as compulsive as those magazines, the unknown forces of her childish sexual fascination drawing her into territory so dangerous? Would her life have been derailed like Wendy's, spiralled down into the chaos of mental problems?

But it had not happened. Wendy had done it instead. Like a sacrificial lamb she had taken the punishment that had rightly been Joanne's. Jo felt ridden with guilt.

Her own life had been easy. Of course it had had its ups and downs, but they were ordinary things, like relationship struggles, or dilemmas about what to do or where to go next. Mostly she had done just what she wanted.

Rationally, Jo thought, neither of them had to suffer. The sensible thing, which had never crossed either of their minds, would have been to tell a grown-up; her mother, or a teacher at school maybe. She hoped that any child in her class would feel able to confide in her if they were ever in that situation. But looking back, the thought of telling an adult would have been unthinkable.

Again her will wanted to change things. Again it cursed the invisible skin of time that separated the present from the past, impenetrable and yet elastic enough that she could be right back there, in those memories, as if it were all happening now.

Her face burned with shame. It buried itself in her hands, which raked through her hair almost before she had noticed her arms had lifted. Fingers clenched. She felt wretched. She hated the feeling. Knowing she could not erase the actions, knowing she had done what she had done, bit into her like a rope around the neck of a tethered beast. It aggravated like the putrid sores she had seen on malnourished creatures that pulled poor wooden carts in the East or carried huge sacking burdens on ill fitting saddles.

She had done this. What use were all her achievements, her qualifications, her CV, so carefully constructed with glowing, and somewhat embellished, accounts of her overseas work? What use was her career, or her family's admiration for her success in securing the job? How easy she had had it growing up, with her comfortable new house and professional parents.

How much of her childhood attitude had been built on pride, looking down on the children from the surrounding area, in which, she could now see, they had been interlopers. And yet it stung so hard because once more it hurt her pride. She had thought herself better than this. She weighed herself and found herself sadly wanting.

****

So the layers of guilt unfold. The pain of facing our actions in their intense, unabridged reality raises welts across our self-image. Guilt and pride. Unavoidably we know the score, and yet, a part of us wants to hide, wants to jettison the interpretation which our conscience is giving us.

Some feelings of guilt are no more than our hurt anger at our own betrayal. Jo struggles with the discomfort of adjusting her image of herself to incorporate the less attractive facets of her actions.

The story does not fit. Just as the facts are subtly preened for public display on the curriculum vitae; not lies, that would not do, but slight re-framing, highlighting the best and most attractive, omitting the unflattering; so too the self presented to the world is edited. And so too, gradually, we come to believe the abridged account we have created.

Bitter at such betrayal, we flagellate ourselves with guilt. We punish angrily the embarrassment we have caused ourselves.

Like wayward children we admonish our untamed aspects for the indiscretions.

Guilt is the face of our impotence. It is the railing of our small inconsequentiality. Jo looks back and sees the child caught in a mire of unknown factors, struggling with forces too big to predict.

She sees the impossibility of knowing and the chance occurrences which shape the course of events. She sees the way that on the one hand so much was unforeseen and out of her hands and yet too, that there is a keel of conscience that directs us in certain directions, even in childhood. But is adulthood so different? Are we as adults any better able to predict a path and know the differences between right and wrong, desire and intuition?

Perhaps, though, the guilt is a soft option. Perhaps we choose guilt because it means taking responsibility. Perhaps the alternative would be to say we have no choice, we are just corks upon the tide of chance. Perhaps in guilt we cling to the last vestiges of identity and to a sense of agency in our lives. Perhaps we cannot face our powerlessness.

But guilt is not comfortable. And worst, it comes to Jo when she sees the effects. She sees the way that her actions have affected Wendy. Of course, this is not the whole story. Wendy is quite right. She made the choice herself to go to the yard that Sunday. She acted within her own history, her own circumstances, her own karma.

History is over-determined. There are always many reasons, many conditions, or perhaps there are none, for to talk of reasons would be to suggest predictability where it does not exist. Whatever, it is undeniable that Jo's behaviour formed part of the net of circumstances, a major block in the wall that created Wendy's prison.

So she feels guilt; guilt at her actions, guilt that it was not her that bore the consequences, guilt that she survived intact. She feels guilt that, in rousing Wendy's envy, she sowed seeds that cemented their lives in different directions: hers towards the decadence of a globe-trotting, middle-class youth, Wendy's to psychiatric institutions and incarceration in her limited world of a London suburb.

But perhaps the last irony is that, despite the different weightings of their lives, at this point, it is hard to say which of the two is doing better in life. Adversity has made Wendy tough and searching into her soul has given her wisdom that perhaps Jo has yet to find. Perhaps too it is only now, in the cauldron of her misery, facing her behaviour in its rawest aspect, that Jo will break through the tangled web of her own defences.

The problem with guilt is that we feel we shouldn't have it. We should be perfect and immune from criticism, especially from our own consciences. It is not so. For we are ordinary, and our nature is to get things wrong. We struggle between uncertainties and sometimes do our best, but often not. This is the rich complexity of our lives.

****

It was half past three when Jo got up. She must have been lying tossing and turning for more than two hours. True, Wendy had been late leaving, and then Jo had pottered round, tidying the tin foil containers and paper wrappings away so that the room wouldn't smell too badly. She had washed the plates in her hand basin in the bathroom. She hadn't wanted to make a noise washing up on the landing so late at night. Then she had put the furniture straight.

After all this, she couldn't put off any longer the moment of going to bed, knowing that once she did go she would no longer be able to protect herself from the churning thoughts. She had been right.

Now there was nothing for it but to get up again. She was not going to sleep.

Jo crept down the stairs. The house was old, and the treads

creaked in places. She hoped she would not wake people. At the same time, she was well aware that others in the building were not always so considerate when they came in late. Passing one door on the first floor she heard loud snores. At least someone was asleep.

Jo wanted to be outside. The fresh air would help to clear her head. The two glasses of wine had long since lost their effect and she wanted some space to let the thoughts jumble themselves into some sort of order. It was chilly and she was glad she had put on her thicker pullover.

Her first instinct was to walk down to the Thames. The park where she had sat the week before was open enough to feel safe even in the darkness. Something about the moving water and the lights that reflected in it was comforting. Walking briskly dispersed the adrenalin, pounding her brain into quietude at least temporarily. The cold air scoured her lungs. Her eyes felt sore and delicate from tears, both from the evening and since she had been in bed. Now they were dry, catching the wind as it blew off the river.

She sat on a bench. It was the same one as she had sat on before, though there were several to choose from. Everything was strangely quiet. In the distance she could hear the occasional movement of a car, separate, a sound that came and went and had direction, not like the steady hum of day-time traffic. Late night taxis, she imagined.

The engines revved heavily, taking the rare opportunity of speeding on London streets. A boat, shifting on its moorings, let out a hollow metallic clanging as its chains rapped against their metal casing. The warehouse windows opposite were dull and unlit, but the dull orange glow of reflected sodium lights made the sky quite light.

Jo watched the water, flowing downstream, turgid and dark. She smelt the pungent and distinctive smell of the river. The tide was running quite fast. She put her hands into the pockets of her coat and hunched down into its collar. Her body felt a bit unreal, disjointed from its surroundings. She yawned. At least part of her knew it should be asleep.

It was easy to sit, watching, not thinking, at least for a while. The walk had exhausted her, and a bit of her would readily have slipped back under her covers and drifted off, at last, into a deep sleep. She got up. Perhaps she should walk home and go back to bed for what was left of the night. After all, she couldn't let herself get too exhausted because she would have to go to work on Monday. It was not like being a student, or when you were travelling, when you could set your own time. The new responsibilities weighed in on her.

She walked back more slowly, weaving her way through the new streets. They were deserted. Some of the houses were in complete darkness, but many had a light on in the hall or top landing. Occasionally she saw a bedroom light on. There was something strangely comforting about knowing that someone else was up at that hour of the night.

As she came to the cul-de-sac, Jo stopped. The cherry trees were big now, their trunks thick and scarred with the lateral markings that characterised their species. There were old cuts too, grown over mostly, from children's pen-knives or other sharp implements. She remembered them as young trees. This was where it had all happened, so long ago now.

Instead of walking on, coming to the main road, and making her way across it to her bed-sit, something made Jo turn into her old street. It was, as she had already remarked, smaller than she remembered. She stood in the middle of the roadway. This was *her* street. That was her house, her window. So many memories; a little girl, straw blond hair in untidy bunches. What did she know?

Then as she stood there, tears began to well up in her eyes once more. They had lost their bitterness. They were sad. Tears for the past, for the potential that had gone, for the possibilities that life had held for all of them and all the lives they might have grown into, as well as the ones they had found.

If only one could go back. If only.

Her thoughts were becoming melancholy, verging on senti-mental, self-pitying. She wondered where Simon was, thought of Philip with all his responsibilities, of her brothers. Even the little girls must be well grown up now, she thought. As far as she knew all of them were doing good things. They had become adults with lives that reflected their childhood promise and were a credit to their favoured beginnings here. Yet there was a narrowing, a reduction in their actualisation. Had they just settled for a conven-tional and secure alternative? Had they set respectability above being authentic to their dreams?

Somehow the promises of those adventurous days had dwindled into the mundane. Life was beautiful, yet desperately disappointing.

Then Jo thought of Wendy, the little girl with frizzy hair and freckles. She remembered her scuffed patent shoes and her shy way of looking up at you, even if she were taller than you. She remembered telling Wendy to wear sensible shoes when she came over. Goodness, she had been bossy. She remembered the way she had looked Wendy up and down that morning when she arrived on the doorstep, and her feeling of critical superiority. She remem-bered taking Wendy to the scrap yard, managing the relationship with Simon and the others, orchestrating their responses to one another.

Tears of remorse started to flow, more urgently than her earlier ones. No longer wallowing in self-pity, she saw at last, clearly, that she had created so much of the situation herself. Of course it was not all her doing, but there was enough that was. Wendy might have made her own choices, but she had also been the victim of Joanne's desires. She had been the foil for Joanne's superiority and the refuge from her self-doubt.

She saw Wendy, wasting away in that hospital in her bitter

struggle to vanquish the demons of her experiences. She saw her frightened and shivering, alone in that hut with that dirty, sweaty hulk of a man.

She saw her, for whatever reason, going back and putting her through that ordeal again and again, for the faint glimmer of self-worth it gave her, long after she in all her superiority and pride had moved on to the grammar school, forgetting her previous friends in her drive to find new and better outlets for her energy.

In that moment, Jo hated herself. She saw only darkness and cruelty, self-serving manipulation and pride. She turned and walked, not back towards her lodgings, but away, along dark unfamiliar streets. She was walking fast. Her breathing was laboured, but she didn't really notice, for her eyes were still awash with tears and sometimes great sobs would break out of her belly, only to be stifled as they broke the air, for fear of being heard.

Her feet were becoming sore, and she had developed a blister on one heel, but this she didn't notice till much later. She just kept walking, her mind full of the miserable regret that gnawed at her but could not be satiated. She had let Wendy down. She had damn near destroyed her. She had ruined her life. She had not even known, had not remembered. She had deliberately made her jealous, played on her weakness and insecurity in some deranged power game.

Paving slabs gave way to concrete and back to paving slabs. Tall tree lined terraced streets unfolded, one on the next. Shops and main roads, crossing places where traffic lights ploughed their steady sequences for occasional early delivery vans, all seemed to pass as features from a train window, seen, but slightly separated from the present reality.

She did not know how long she had been walking, or where she had come to, so deeply was Jo caught in her feelings, but gradually she became aware that it was beginning to get light. There was more traffic, and the chill grey dawn was penetrating her body with its special cold.

She was on a slight incline, a main road of sorts, red tarmac rising towards a close horizon with a row of houses on one side and some dark sycamore trees on the other. On the corner, near at hand, stood a large red sandstone building; a church. It had a big wooden notice board outside. St Barnabas it said.

The door was slightly open. Jo was surprised. She had not expected to find anywhere open at that time of the morning. It must still be early. She sidled up to the door and peeped inside.

The inside of the church was dark, but there was a light on up at the front by the altar, shining onto the huge crucifix. Above it in the darkened apse a small red dot of light held constant vigil. There were several people there and she realised that she must have stumbled in on early morning mass. A priest in vestments was standing at the low wooden rail that marked off the sanctuary area, reading something from a small book that he held in his up-stretched hand. His other hand was held aloft in a gesture of blessing. Three people were in the front row of chairs, all women, and all elderly. Jo slipped into one of the pews at the back, behind a pillar.

The priest came to an end, and then, after turning and bowing to the altar and making the sign of the cross, walked up the central aisle to the main door. He was a stocky man, red faced and middle aged. The women followed him. Jo heard conversation in the porch-way. Then the door closed. They had not seen her. The church was empty.

Jo sat in the pew for some time. Her face felt sore and she ached from crying. She was conscious of the puffiness around her eyes. She put her face in her hands. Her cool palms felt comforting against her cheeks. She didn't know why she had come into the church. She wasn't religious and didn't even know what sort of church it was. She just felt drawn to be there. It was quiet and comforting, a place of refuge. Instinctively she knew it was where she needed to be.

"I'm sorry, oh God, I'm sorry," she found herself saying.

The words echoed from her lips with no impetus from her own side. She found herself repeating them again and again. The call on God was an expletive rather than any urge to prayer, and yet, this too was strangely comforting.

Eventually, even the words subsided. Jo lifted her face from her hands and looked up. She found she had been kneeling. Light was flooding into the church through a window high up in the nave. It was a fine day and the sun was golden as it streamed in, creating a pool on the patterned tiles of the floor.

There was a slight noise behind her, and looking round, Jo saw a young priest in a black cassock coming into the church by the main door. He had fair hair, tousled as if it had not been properly combed, and a round boyish face. He looked serious.

The young man had seen her too. He came over.

"Hello, can I help?" he asked.

As he came up to her, he must have seen her tear stained face, red and blotchy, and her puffy eyes, but he did not remark on them. He just stood, smiling slightly.

Jo looked up. A strange impulse to confess flashed across her mind. Part of her wanted to tell him her sins and ask absolution, but in the same instant she knew she did not need to. Behind the young man, the light shone brightly, throwing him into silhouette. Suddenly she wanted to be outside.

She smiled. "No, its fine, I was just going home," she said.

****

And so it was. Nothing could take her guilt away because nothing needed to. Etched in her being, like the veins in an old gnarled piece of timber, the past gave framework to the present in all its complex motivations.

Only when we accept our darkness can we feel the light that

surrounds us, the light that extends for ever and ever and does not judge us, but loves us for our complicated shades of grey, black, purple and vermilion in all their dappled splendour.

Postscript

This book has been a journey, an exploration. Through the unfolding of the story, I have found my own experiences, and those of people I have known, mirrored and transformed in so many ways.

The fund of human experience is vast, yet limited, patterns repeat, yet each person's particular life unfolds in a way that is unique. I have come to know Jo, Wendy and the others who fill these pages as friends. They have surprised me. They have shown me facets of experience which were new, and ways in which their ways of thinking and acting differed from one another and from my own. I have come to love them.

The book has moved between narrative, analysis and commentary, and in writing it I have tried to reflect and describe, drawing out salient aspects of the story for our journey into guilt. In this I have deliberately not drawn strongly on theoretical expositions. I have preferred to leave space for interpretation and discussion by the reader.

Those who wish to know more of my theoretical ideas, which perhaps, but not necessarily, create something of the backdrop to this book, can read my other books. There you will find descriptions of the processes which create our mental structures, and also in particular of the spiritual framework from which ideas on guilt, love and our ordinary nature derive.

Whilst I was writing this book, a member of my community asked if I would write an article on guilt for our community's newsletter. I did. This piece explored some of the perspectives on guilt which lie behind this book, and so may be of interest to the reader. I therefore include a slightly abridged version of the article here.

Beyond Guilt

Why do so many people feel guilty? As someone who often listens to others talking about their lives, I hear again and again the anguish of regret. Why did I do it? Why did I not do it? Why did I not see; not hear? How could I be so silly? Why am I not good enough? The voices plead for answers.

And in the night, the ghosts of memories flock in to terrorize the wakeful with thoughts of what might have been, or worse, what was.

We all have regrets. Some regrets are justified. Recognition that we messed up, that our behaviour was thoughtless, selfish, cruel, unethical, is not easy to face. How can we readily accept such self-condemnation? Yet other guilt is darker, less clearly located, a sense of brooding unease that permeates our being as if the night itself had seeped into our soul.

To lie, eyes staring awake, heat rising in the breast, mind swimming downward in the spiral of a drowning man, is to know guilt. Breath caught in the between space of "if only". Heart beating out its jagged rhythm across the darkness, it descends, tightening its grip.

Of course we are right.

The dark intimations of fallibility are quite correct. How could it be otherwise? Are we not ordinary beings?

The truth shines like a light into our darkness, like the soothing hand on our forehead that tells us that the dream has passed. Of course we do things badly sometimes. Of course we let people down. Of course... How awful if it were otherwise.

Being ordinary is a great liberation, the relief of ordinariness. So much of our feeling of guilt comes from our expectation that we should be extraordinary. Not only do we mess up and feel regret, we then feel deeply ashamed that we have proved our failure as perfect beings. We squirm with humiliation at the prospect that others might see our imperfection. We struggle to hide beneath a mirage of niceness, whilst layers of resentment and anger bubble up at our exposure.

So, guilt is many layered. Sometimes it reflects the reality. We did do wrong. Often it is more a feeling response, arising in us from the perception of judgement. We judge ourselves. We imagine that others judge us. Sometimes they do. Crazy, that in a world of ordinary humans, so much expectation of never doing wrong should abound.

Understanding guilt requires an understanding of our nature. Conditioned beings, in particular we nurse our conditioned identities; we rely on certain continuities. Identity is our protection. Good or bad, it wards off the uncertainty of life.

For some, the self is seen as something to be perfected; it is paraded before others like a stately car, all shining chrome and gleaming bodywork, polished to the point where nothing out of place detracts from the pleasing image.

So, for some, willing themselves close to perfection, guilt manifests in burning anger that their behaviour is less than exemplary. Slip ups scratch the smooth surface of such lives. Anger that arises then, itself gives rise to further guilt. We have so let ourselves down, how could we? And now, these feelings boiling in the mind that should be calm and tranquil. Guilt multiplies.

Other times, guilt is the habit. Reflecting our doleful image of our imperfection, we wallow in its confirmation. We invite condemnation because it sustains our existence. We cling to guilt in the relief that we cannot do worse for we are already sunk. No possibilities. No pressure.

Heroic misery blankets our reality. They cannot kick us further now, for we have already surrendered to their criticism.

Whether the perfect self or the utter failure, these constructed identities protect us from the raw impermanence of life. To accept the reality of our human condition, means casting ourselves into a sea of uncertainty. We cannot do it of our own volition. We need faith.

So we return to our ordinariness. If we can realise that we are acceptable *just as we are,* we can face the ordinary misdemeanours of our lives. Of course we get it wrong, but it is not necessary to compound the suffering with pretence. We are not perfect and we do not need to be. Nor do we need to cling to the bad, which inevitably arises from time to time, in order to safeguard ourselves from condemnation.

With recognition of this ordinariness comes true relief. The paradigm is one of relaxation; of refuge. No longer locked in criticism of self, we have less reason to feel critical of others, though, of course, as ordinary humans we are by no means perfect in either respect! Getting to this point of acceptance, however, requires us to cross a line which is not always easy to negotiate.

Most importantly, the message of ordinariness is one of radical non-judgementalism, or, put another way, it means accepting that we are acceptable just as we are, warts and all. This is the challenge. Most of us would prefer to be accepted as we'd like to be. We want to believe we are really only the nice bits, and that the rest of our behaviour is just a series of unfortunate anomalies.

If we can make the crossing, however, we no longer have to fortify ourselves as much. The deep honesty which comes from recognising our humanity in all its colourful, and sometimes dismaying, guises releases a layer of pretence and we step into the world lighter. Accepting that, yes, sometimes we *are* guilty.

We no longer have to persecute ourselves, however, by floundering in the feelings of guilt. We do not need to endure the torture. We can make recompense, learn, and then let go because our egos are not threatened by knowing that we have slipped up yet again. That is true freedom.

First published in *Running Tide Magazine*, Spring 2008
Amida Trust
12 Coventry Rd
Narborough, LE19 2GR
www.amidatrust.com

BOOKS

O is a symbol of the world, of oneness and unity. In different cultures it also means the "eye", symbolizing knowledge and insight. We aim to publish books that are accessible, constructive and that challenge accepted opinion, both that of academia and the "moral majority".

Our books are available in all good English language bookstores worldwide. If you don't see the book on the shelves ask the bookstore to order it for you, quoting the ISBN number and title. Alternatively you can order online (all major online retail sites carry our titles) or contact the distributor in the relevant country, listed on the copyright page.

See our website **www.o-books.net** for a full list of over 400 titles, growing by 100 a year.

And tune in to myspiritradio.com for our book review radio show, hosted by June-Elleni Laine, where you can listen to the authors discussing their books.

mySpiritRadio

This book is a journey; an exploration into those areas of life which both fascinate and repel us. Through the weaving together of an account of a group of young people, fine grained analysis of the emotional and ethical basis of guilt, and illustration draw from a variety of life circumstances, the reader is drawn into the complexity of a subject which troubles many people in the modern world. The book deals sensitively with some of the most challenging areas of human experience, confronting the reader with situations in which there are no easy answers. Yet the writing retains a joy in life. At times both humorous and emotive, it reveals the beauty of the everyday and the pathos of the ordinary. A book that crosses boundaries, this is one of the few books on the topic which will have you reading into the small hours of the morning, eager to discover the secret worlds of the characters whose lives illustrate its themes.

Caroline Brazier has been a psychotherapist for twenty years, and is course leader of the Amida Psychotherapy Training Programme. A resident member of a Buddhist community, she divides her time between travelling, writing and teaching. She has three adult children.

"Caroline Brazier has produced a 'tour de force'. Her book is part novel, part autobiography, part commentary but, above all, it is a deeply spiritual exploration of perhaps the most elusive and yet most universal of all states of being. Guilt feelings, appropriate and inappropriate, afflict us all and in these pages we see how they can cripple lives and lead to self-deception and gross self-denigration. This gentle, sensitive and yet ruthlessly honest book combines the gifts of the talented story-teller, the insightful therapist and the wise spiritual traveller. It will make you laugh and weep and it will also compel you to re-visit much of your own experience with heightened awareness and awakened conscience."
Brian Thorne, Emeritus Professor of Counselling, University of East Anglia

"an amazing dissection and re-weaving of guilt and all its pained relatives. It is perhaps the most complete "anthology" of the permutations of guilt that I have ever seen, subtle, complex, multi-faceted and nuanced, layer upon layer of yet another meaning of the effects of guilt... provided through the eyes and heart and intellect of a very astute and brilliant adult author, psychologist, spiritual companion and human observer. I was truly amazed. I loved the interweaving of the story line/narrative as it grew in suspense and at different life stages and from different perspectives of the same event by different people... I shall surely never see guilt in the same way again, and I will listen with even more compassion to those so suffering from its stings."
Dr Gay Barfield, educator, author & former founder and co-director with Carl Rogers of the Carl Rogers Institute for Peace.

BOOKS

Psychology
UK £11.99
US $24.95

www.o-books.net

US $24.95
ISBN 978-1-84694-160-3

9 781846 941603